A SURVEY OF
LLOYD'S SYNDICATE ACCOUNTS
FINANCIAL REPORTING AT
LLOYD'S IN 1985

RESEARCH STUDIES IN ACCOUNTING
BV CARSBERG, SERIES EDITOR

Bhaskar, KN, Williams, BC
**THE IMPACT OF MICROPROCESSORS ON THE SMALL
ACCOUNTING PRACTICE**

Bromwich, M
THE ECONOMICS OF ACCOUNTING STANDARD SETTING

Carsberg, BV, Page, MJ (Joint Editors)
CURRENT COST ACCOUNTING

Carsberg, BV, Page, MJ, Sindall, AJ, Waring, ID
SMALL COMPANY FINANCIAL REPORTING

Glynn, JJ
VALUE FOR MONEY AUDITING IN THE PUBLIC SECTOR

Kirkman, PRA
**INFLATION ACCOUNTING IN MAJOR ENGLISH-SPEAKING
COUNTRIES**

Macve, RH
A SURVEY OF LLOYD'S SYNDICATE ACCOUNTS

A SURVEY OF
LLOYD'S SYNDICATE ACCOUNTS
FINANCIAL REPORTING AT
LLOYD'S IN 1985

RICHARD MACVE

Julian Hodge Professor of Accounting,
The University College of Wales, Aberystwyth

Prentice/Hall International

Englewood Cliffs, NJ   London   Mexico   New Delhi   Rio de Janeiro
Singapore   Sydney   Tokyo   Toronto

In association with

THE INSTITUTE OF
CHARTERED
ACCOUNTANTS

IN ENGLAND & WALES

The Institute of Chartered Accountants in England and Wales

British Library Cataloguing in Publication Data

Macve, Richard
  Survey of Lloyd's syndicate accounts. –
  (Accounting research)
  1. Lloyd's of London   2. Syndicates (Finance)
  – Great Britain
  I. Title   II. Institute of Chartered Accountants
  in England and Wales   III. Series 368'.012'094212
  HG8039

  ISBN 0-13-878273-3

This book consists of a research study undertaken on
behalf of The Institute of Chartered Accountants in
England and Wales. In publishing this book the Institute
considers that it is a worthwhile contribution to
discussion but neither the Institute nor the Research
Board necessarily shares the views expressed, which are
those of the author alone.

No responsibility for loss occasioned to any person
acting or refraining from action as a result of any
material in this publication can be accepted by the author
or the publisher.

Prentice-Hall Inc., Englewood Cliffs, New Jersey
Prentice-Hall International (UK) Ltd, London
Prentice-Hall of Australia Pty Ltd, Sydney
Prentice-Hall Canada Inc., Toronto
Prentice-Hall Hispanoamericana SA, Mexico
Prentice-Hall India Private Ltd, New Delhi
Prentice-Hall of Japan Inc., Tokyo
Prentice-Hall of Southeast Asia Pte Ltd, Singapore
Editora Prentice-Hall do Brasil Ltda, Rio de Janeiro

Printed and bound in Great Britain for
Prentice-Hall International (UK) Ltd,
66 Wood Lane End, Hemel Hempstead,
Hertfordshire, HP2 4RG, by SRP Ltd,
Exeter

1 2 3 4 5 90 89 88 87 86

ISBN 0-13-878273-3

CONTENTS

FOREWORD

by Ian Hay Davison
Deputy Chairman & Chief Executive of Lloyd's

The years 1980 to 1985 have been years of major change at Lloyd's, spanning as they do the period from the publication of Sir Henry Fisher's Report on 'Self-regulation at Lloyd's to the date on which syndicate accounts, on public file, were required to show a true and fair view. Accounting was not, of course, the only matter dealt with by Sir Henry Fisher and has not been, by any means, the only focus of attention of the new Council of Lloyd's, which has put its hand to an energetic and far reaching programme of reforms between 1982 and 1985. These reforms have covered many aspects of the Market at Lloyd's, but in no respect have they produced such a far reaching change as in the accounting area.

As Professor Macve points out in his initial chapter, "the biggest change has probably been the change in climate – openness and disclosure are now the order of the day as against exclusiveness and secrecy." Such a change was inevitable given the dramatic growth in the number of members of Lloyd's and the substantial increase in the portion of the total membership who now have no working connection with the Market. Better accounting was overdue and Lloyd's has turned to with a will to improve its accounting arrangements.

Professor Macve's excellent book charts the course of the accounting changes introduced in the first three years of the new Council of Lloyd's which was brought into being by the Lloyd's Act 1982. Accounts of syndicates now conform, in most respects, to the requirements of the Companies Acts. Names are now provided by agents appointed by the Names to act on their behalf with comprehensive, well prepared and properly audited accounts of their stewardship. As a result, as I know from many conversations with Names, they feel much better informed and are much better advised about their underwriting affairs.

Professor Macve's admirable analysis of the accounting reforms at Lloyd's, based on a detailed examination of the accounts now placed on public file at Lloyd's, provides an excellent introduction to the subject of accounting for syndicates and at the same time provides a useful commentary to those familiar with the accounting problems of underwriting, but who wish to improve the presentation of their underwriting figures. Professor Macve's book will, I am sure, be required reading for underwriters, agency directors and syndicate auditors at Lloyd's and for those in a wider circle outside Lloyd's who wish to marvel at the progress made in such a brief period in changing the accounting arrangements for the world's greatest insurance market.

PREFACE

In this survey I aim to present an explanation and illustration of the annual reports of Lloyd's syndicates, which are now publicly available. The reports upon which the survey focuses are 'the 1984 reports', i.e. those filed in 1985 for the year ended 31 December 1984, which were the first reports subject to the requirements of the Syndicate Accounting Byelaw (No.7 of 1984). They normally contained the syndicate underwriting accounts showing the result for the 1982 year of account (the 'closed year') and the progress to date of the two 'open' years (1983 and 1984), together with the syndicate balance sheet at 31 December 1984 (and I often refer to these four statements collectively as 'the 1984 accounts'). Comparisons are made with the 1983 reports, which were the first to be made public but for which many of the detailed requirements were not yet mandatory.

This survey is not intended to be either a 'league table' of syndicates' results or a textbook of Lloyd's accounting and market practices, but I have provided some background discussion of the disclosure and measurement issues and explanation of the relevant Lloyd's byelaws, as well as analyses and illustrations of practices, in order to bring out the points of interest that arise, particularly when one compares accounting at Lloyd's with accounting for other enterprises. The structure of the survey is similar to that of the ICAEW's surveys of published accounts (e.g. Tonkin & Skerratt, 1984). It is based on all the 457 1984 annual reports filed at Lloyd's in 1985, although much of the detailed analysis focuses on a random sample of 100 of these reports (for details see Appendix IV). I have not, however, discussed the special factors relating to the short-term life insurance syndicates at Lloyd's because they constitute a very small proportion of the market's business.

Chapters 1 and 2 outline first the developments in syndicate accounting and reporting that have been taking place at Lloyd's, and second certain other aspects of accounting and reporting in relation to Lloyd's which provide the context within which these developments should be viewed.

Chapters 3 to 17 comprise the main body of the survey, in which I review first the syndicate accounts; then the statements of disclosure of interests that managing agents are required to include in the annual report; then the additional reports (underwriters' and managing agents' reports) for which filing is now required; and finally the auditors' reports (which will have to give a 'true and fair view' opinion on the 1985 and subsequent annual reports, and in fact did so on the majority of the 1984 reports).

I have included some examples, in some cases to illustrate the 'standard' practice, in others to show how particularly effective disclosures and presentations have been made. The examples chosen are not necessarily the 'best' as in many cases they could have been chosen from any one of a number of reports.

In the final chapter I discuss some important issues that either have to be faced over the next few years, or in my opinion ought to be addressed in considering the future development of syndicate reporting.

Where appropriate I have given references to suitable further readings, the full titles of which are given in the Bibliography in Appendix VIII. I have made use of some abbreviations and short-form references: some in widespread use, some of my own (see Appendix IX). I have generally referred to underwriting members of Lloyd's as 'Names' (and used 'he' and 'his' for brevity with regard to Names of either sex).

As the new reporting requirements have been implemented in stages and as other reforms of the market's practices are still being implemented, it may be appropriate to repeat this survey to provide an updating and monitoring of how syndicate reporting 'settles down' in the new environment at Lloyd's. I shall be grateful for any suggestions from readers as to how the coverage and presentation could be made more useful in a future edition.

RICHARD MACVE

Aberystwyth
December 1985

ACKNOWLEDGEMENTS

I am grateful to the ICAEW's Research Board and to the Council of Lloyd's for sponsoring this survey. I would like to thank the members of the Regulatory Services Group and of the Accounting and Audit Review Department at Lloyd's (in particular Michael Stephen, Cathy Shorthouse, John Evans and Jane Rose) for providing me with the necessary material from the central file and with a great deal of other helpful information about Lloyd's and the recent developments in disclosure and accounting requirements. I am also grateful to a number of people who have given me their time to discuss aspects of the survey, including:

Brandon Gough, member of the Council of Lloyd's and Chairman of its Accounting & Auditing Standards Committee; former Chairman of the CCAB Auditing Practices Committee

Ian Hay Davison, Deputy Chairman and Chief Executive of Lloyd's

Terence Pitron, Former Chairman of Lloyd's Aviation Underwriters' Association

John Rew, Former Deputy Chairman of the Association of Lloyd's Members; Joint Editor of 'Lloyd's League Tables – 1982'

Partners and staff of the following firms of panel auditors:
Arthur Young
Deloitte Haskins & Sells
Ernst & Whinney
Littlejohn de Paula
Neville Russell
Peat, Marwick, Mitchell & Co.

Christopher Napier, Robin Oakes and colleagues in the University of Wales, particularly David Gwilliam, gave me very helpful criticisms and comments on an earlier draft.

None of the above would of course necessarily agree with the views expressed in this survey, nor are they responsible for its remaining faults.

Special thanks are due to Kate Oultram for her research assistance, to Eileen Evans, Jennie Macve and Jean Matthews for their help with typing and wordprocessing, and to Giles Wright, Maggie McDougall and Ruth Freestone at Prentice-Hall.

ACKNOWLEDGMENTS

EXECUTIVE SUMMARY

I. Scope of this Study

The 1983 annual reports of the Lloyd's syndicates were the first to be made public. Most of Lloyd's detailed regulations on the form and content of syndicate reports ('the syndicate accounting rules') were finalised when the Syndicate Accounting Byelaw (No.7 of 1984) ('SAB') was issued in October 1984, and the 1984 reports are therefore the first to have been issued under these rules. The only major change still to come into force – and which will apply to the 1985 and subsequent reports – is the requirement for the auditors to give a 'true and fair view' opinion: but in fact the majority of the 1984 reports already carried such an opinion, so that the pattern for the future is now essentially in place.

This survey analyses the disclosures provided and the accounting practices followed in the 1984 reports (i.e. those for the year ended 31 December 1984), which had to be filed with Lloyd's by 15 June 1985. While it focuses on the accounting and reporting requirements that are now in force, it also covers some of the history of the various recommendations and requirements that have been issued by the Council of Lloyd's, and the stages of their implementation, and in particular comments on comparisons between the 1984 and 1983 reports.

2. Syndicate Accounts: Names, Policyholders and the 'Public Interest' (Chapter I)

The 'users' to whom syndicate accounts are of most concern are:

- current and prospective Names
- customers and creditors: the insureds
- competitors
- Government agencies
- the 'public interest'

The main pressure for accounting reform has resulted from the rapid growth in the number of Names at Lloyd's (which has more than tripled over the last ten years) and their increasing remoteness from direct contact with the operations of the market. This pressure has been reinforced as a result of the 'scandals' affecting Names.

The situation differs from that of the insurance companies. There the increase in regulation and demand for information in recent years has been primarily a result of the DTI's concern for the security of policyholders.

The new climate of openness and disclosure also serves the 'public interest' in helping to explain and justify the economic role of Lloyd's.

3. Objectives of Accounting Reforms (Chapter 1)

Accounts are required for three main purposes:

– accountability or 'stewardship' of agents
– sharing of results
– information as a basis for decisions

The objectives of the accounting reforms have been to enforce the accountability of the agents who manage Lloyd's syndicates by ensuring full disclosure; to see that clear and fair rules are used for sharing results; and to improve the quality and quantity of the information available about the performance and prospects of the syndicates. Names need to be able to make comparisons between syndicates. Their members' agents are important intermediaries in analysing and interpreting the extensive accounting information provided for them.

The model that has been adopted has been that of the audited reports and accounts of UK companies, that are required under the Companies Act to give a 'true and fair view' of their financial affairs. In applying this model to Lloyd's syndicates' accounts (which involves the application of the SSAPs of the UK professional accounting bodies) it has been necessary to adapt it for certain unique aspects of Lloyd's business and market practice. In particular the 'three year' accounting system at Lloyd's means that a true and fair view can only be said to be given of the 'closed year' result and of how this has been shared among the syndicate's members.

4. Requirements for the 1984 and 1983 Reports (Chapter 1)

When the transitional reporting provisions have fully worked through (i.e. by the accounts to December 1985, when the 1983 underwriting account will 'close') the essentials of the reporting requirements, as set out in SAB, will be that the Lloyd's central file will have available for public inspection, for a typical syndicate:

1. an underwriter's report
2. a managing agent's report
3. an annual report comprising:
   (a) underwriting accounts for three years (one 'closed' and two 'open')
   (b) balance sheet
   (c) notes to the accounts
   (d) disclosure of material interests
   (e) 'seven year summary' of past closed years' results
4. auditor's report on the annual report which will give the auditor's opinion on whether or not the accounts give a true and fair view of the result of the closed year, and otherwise comply with the Lloyd's syndicate accounting rules (as set out principally in SAB). This will cover the fair presentation of the information in point 3d (Disclosure of Interests), as required by Byelaw 3 of 1984, and the consistency of the information in points 1 and 2 with that in 3.

The transitional stages are:

– For the 1984 reports the requirement for a 'true and fair view' was not yet obligatory;
– For the 1983 reports:
   Points 1 and 2 were not required to be filed, although they had to be prepared for Names and were recommended as 'voluntary' information to be included in the central file.

Point 3 did not have to include 3d and 3e above. However the filing of a separate Disclosure of Interests statement by each agent (or a 'nil' return) was required by the Disclosure of Interests Byelaw, although it did not have to be audited. The 'seven year summary' was a recommended attachment to the accounts (but did not have to be audited). The *minimum* required filing with regard to the 1983 reports for a typical syndicate was therefore:

3. an annual report comprising:
    (a) underwriting accounts ('closed' for 1981, and 'open' for 1982 and 1983)
    (b) balance sheet at 31 December 1983
    (c) notes to the accounts
4. audit report on point 3.
5. (=3d) Disclosure of Interests statement (unaudited).

No particular format or accounting policies had been specified, but there was available the 'Lloyd's Accounting Manual (Provisional)' [referred to hereafter as PAM], which contained recommendations on best practice and specimen reports.

Measuring the speed of change is difficult because accounts were not publicly available before the 1983 reports. Nevertheless, it appears that the rules largely reflect existing 'best practice' and that the radical new element is publicity. However, one response to the implementation of SAB's regulations on form and content has been a tendency, already emerging in the 1984 reports, to abandon some useful additional presentations of information that were previously given and to standardise SAB's minimum requirements as a norm.

5. The Context of Syndicate Accounts (Chapter 2)
The reports and accounts of the individual syndicates are only one aspect of the preparation of publicly available financial information about Lloyd's. The information relating to each syndicate is aggregated to produce statutory returns for the DTI of the insurance business transacted at Lloyd's (analysed by class of business). These are also available to the public in a 'glossy' format, like that of a company's annual report to its shareholders, as 'Lloyd's Global Accounts'. Of major importance in regard to the security of policyholders is the annual solvency examination, of which the results are summarised in the returns prepared for the DTI confirming the adequacy of each Name's means to meet his liabilities at Lloyd's. As substantial proportions of Names' 'equity' and 'risk capital' are held in reserves and private wealth that are outside the syndicate accounts it is particularly important to make clear just which items the accounts do and do not include, as compared with a company's accounts.

6. The Accounting Entity (Chapter 3)
The normal presentation of accounts is one set per syndicate. The main exceptions are those where investment funds are administered separately for different subgroups of Names on the syndicate (e.g. for 'US' and 'other' Names) and either the results in the underwriting accounts are analysed between these subgroups, or sometimes separate sets of accounts are provided for each subgroup. Where the funds for different subgroups are managed by different (quasi) managing agents each agent normally prepares a set of accounts relating to the Names in that subgroup. Separate accounts may also be prepared in respect of Names participating through different members' agencies.

Where two or more syndicates have the same Names with the same participations (including 'incidental' and 'mirror' syndicates) their accounts are usually combined, although occasionally the results are shown separately for each syndicate. Although other combinations of figures were sometimes given for the 1983 accounts, this is now expressly prohibited.

Given the element of choice, it is important to make clear just which combinations or subdivisions of syndicate figures are being presented.

7. Accounting Formats (Chapter 3)

A significant change introduced in the last two years has been the presentation of premiums in the underwriting accounts split between 'gross' and 'reinsurance'.

There have been some further changes as between the formats *recommended* for the 1983 accounts and those *required* for the 1984 (and subsequent) accounts. In particular under the current requirements, the syndicate allocated capacity is shown in the underwriting accounts. This is particularly important both because of the Lloyd's rules relating to the amount of premiums that Names may write, given the size of their Lloyd's deposits and other means, and because it is the key to explaining individual Names' share of the result. While all the 1984 accounts met this requirement, only a quarter of the 1983 reports had given this information in the accounts or notes.

The revenues and outgoing are normally just presented on a cumulative basis for each of the three underwriting years (one closed and two open), together with comparative figures. In my opinion, further consideration needs to be given as to whether it would be useful also to present:

(a)   calendar year figures (see sections 11 and 14);

(b)   further analysis of the 'pure' result of the closed year and of how the prior years have developed (see section 12).

8. Accounting Policies: General (Chapter 4)

The major differences between the accounts of a Lloyd's syndicate and those of a company reflect the facts that:

(a)   a syndicate is a venture whose constitution lasts for only one year, and the rights and obligations of its Names are normally liquidated by cash settlement when the result of that year's underwriting is determined;

(b)   by Lloyd's market practice the results of each year are only 'closed' at the end of three years;

(c)   by Lloyd's market practice, risks are normally allocated to the Names on the syndicate in the year in which the policy is signed through the Lloyd's Policy Signing Office, and therefore not necessarily to the Names on the syndicate in the year in which the underwriter accepted the risk or to which the risk relates;

(d)   the liability of each Name is unlimited and is several, not joint with the other Names on the syndicate.

It had been envisaged when PAM was issued in 1983 that the peculiarities of Lloyd's would require the issue of specialised 'Statements of Lloyd's Accounting Practice'. It was later decided, and embodied in the requirements for the 1984 and subsequent accounts, that agents and auditors should apply the general SSAPs insofar as they are applicable to Lloyd's, other matters being specifically dealt with in the accounting rules prescribed in the relevant byelaws. However, SSAP2's statement of the 'fundamental accounting concepts' applicable to all accounts intended to give a true and fair view is specifically modifed in SAB to recognise:

(a) that the 'going concern' assumption does not apply to Lloyd's syndicates, and
(b) that the 'accrual' and 'prudence' concepts only apply to the closed year, the open year accounts and the balance sheet being merely 'on account' statements of the accumulating revenues, expenses, assets and liabilities of those years, and giving no indication of their ultimate surplus or deficiency.

For these reasons it is regarded as appropriate for the requirement for a true and fair view to apply only to the closed year of account.

SSAP2's 'consistency' concept requires that the effect of any changes in accounting policy be quantified.

In addition to the concepts in SSAP2, it is emphasised in SAB that a fundamental objective in preparing the accounts must be that of maintaining 'equity' between the Names on a syndicate in different years: in particular with regard to the determination of the 'reinsurance to close' which transfers the outstanding rights and liabilities of the closing year to the Names of the subsequent year. Because of the finality of this transfer SAB does not state (as SSAP2 does) that 'prudence' prevails over 'accruals' where there is a conflict. How 'equity', 'accruals' and 'prudence' are to be balanced in practice will inevitably be a matter for professional judgement.

In my opinion it is desirable that explanations about the non-applicability of 'going concern', and about the fundamental importance of the objective of 'equity' should be included in the notes to the accounts: such explanation was rare in the 1984 and 1983 accounts.

9. Underwriting Transactions (Chapter 5)
Compliance with PAM's recommendations on accounting policies was already high in the 1983 accounts, the main exceptions being with regard to the methods of accounting for premiums and claims, where a high proportion of syndicates appeared to follow alternative practices. However, because compensating adjustments should be made to the calculation of the reinsurance to close, these alternatives should have no effect on the overall determination of the result of the closed year (although this was not generally made clear).

In my opinion the criterion for choice of method should be that of providing the most useful basis for the underwriter's statistical analysis: but although under the rules in force for the 1984 (and subsequent) accounts some variety of practices is permitted, SAB does not permit the allowance for closing year accruals to be made in the calculation of the reinsurance to close.

In nearly half the 1984 reports examined there appeared to be a different accounting policy being used as compared with 1983; but mention of any change was very rare (as was any explanation that the change would have had no effect on the result).

10. Reinsurance to Close (Chapter 6)
Estimates of outstanding insurance liabilities are required for two purposes:

1. To calculate the reinsurance to close in order to settle the result of the closed year.
2. To estimate whether the balances on the open years are likely to be sufficient to cover the future development of their premiums and claims (including the further development of the closed years reinsured into them).

Essentially it is the comparison of the liabilities detemined under point 2 with their available assets (including personal assets) that determines the 'solvency' of the Names, and Lloyd's, with the approval of the DTI, lays down certain minimum requirements for the calculation of these liabilities. However, the primary objective with regard to giving a true and fair view of the result and to determining the reinsurance to close is to arrive at an equitable amount, based on the information available, at which the outstanding liabilities of the closed year should be transferred to the Names in subsequent years – it is therefore important that the amount should not only be adequate but also not be excessive. The Inland Revenue shares this concern.

Although there had been a marked improvement as between the 1983 and 1984 accounts, some of the wordings used in the notes to the accounts to explain the calculation of the reinsurance to close still appeared to be more appropriate to a 'solvency test' than to the determination of an equitable result. In my opinion, agents and auditors should give further attention to how the objective and basis of the estimate is described. In addition, and in common with the rest of the insurance industry, Lloyd's syndicates also need to examine in particular the criteria for determining:

(a) how future expenses are allowed for in estimating outstanding liabilities
(b) how estimates of future inflation are incorporated
(c) to what extent the future investment income to be earned on the amounts provided should be incorporated into the calculation (i.e. should the liabilities be 'discounted' and how should the investment returns then be accounted for?)
(d) to what extent the assumptions made about these and other factors underlying the calculation should be disclosed.

11. Other Assets, Liabilities, Income and Expenses (Chapters 7 to 10)
In general the treatment of these items (including translation of foreign currency items and taxation) is highly standardised, and as only short-term, liquid assets are normally held, they present few valuation problems.

As expenses may be allocated over the three years of account, and are usually not accrued for open years, it is often not obvious at what level the expenses are running on a calendar year basis. In particular it is, in my opinion, desirable that the amount of the estimated audit costs in relation to the current annual report be stated; and to be comparable with companies the remuneration of the underwriter and information about the number of highly paid employees could also be disclosed. There is also still scope for fuller and clearer explanations to be given of the bases of allocation between managing agent, managed syndicates and individual underwriting years, and of the extent to which expenses have been accrued.

12. Extraordinary and Exceptional Items and 'Pure Year' Accounting (Chapter 11)
Given the nature of insurance business and the three-year accounting system at Lloyd's, it is generally not appropriate to identify transactions and events under these categories. However it had been recommended for the 1983 accounts that, where material, the impact of the development of the previously 'closed' years on the result should be disclosed as an 'exceptional' item and about 10% of syndicates gave this information that year. There is now no such requirement and fewer syndicates gave the information in the 1984 accounts. Given the size of some of the

adjustments that are made to prior-year estimates it is, in my opinion, desirable that at least this much information about the 'pure' closed year, and preferably information about individual prior years, should be given (as is required of insurance companies in their DTI returns) if the readers of the accounts are to be able sensibly to interpret the results and understand the margins of error within which estimates have to be made.

13. The 'Seven Year Summary' of Past Results and 'Inflation Accounting' (Chapter 12)

A seven year summary is now required as part of the audited annual report. About one-third of the 1983 reports had already included such a summary, which was recommended for that year but not yet mandatory (and did not have to be audited). The statement shows for each year, first the syndicate's allocated capacity for writing premium income, the number of Names on the syndicate and the aggregate syndicate net premium written; and second, the amounts of premiums, claims, income, expenses and net result attributable to a Name having a stated 'standard share' on the syndicate. It thus provides the most comprehensive measure available for comparison of results over a period of years.

There is no requirement for syndicates to prepare any statements showing the effects of inflation. However, as the results in the seven year summary are expressed in terms of a standard share of allocated premium income they permit Names to make their own allowances for the effects of inflation in interpreting the results. A useful feature of some of the statements provided (although regrettably fewer in the 1984 than in the 1983 reports) was the expression of individual items (e.g. expenses) as a percentage of the premium income written, which made it easier to see the trends in the figures.

In my opinion, the question of whether any further restatement of figures is desirable to indicate the impact of inflation deserves further research, both by Lloyd's and by the rest of the insurance industry.

14. 'Source and Application of Funds' Statements and Calendar Year Accounting (Chapter 13)

There is no requirement to provide such statements with the accounts and the general opinion at Lloyd's is that they would provide no useful information, although one agent's syndicates did include them in each year. In my opinion, they could be designed to meet the objective of complementing the underwriting accounts by displaying the calendar year figures for the movements of syndicate funds (distinguishing cash flows from accruals) and deserve further consideration.

15. Disclosure of Interests (Chapter 14)

A number of institutional reforms are being implemented at Lloyd's to reduce potential conflicts of interest between managing agents and Names (e.g. divestment of brokers and managing agents, banning of related party reinsurance and restriction of 'multiple syndicates'). In addition, the Disclosure of Interests Byelaw (No.3 of 1984) requires fair presentation in relation to each syndicate of any material interests of relevant parties in any transaction or arrangement affecting Names on that syndicate. For the 1984 and subsequent reports SAB also requires details about other syndicates managed in the same market.

The disclosures were subject to audit in the 1984 reports, but not in respect of the 1983 reports when compliance was weakest in this area of reporting. Not only had a number of agents failed to file a statement with their 1983 accounts (even if they had nothing to disclose, a 'nil' return was required), but there was little financial quantification of relevant transactions, interests and their effects (expected for 'fair presentation' under the Byelaw). In part this may have reflected the comparatively late date at which the relevant Byelaw was issued (in April 1984) and the changes in the proposals that had been made during consultation with the market. On the other hand, there also appeared to be a tendency on the part of many agents to disclose all possible interests and arrangements where there might be held to be a conflict of interest even though any financial impact was negligible. The standard of reporting in the 1984 reports was considerably better. To what extent this reflects a learning process by agents, and to what extent it reflects the role of the auditors in ensuring meaningful disclosure by agents, it is not possible to tell. However, there is still a need for greater attention to be paid to setting out clearly the financial implications of the items disclosed.

16. Managing Agents' and Underwriters' Reports (Chapters 15 and 16)

Full understanding of the performance of a business, and of the nature and risks of its activities, requires more information than the financial accounts alone can reveal. In the case of Lloyd's syndicates much of this kind of information is provided by the managing agents' and underwriters' reports.

Agents were *required* to prepare for Names, but only *recommended* to file, these statements in respect of their 1983 reports. From the 1984 reports onwards filing is *required* and there have been some changes in the information to be provided.

The reports filed 'voluntarily' in respect of 1983 and as a requirement in respect of 1984 varied widely in informativeness. The recommendations in PAM had included the quantified analysis of premium income and results by various 'segmental' classifications of the syndicate's business: e.g. category of business; type of acceptance; geographic origin; currency. Relatively little of such quantified analysis was generally provided in either year. There is considerable disagreement in the market about how best to explain the risk characteristics of the business written, bearing in mind the competitive sensitivity of much of the information and the fact that, in contrast with many other industries, the underwriter has considerable scope to change his portfolio of business written from one year to the next. The division of the market into marine, non-marine, aviation, motor, etc. is itself a 'segmentation' of business and results, and in my opinion further research is needed as to how much more detailed the analysis that is provided on public record should be.

While underwriters usually discussed the prospects of the open years, and often gave some indication of whether they expected a profit or a loss, or a better or worse result than in previous years (usually being more specific about the first open year than the second), quantified forecasts were only rarely given, mainly where losses were anticipated. Whether it is possible to provide more detailed forecasts and if so whether they should be given and in what form, also, in my opinion, deserves further consideration.

17. Audit Reports (Chapter 17)

With the introduction of the mandatory disclosures and accounting rules, qualifications in audit reports were more frequent on the 1984 than on the 1983 accounts.

Although auditors are not *required* to give a 'true and fair' opinion until the 1985 accounts are filed in 1986, this was recommended for the 1984 accounts where possible and was given in the majority of cases. The scope of the audit was extended for the 1984 accounts to cover the disclosure of interests statements; the consistency of the managing agents' and underwriters' reports with the accounts; and the incorporation of the seven year summary into the annual report. (A few auditors had given opinions on some of these matters, and some a true and fair opinion, in respect of the 1983 accounts.)

As syndicates frequently provide detailed analyses of investment holdings it is desirable that the auditors include these in the scope of their report.

18. The 'True and Fair View' (Chapter 17)

Auditors now generally accept that there is no reason in principle why a true and fair opinion cannot be given in respect of Lloyd's syndicates, although there are a number of practical difficulties to be overcome.

Even in regard to giving an opinion only on the closed year, the uncertainties involved in calculating the 'reinsurance to close' may lead to more accounts having to 'run-off' to avoid unacceptable qualification. There has also been the question of whether the records kept at the underwriting box are adequate, and in a suitable form, to provide the basis for the audit of the syndicate accounts. A quarter of the 1984 accounts and nearly a fifth of the 1983 accounts included in the notes a statement to the effect that the underwriter relied on the LPSO for the accuracy of the processing of transactions. SAB's requirements about accounting records, and the arrangement for an auditor's opinion on the LPSO system itself, should remove many of these difficulties, and a 'true and fair view' opinion is required not later than in respect of the 1985 syndicate accounts to be filed in 1986.

The final question is whether the objective should be to have a 'true and fair view' opinion on the accounts as a whole. This would be likely to require the following additional reforms:

(a) A view would need to be taken on the likely outcome of the open years. This would not necessarily imply 'one-year accounting' – adjustment need only be made if losses are forecast, which is the practice followed by many insurance companies (and occasionally by syndicates in unusual circumstances). It would, however, be a significant change from the present three-year accounting system, and since it would not improve 'solvency' protection (as allowances for open year deficiencies are already made for that purpose) and there would be accounting difficulties (as Names' assets to cover open year deficiencies may be held in deposits and reserves outside the premiums trust funds appearing in the syndicate's balance sheet), there would seem to be no clear advantage from such a change unless the three-year accounting system is to be abandoned altogether (i.e. profits may be recognised as well as losses after one year). As any such revolutionary change would in turn require reappraisal of the timing of distribution to Names, and of the related tax arrangements, in my opinion the way forward is to start by considering whether disclosure of any estimated deficiencies on open years should be given in the accounts.

(b) The market's normal practice of allocating risks to Names by LPSO signing date would give rise to further difficulties. Even though the accounts properly reflect the allocation that has actually occurred, they would be incomplete if they did not account for all risks accepted by the underwriter to the end of the accounting year. Perhaps some kind of preliminary account for the new underwriting year would have to be included. In fact it now seems likely that this practice may be changed (subject to the problem of maintaining the consistency of the underwriting statistics) to avoid any danger of manipulation of the allocation of business from one year to another, and if so, this difficulty would disappear. Otherwise, it may be appropriate for some explanation to be included of the extent to which risks have been accepted that are not yet reflected in the accounts.

However, one may argue, on a very different tack, that 'true and fair' is always understood in the context of the accounting practices customarily applied, and that provided Lloyd's accounting policies are clearly understood, and clearly explained in the accounts, no further change is necessary (one audit firm already gives an overall 'true and fair view' opinion on the accounts as a whole).

19. Conclusions – and the Future (Chapter 18)
Significant changes have been taking place in accounting and reporting at Lloyd's. Whether accounting reforms can prevent future 'scandals' cannot be definitively answered, as there is often no clear relationship between a requirement for disclosure of a particular kind of information, or a requirement for the adoption of a particular accounting method, and ensuring that clever and determined individuals are unable to conceal their activities and reap illegal or unacceptable rewards. Every new rule creates a new loophole. There is, however, a new climate of openness at Lloyd's which should discourage abuses and enable the economic role of the market to be better understood. On the evidence of the survey I have undertaken the reforms of syndicate reporting have in general been successfully implemented.

These developments will put Lloyd's syndicate accounts in many respects ahead of ordinary company accounts with regard to providing useful information. Given the up-to-date valuations of assets, and the necessarily 'forward looking' approach to estimating the reinsurance to close, the accounts are largely free of most of the limitations of 'historical cost accounting'. They aim to provide both a realistic picture of how the syndicate's insurance venture for a given year has turned out, and an equitable basis for dividing the result between the Names who participated in it.

There are however, additional improvements in accounting and reporting practice that should be considered, which are suggested in the chapters of this survey and are summarised here:

(a) There should be fuller explanation of the way in which the fundamental accounting concepts underlying the preparation of accounts are modified for Lloyd's syndicates (in particular in regard to the non-applicability of the 'going concern' concept and the importance of 'equity' between Names).

(b) Explanations of how underwriting transactions are accounted for should be clearer and, in particular, should explain why the closed year result is unaffected by the choice of accounting method.

(c) There should be more emphasis on explaining the factors that have entered into the calculation of the reinsurance to close as a 'best estimate' and less on the considerations that are relevant to assessing adequacy of reserves for solvency purposes.

(d) Further information could be given about expense allocations, the extent of accruals, and the various charges that have arisen during the calendar year. In particular, an estimate of the current audit cost should be given (whether or not it has been accrued). Executive remuneration could also be disclosed.

(e) There should be disclosure of the way in which prior closed years have subsequently developed, at least in their total effect on the current result if not by individual years (as is required in the DTI returns of insurance companies).

(f) The use of ratios and percentages in the seven year summary should be extended.

(g) There should be further consideration of how to provide the calendar year information that would be provided by a Source and Application of Funds statement.

(h) Any analysis of individual investment holdings, where provided, should be included in the scope of the audit report.

There are also other, more fundamental items that are not yet on the agenda:

– Consideration should be given to providing a note of any estimated losses on open years.

– In common with the rest of the insurance industry, Lloyd's needs to research the best treatment of future expenses and future investment income in assessing how much to provide for future liabilities in the 'reinsurance to close'; and how the impact of inflation on results might be measured.

– 'Pure year' accounting; greater segmental analysis; fuller explanation of assumptions; and provision of forecasts for open years, should also be on the list of topics to be considered.

Above all it is important that agents should not feel constrained by the Council's accounting and disclosure rules, but should recognise that these embody only the minimum required standards. Individual agents should continue to experiment with supplementary disclosures and imaginative presentations of information.

Once the market has digested the effects of the present 'catching up' under the new regime of disclosure introduced so far, it will be interesting to see if Lloyd's becomes converted to the idea of being a leader in setting the standards of accountability to which companies should also aspire.

A SURVEY OF
LLOYD'S SYNDICATE ACCOUNTS
FINANCIAL REPORTING AT
LLOYD'S IN 1985

CHAPTER I

DEVELOPMENTS IN DISCLOSURE

It is often said that Edward Lloyd's most important service when he opened his coffee house, sometime around 1687, was the provision of reliable information about shipping movements to those who met there, and who were previously prey to wild and speculative rumour. Insurance is inherently about risk and uncertainty; but the risk and uncertainty are handled most efficiently where up-to-date, relevant and reliable information is to hand to assist the necessary exercise of judgement. Investment is also about risk and uncertainty, and there is a widely held belief in societies such as our own that investors too should have up-to-date, relevant and reliable information. Determining how much information, and of what kind, raises a host of theoretical and practical problems (see e.g. Macve, 1981), some of which are discussed below. But for investors in companies there are the requirements of the Companies Acts, the Stock Exchange and Accounting Standards which regulate not only the financial reporting that is to be provided directly to individual shareholders but also what is to be publicly filed and available to all for a small fee.

Public filing implies that there are other parties, besides existing investors, who have an interest in and a right of access to information about an organisation's financial position, as well as about certain other aspects of its affairs. (Management, of course, has both a direct interest and direct access.) Studies such as *The Corporate Report* (ASC, 1975) and the 'Sandilands Report' (1975) in the UK, or the pronouncements on Statements of Financial Accounting Concepts by the Financial Accounting Standards Board in the USA (e.g. FASB, 1978), have suggested that these other interested external groups do or should comprise:

Future investors
Bankers and other lenders
Creditors
Customers and suppliers
Competitors
Employees and unions

Government (as taxing authority and regulator for the public interest)
The public at large

In addition there are the financial analysts, professional advisers, the press, researchers and educators etc. who may be seen as intermediaries, acting on behalf of or in the interests of these other groups. In the case of Lloyd's, the 'members' agent' is an important intermediary with a responsibility for advising Names.

In the case of insurance companies one of these groups whose interests have long been specially recognised has been the policyholders (the 'customers'). The objective of much of the regulatory activity in regard to insurance carried out by the Government, through the Department of Trade and Industry, is the protection of policyholders; policyholders are entitled to a copy of their insurance company's audited annual accounts and DTI returns. In the case of Lloyd's the auditors confirm the 'solvency' of each Name (for which it is his overall wealth that is relevant) but even the DTI only receives detailed statements relating to the business of Lloyd's as a whole. The detailed accounts of the individual syndicates have traditionally been regarded as a private matter between principals and their agents or stewards. The 1983 accounts were the first to be made public.

The managing agent of a syndicate organises the underwriting on behalf of the various 'Names' on the syndicate and has an obligation to account to them (as individuals – because their liability is several, not joint) for the balance of profit or loss on their activities and for any other payments and receipts he makes on their account. Under Lloyd's market practice, the results of underwriting in 1986 will not normally be finally determined until the end of the 1988, and, if profitable, a cheque for the net result, after including investment returns and deducting expenses (and some payments in respect of taxation), will then be sent in 1989 to each Name on the syndicate. While many agents may have provided their Names with comprehensive information in the past, there has traditionally been no necessary assumption that a Name would need to know either about the affairs of the syndicate as a whole, or of other syndicates in which he had no participation.

Traditionally, Lloyd's has been regarded as an exclusive club, whose members would prefer to operate largely on a basis of mutual trust and respect, and often with fairly close personal knowledge of each other. In recent years it has become considerably less exclusive. The number of Names on syndicates has gone up from 2743 in 1950, through 3917 in 1955, 5828 in 1965 and 7666 in 1975 to over 26,000 in 1985, and it is still rising fast. (The largest syndicate for underwriting year 1982 comprised more Names than the whole of Lloyd's thirty years before.) Approximately 15% are overseas Names, of whom the majority are US residents. Inevitably the widening gap between those who work at Lloyd's and the passive risk-takers has made informal, personal communication of information increasingly difficult, while the substitution of regular formal reporting has in the past largely been left to develop according to individual need, or when professional advisers, such as syndicate auditors, have urged improvements on their clients.

There has been little pressure from the DTI, compared with its pressure on the insurance and reinsurance companies. While there has been increased regulation, with demands for ever more detailed information and the introduction of the Policyholders' Protection Act 1975, in attempts to improve the Department's ability to monitor the solvency of the companies and protect policyholders (see e.g. Harte and Macve, 1986), the concern over Lloyd's in recent years has not been so much for policyholders (as all legitimate claims have been paid) but for the protection of the Names. (The DTI's monitoring on behalf of policyholders is described further in Chapter 2.)

Lloyd's self-examination began in earnest with the setting up of a working party in 1978 under Sir Henry Fisher (see Cockerell, 1984). The desire for reform was spurred on by the subsequent relevations of breaches of trust and fraud by a number of agents and underwriters, in a series of cases that have made press headlines (see Hodgson, 1984). While undertaking the investigations into these scandals, Lloyd's has been proceeding with the introduction of a number of sweeping reforms of its organisation, rules and disciplinary procedures. The aspect of reform that is reflected in the contents of this survey is the new approach to syndicate accounting and reporting.

The primary goal that has been adopted in regard to the annual accounts and reports of syndicates has been to make them comparable (as far as is possible given certain unique aspects of Lloyd's business and market practice) with those expected of a company under the Companies Acts – and in some respects going beyond what is required of insurance companies, who are still exempt from some of the requirements that apply to 'normal' companies (CA1985, Section 257. See also Macve, 1977).

This objective is captured in the requirement that the accounts shall give a 'true and fair view' (albeit only in regard to the closed year). This was encouraged for the 1984 accounts but it is not necessary for the auditors to include an opinion on this in their report until the 1985 accounts. (Some of the particular problems in applying the 'true and fair' standard are discussed in Chapter 17.) 'True and fair' in this context should be understood as meaning essentially 'to the same standard as a limited company's accounts' and, as Counsel advised the ASC (*Accountancy*, November 1983, pp.154–156), that in turn means to the standard, and according to the accounting policies, that may normally be reasonably expected from a set of company accounts. The intention is that accountants and auditors should treat accounting for, and audit of, Lloyd's syndicates in the same manner as they approach company accounting and auditing, although allowing for any special peculiarities of the business and the reporting entity. This may be distinguished from the traditional 'Lloyd's audit', the sole purpose of which is to ensure that the assets deposited by Names are adequate to cover the extent of their known and likely liabilites on their underwriting. (Further discussion of this 'solvency audit' is given in Chapter 2.)

In addition to the financial statements there are also new requirements for disclosures of interests (see Chapter 14) and for discussion of results and plans in reports by the Managing Agent and Underwriter (see Chapters 15 and 16).

The speed of change at Lloyd's appears to have been rapid. The Fisher Task Group 4 reported on recommended developments in syndicate accounting (including suggested accounting rules) in December 1982. 'Lloyd's Accounting Manual (Provisional)' (referred to here as PAM), was issued in November 1983 and contained recommendations on best practice and a specimen annual report (and formed the basis, albeit with some important changes, of the final accounting rules). Byelaw 2 of 1984, requiring central filing of the 1983 accounts, were passed on 13 February 1984 and Byelaw 3, requiring filing of Disclosure of Interests in respect of the 1983 accounts, was passed on 9 April 1984. Filing of the 1983 reports was required by 15 June 1984. 'The Syndicate Accounting Byelaw' (Byelaw 7 of 1984, referred to here as SAB), setting out the final mandatory accounting rules for the 1984 reports (which had to be filed by 15 June 1985), was passed on 8 October 1984.

It is, however, difficult to measure the speed of change because accounts were not previously filed, so no ready basis of comparison is available. However, based on my discussions with a number of firms of Chartered Accountants involved in Lloyd's audits, my impression is that, as with most accounting and auditing reforms, it has been largely a matter of bringing everyone up to the standard already adopted by the leaders. Some firms have shown me their pro-formas for Lloyd's accounts that were in use in prior years and which are essentially similar to those now mandated for all. Many Names would already expect to receive an underwriter's and managing agent's report containing some information about the year's business activity and results. The major change in accounting presentation has probably been that, whereas it was traditionally customary only to give net premium income figures, there is now a requirement to show gross, reinsurance and net premiums, as well as the syndicate's allocated premium capacity. The 'Disclosure of Interests' statements are also new, both in so far as they go beyond what agents are obliged to disclose to Names directly under the general law of agency, and also require *public* disclosure of these matters, and because they remind those agents who have previously overlooked these obligations of the need for full accountability to their principals. The biggest change has probably been the change in climate – openness and disclosure are now the order of the day as against exclusiveness and secrecy.

The other important aspect of the new reporting requirements is that they impose a uniform minimum standard on all syndicates. However one side-effect of this appears to have been that a tendency has already emerged for syndicate reports to adopt a uniformity of treatment and presentation that is limited to the requirements of the byelaws. Subsequent chapters comment on ways in which some useful varieties of presentation or additional disclosures that syndicates have previously provided – and which could still be provided while complying with the byelaws – have largely disappeared.

When the transitional reporting provisions have fully worked through (i.e. by the accounts to December 1985, when the 1983 underwriting account 'closes') the essentials of the reporting requirements, as set out in SAB, will be that the Lloyd's central file will have available for public inspection, for a typical syndicate:

1. an underwriter's report
2. a managing agent's report
3. an annual report comprising:
   (a) underwriting accounts for three years (one 'closed' and two 'open')
   (b) balance sheet
   (c) notes to the accounts
   (d) disclosure of material interests
   (e) 'seven year summary' of past closed years' results
4. auditor's report on the annual report which will give the auditor's opinion on whether or not the accounts give a true and fair view of the result of the closed year, and otherwise comply with the Lloyd's syndicate accounting rules (as set out principally in SAB). This will cover the fair presentation of the information in 3(d) (Disclosure of Interests), as required by Byelaw 3 of 1984, and the consistency of the information in 1 and 2 with that in 3.

The transitional stages have been:

– For the 1984 reports (i.e. the reports filed in 1985 which are the subject matter of this survey) the requirement for a true and fair view was not obligatory.
– For the 1983 reports (the first to be made public): 1 and 2 were not required to be filed, although they had to be prepared for Names and were recommended as 'voluntary' information to be included in the central file; 3 did not have to include 3(d) and 3(e) above. However the filing of a separate Disclosure of Interests statement by each agent (or a 'nil' return) was required by the Disclosure of Interests Byelaw (No. 3 of 1984), although it did not have to be audited. The seven year summary was a recommended attachment to the accounts (but did not have to be audited).

The *minimum* required filing that year for a typical syndicate was therefore:

3. an annual report comprising:
   (a) underwriting accounts ('closed' for 1981, and 'open' for 1982 and 1983)
   (b) balance sheet at 31 December 1983
   (c) notes to the accounts
4. audit report on 3

5. (=3d) Disclosure of Interests statement (unaudited).

For these 1983 reports no particular formats or accounting policies were specified, but PAM's recommendations were available.

The detailed chapters of this survey comment inter alia on the accounting methods adopted by syndicates in their 1984 accounts, and some of the consequences of the transition from the recommendations that related to the 1983 accounts to the final requirements that are now in force, and under which the 1984 accounts were prepared.

OBJECTIVES OF FINANCIAL REPORTING

The primary objective of the new requirements for fuller disclosure is to ensure proper accountability to Names of the honest stewardship of their agents. To this is linked the requirement for disclosure of interests. As with company accounts, two further major purposes of preparing accounts are, first, to show how the results are to be divided between participants, and second to report on progress and performance in order to aid decisions on future investment plans.

With regard to the division of results, the preparation of syndicate accounts has an even more important role than in the case of a company. While company accounts provide the basis on which the legal dividend rules impose ceilings on distributions, the syndicate accounts determine the precise amount of the division between Names. Moreover, there is no alternative mechanism for sharing the results equitably. In a listed company, if the dividend distribution is too cautious or profits are ploughed back, investors may get their returns in share price appreciation. If a Name leaves a syndicate at the end of an underwriting year, the cheque he receives when the account closes is his final settlement. It is important that the basis of division should be as clear and fair as possible.

In company accounting there often appears in practice to be a conflict between the objective of using the accounts as a basis for determining the amounts divisible under dividend rules or other legal contracts (where 'prudence' is at a premium) and the objective of measuring performance (which requires an often highly subjective view of likely future outcomes) (e.g. Edey, 1978). In Lloyd's syndicate accounting the attempt has to be made to bring the two objectives closer together. Three factors which help are, first, the three year accounting system which allows more time for the true situation to emerge; second, the valuation of assets at current values, which provides a proper basis for 'handing over' the business from one year's Names to their successors; and third, the estimation of the necessary 'reinsurance to close' (which closes the account after its third year and provides for outstanding liabilities), which is essentially a forward looking, subjective, expert judgement of likely future outcomes and reflects as much knowledge as is available about how the business is progressing and is likely to progress. The price that has to be paid to obtain this more realistic appraisal is the delay of two years before a view is taken and the underwriting account is closed: whereas with companies a view is normally taken on their position as at the end of the latest accounting year.

Appraising performance is, however, not just a matter of measuring individual results – it normally requires comparisons both over time and between similar business entities. While the new filing requirements ensure that Names are receiving information about their own syndicates' current and past performance, they also ensure that the details of other syndicates' results are available for comparison. Some comparisons have previously been possible. For example, the Association of Lloyd's Members (ALM), a voluntary association of Names, has been publishing annual 'league tables' of syndicate results, based on the accounts its members have received. Now the underlying information about all syndicates is available, not only for league tables (e.g. Rew & Sturge, 1985), but for anyone to obtain from the central file, for a fee of £5 for a copy of each syndicate's file.

In regard to the needs of other users, the new requirements probably add little to the protection of creditors and policyholders, who are covered by the existing arrangements for the 'solvency audit' (see Chapter 2) and by the other aspects of Lloyd's rules which provide the necessary assurance that Names have adequate means to meet all their insurance liabilities. The general availability of all syndicate accounts will, however, provide some additional information to competitors both inside and outside the Lloyd's market, and the process of agreeing the new rules has illustrated the conflicts, and the need to strike a balance, between disclosure and commercial confidentiality, for example in regard to the level of detail expected in underwriters' reports (see Chapter 16).

It is not possible for me to comment on how far the syndicate accounts may be of direct relevance to the interests of employees of managing agents or of the other organisations associated with the Lloyd's market; but both they and the public at large have an important 'indirect' interest in the disclosure of syndicate results. The new accounting requirements are one part of a package of reforms being instituted at Lloyd's in order to protect its reputation as one of the world's leading insurance markets. Lloyd's is a major contributor to Britain's invisible earnings and there is surely a high degree of 'public interest' in seeing that its self-regulation is effective. Apart from any direct interest in the individual results of syndicates, the availability of their accounts, together with the related disclosures, is an important means for letting the public see how that self-regulation is operating.

CHAPTER 2

THE CONTEXT OF SYNDICATE ACCOUNTING

In assessing the significance of the requirements for publication of syndicate accounts it is necessary to be aware of the other purposes for which accounting information is prepared at Lloyd's for 'external' users, based essentially on the same underlying information as the syndicate accounts. These are:

1. Names' personal accounts
2. the preparation of Lloyd's Statutory Statements of Business and 'Global' Accounts
3. the 'solvency audit'.

I. NAMES' PERSONAL ACCOUNTS

The syndicate accounts that are now filed for public inspection normally give aggregate results for the syndicate as a whole (or for identifiable subgroups of Names) arrived at after charging syndicate expenses. In addition the managing agent will prepare for each Name a personal account showing his individual share of the result of the syndicate and deducting his personal expenses (such as profit commission, agent's salary, Lloyd's subscriptions and contributions to the Central Fund), to calculate his net balance. The Name's member's agent will combine the information from these personal accounts to determine how his results from each syndicate are to be dealt with (e.g. paid to him; used to cover closed year deficiencies on his other syndicates; added to his reserves). These personal accounts are private and are not filed in the central file.

2. LLOYD'S STATUTORY STATEMENTS OF BUSINESS AND GLOBAL ACCOUNTS

The information relating to each syndicate's underwriting and other income and expenses is aggregated to produce the statutory returns (analysed by class of business) of the insurance business transacted at Lloyd's, which have to be made to the DTI (although these statements themselves are not audited). Lloyd's has adopted the practice of also making these returns available in a 'glossy' format analogous to that of a listed company's annual report. This is done not only to provide a more readable overall view of Lloyd's business and the security behind its policies for the benefit of, for example, overseas insurers who reinsure at Lloyd's, but also so as to be able to take advantage of the public relations opportunities that ordinary companies readily appreciate are provided by this medium.

The latest report is available under the title 'Lloyd's Global Accounts 1984' and presents the aggregate accounts for each class of business in a more readable form than the basic statutory returns, with clear explanations and accompanied by commentaries from the Chairman of Lloyd's and the respective Chairmen of the various underwriters' associations.

The aggregate figures for all classes of business combined, with the notes thereto, are reproduced here as Appendix V. Essentially these are the totals of the figures appearing in the 1984 syndicate underwriting accounts covered by this survey. In recent years (starting with the 1982 'Globals') more detail has been provided than in the past of individual classes of business, as well as the amount of the reinsurance to close, so that the breakdown of the figures now corresponds fairly closely to what appears in individual syndicates' accounts. However, premiums are still shown net. Although an analysis between gross and net became mandatory for syndicates' own 1984 accounts (and was in fact already provided by all syndicates in their 1983 accounts) aggregating these figures in the Globals would be of little use unless 'consolidation adjustments' could be made to eliminate reinsurance within Lloyd's, which would otherwise be included in both figures.

The 'Global Accounts' also contain a statement explaining the security behind Lloyd's policies (which is reproduced here as Appendix VI). This treats the aggregate of the balances on the open years (including the reinsurance to close received from the 1982 account) as comparable to the 'technical reserves' (i.e. outstanding liabilities) of insurance companies. However, since this item in the statement is merely the aggregate of the open years' balances in the individual syndicate accounts, which do not include any provision for possible losses on the open years' underwriting, it does not appear to be the most relevant figure for this comparison. A more relevant figure would be the 'provision for estimated future liabilities' as used in Form 9 of the statutory returns to the DTI (see Appendix VII), which is arrived at from the results of the 'solvency audits', including allowance for any open year deficiencies as calculated on the approved basis (as explained below).

3.   THE 'SOLVENCY AUDIT'

Each year it is necessary for the DTI to be satisfied that each Name at Lloyd's will be able to meet his insurance liabilities, for which he is severally liable with unlimited liability. Each Name may participate in several syndicates (as arranged by his 'member's agent'). The assessment of insurance liabilities in regard to each syndicate is examined by the syndicate auditor. This work requires an assessment of whether there is any deficiency in the accumulated balances of premiums less claims etc. on the 'open' years to cover the likely development of their liabilities, which in turn requires an assessment of the adequacy of the 'reinsurance to close' that has been estimated as needed to cover the outstanding liabilities of the 'closed' account, and which has (normally) been transferred to the succeeding 'open' year of account of the same syndicate. To assist syndicate auditors in making these assessments, they are provided with the *Instructions for the Guidance of Lloyd's Auditors* (which are approved each year by the DTI) and which lay down minimum acceptable calculations of future liabilities (see also Chapter 6). If the closed year shows a loss, or there are deficiencies on the open years, then the Names will have a liability in respect of that syndicate.

The individual Name's liabilities, if any, in regard to each of his syndicates are combined (according to certain rules of set-off) and compared with his assets at Lloyd's. These comprise his 'Lloyd's deposit' (i.e. the amount he must deposit with Lloyd's as a precondition for underwriting, equal to 25% of his premium limit) together with any 'personal reserves' and 'Special Reserve Funds' that he may have built up (i.e. reserves that comprise the specified trust funds that are set up for Names either on the recommendation or requirement of their agents, or to take advantage of certain Inland Revenue concessions). The auditors obtain confirmation of these funds and if, after 'earmarking' as much of them as Lloyd's rules allow, the Name still has a net deficiency he must deposit additional sums. The auditors will then confirm to Lloyd's that all the Names for which they have conducted the audit are able to meet their liabilities.

Thus, in addition to the information that will appear in the syndicate accounts, an assessment of any deficiency on the open years and a calculation of Names' assets at Lloyd's also enter into the annual 'solvency audit'. This information, aggregated over all Names, and with the addition of Lloyd's own funds, appears in the statutory returns to the DTI in 'Form 9' (reproduced here as Appendix VII), although this aggregate statement is not itself audited.

Not only do Names have to deposit certain sums, and (voluntarily or by agreement) build up reserves at Lloyd's, they are also required to have a certain overall level of wealth in approved forms (their 'means'), which has to be certified on admission, and also whenever their premium capacity is increased, or periodically at the request of the Council. This information also appears in 'Form 9' in order to assess the total wealth available to provide the 'solvency margin' necessary to support the level of business being written at Lloyd's. (An explanation of the significance of these items is also given in Appendix VI.) This means that a large proportion of what, in a company, would be the 'free reserves and equity capital' is, in the case of a Lloyd's syndicate, held outside the funds that are included in its balance sheet. According to the Global Accounts and 'Form 9' only 63% of the total assets shown as available at 31 December 1984 to meet Names' liabilities were held in the syndicate accounts.

It is therefore important, in interpreting Lloyd's syndicate accounts, to be clear just what items they do and do not include, as compared with a company's accounts. Some of the 1983 reports included statements such as the following in the notes to the accounts:

NAMES' RESERVES:

Particulars of Reserve Funds are supplied to Names individually and are not included in the Syndicate Balance Sheet, but nevertheless form an integral part of the Names' underwriting interests.

While such explanations may have been primarily for the benefit of Names, they would also be helpful to other readers of the accounts. Unfortunately (as they are not required by SAB) they appear to have fallen victim to a tendency to uniformity and have not reappeared in the 1984 accounts (see also Chapter 8).

CHAPTER 3

THE ACCOUNTING ENTITY AND FORMATS OF ACCOUNTS

INTRODUCTION AND REQUIREMENTS

SAB specifies that, in relation to each syndicate, its managing agent must prepare for each 'Name' an annual report (including the underwriting accounts, balance sheet, notes and 'seven year summary' as well as the prescribed disclosures of interests). Thus the accounts may be filed separately in respect of each underwriting member or may show the combined figures for all or some of the syndicate's members.

If the investment portfolios of any subgroups of members are separately administered, the underwriting accounts must show how their separate administration has been conducted (although a combined balance sheet for the syndicate as a whole may still be prepared). A common example is where funds are managed separately for US resident Names. There are also special provisions to fix the responsibility where funds are administered by different ('quasi') managing agents, to ensure that an annual report is prepared.

These arrangements recognise that the legal entity is the individual underwriting member (who is severally liable for his underwriting commitments) and that the 'syndicate' is a creation of underwriting and administrative convenience. Normally it also makes a convenient accounting unit because all the individual Names share in the insurance underwriting in agreed proportions, although investments and expenses may be attributable on different bases to different subgroups, or have to be allocated from the management of several syndicates.

It is for this reason that, where two or more syndicates have the same members with the same participations (including 'incidental' and 'mirror' syndicates), Schedule 1 para.3(c) of SAB allows them to be grouped together in the set of accounts: although where the class of business is substantially different, or they have different underwriters, it may be more appropriate to give separate results.

No other 'consolidation' of syndicates is now allowed – so that where the funds of several syndicates are managed on a group basis a separate balance sheet is also now required for each syndicate (if necessary by allocating the funds). This rule was not spelt out for the 1983 annual accounts and in some cases, although separate underwriting accounts were given for each syndicate, their balance sheet for that year was combined with that of one or more other syndicates.

Another practical fiction is, of course, that the syndicate is a continuing entity. In fact each syndicate lasts for only one year. In the following year the Names on a syndicate may differ and/or their participations may change. Nevertheless, for accounting and administrative purposes the individual syndicates (identified by a number) are usually treated as an entity and accounts are prepared on that basis.

Syndicates may have 'multiple' numbers. This is usually because, say, a marine syndicate writes certain categories of business under different numbers, for administrative convenience, or also writes 'incidental' non-marine business under another number (the constitution of the incidental syndicate being identical to that of the main syndicate). In other cases they may reflect 'historical accidents', e.g. where syndicates which used to be independent have been merged or a new syndicate has taken the place of a previous syndicate after some reorganisation. While these additional and 'old' numbers may appear in the syndicate's title, the listing in this survey confines itself to the single leading number by which the syndicate may be identified (see Appendix I for a full listing).

As regards the format of the syndicate accounts, SAB has imposed a standard format, in a similar manner to the way in which the Companies Act 1985 requires a standard format for company accounts (although insurance companies are at present exempt pending a proposed directive from the EEC). As with the CA1985 formats there is flexibility in that certain detailed items may be relegated to the notes. An example of a syndicate using the maximum flexibility available under the format layout for (a) the balance sheet and (b) the underwriting accounts is given in Example 3 below. Some variations are required where the underwriter has decided not to close an account but to 'run it off' for a further period until a result can be determined (see Chapter 6). Comparative figures are required.

PAM had proposed a slightly different format, and although at the time the 1983 accounts were filed there was no mandatory requirement to follow this, in practice most syndicates did.

The major differences from PAM's recommendations that are now required, starting with the 1984 accounts are:

1. In the underwriting accounts:
   (a) The account begins by showing the syndicate allocated capacity.
   (b) An analysis of the reinsurance to close is required to show the proportion due from/to whole account quota share reinsurers.
   (c) The balance of premiums less claims (including reinsurance to close) is described as 'underwriting result/balance' rather than 'technical result/balance'.

    (d) The final balance, after investment income, expenses etc., is described
         as 'profit/loss/open year of account balance' rather than 'underwriting
         result/balance' or 'net result/balance'.
2. In the balance sheet, the balance due to/from Names in respect of the
    closed year is deducted/added before arriving at 'total assets less
    liabilities', so that the net assets represent the funds accumulated to date
    in respect of the open years.

It is particularly important that the syndicate allocated capacity be stated
both because of the Lloyd's rules relating to the amount of premiums that
Names may write, given the size of their Lloyd's deposits and other means
(see also Appendix VI), and because it is the key to explaining individual
Names' share of the result (see also Chapter 12). Example 6 below gives an
explanation of its significance.

ANALYSIS

Composition of Accounts

Generally, one set of accounts was filed in 1985 and 1984 for each syndicate
by its managing agent or one of its joint managing agents (with any mirror or
incidental syndicates' figures combined with those of the main syndicate).
The variations were:

(a) Where 'quasi' managing agents had administered the funds of subgroups
     of Names on the syndicate a set of accounts would usually be filed for
     each subgroup, normally (but not always) explaining what proportion of
     the total syndicate figures were included (see Example 1). (This resulted
     in eleven additional 1984 reports (1983: thirteen) for the purpose of this
     survey.)

(b) In the case of three syndicates (1983: four), separate 1984 accounts were
     filed for subgroups of Names participating in the syndicate through
     different members' agents (see again Example 1). (For the purpose of the
     analysis in this survey, these syndicates have been treated as if only one
     report had been filed.)

(c) In the case of ten syndicates (1983: eleven) separate 1984 accounts were
     filed for their US and 'other' subgroups of Names (see Example 5). (More
     normally, however, the insurance underwriting figures were given for the
     whole syndicate and the account was then split to show the different
     investment income, expenses etc. accruing to the two groups of Names
     (see Examples 2 and 4).) (For the purpose of the analysis in this survey
     these syndicates have been treated as if only one report had been filed.)

(d) In the case of three syndicates (1983: four) separate 1984 reports (or
     separate figures within the report) were provided for their mirror or
     incidental syndicates (and these additional reports have been analysed in
     this survey).

(e) In eight cases, involving 22 syndicates, combined 1983 reports giving, for example, one balance sheet for a group of syndicates under common management had been filed. This was not permitted for the 1984 (or subsequent) accounts. In a number of other cases in both years, while the individual syndicates' accounts were given, they were bound together in one set, e.g. with one set of notes and one audit report. (Except where stated, these cases have been analysed as if there was a separate report for each syndicate.)

As a result of these variations the analysis in this survey covers the 1984 reports relating to 446 syndicates (1983: 455) – including the three (1983: four) in (d) – and, with the addition of the eleven (1983: thirteen) reports in (a) covers a total of 457 (1983: 468) annual reports (see Appendix I).

Formats

A   Underwriting Accounts

While the 1984 accounts were almost wholly standardised in following SAB's prescribed formats, in the previous year (before they became mandatory) there was still considerable variation of layout. A major change from widespread previous practice has been that premiums and claims are now analysed into 'gross' and 'net'– i.e. the reinsurance element is shown separately. Even in their 1983 accounts no syndicate continued to give just the net figures (although it was not mandatory to follow PAM), but a number presented the net figures on the face of the account and the analysis in notes (which was no longer permitted for the 1984 accounts). On the face of the underwriting account it was fairly common in the 1983 accounts for the order of investment income, profit or loss on exchange, and syndicate expenses to be varied from that in the format, and in a few cases profit or loss on exchange would be shown before stating the subtotal for underwriting result/balance (or what was 'technical result/balance' in the recommended format for the 1983 accounts).

There were some exceptions in 1984: Example 2 is a case where the auditors agreed with the variation, and Example 5 where they did not (in respect of the open year account). It is, of course, perfectly compatible with SAB to add information about percentages of account items to the prescribed layout (as with the closed year in Example 5) and it would be useful if more reports did so.

With regard to the information required in the 1984 accounts that differed from PAM's recommendations for 1983 (see pages (13) to (14) above):

• (a) All syndicates gave the information about syndicate allocated capacity, as required, in their 1984 accounts, whereas only about a quarter of the 1983 reports had included it in the accounts or notes. Some syndicates also gave explanations of its significance (see Example 6).

- (b)   Few syndicates gave an analysis of the reinsurance to close to show the amount relating to whole account quota share reinsurance in either year. Of the random sample of 100 reports, 9% in 1984 and 5% in 1983 gave this information. While this may indicate that few such arrangements are in force only 3% of the sampled reports (1983: 1%) specifically stated that there was no such quota share reinsurance. See Example 3 to Chapter 6.
- (c) and (d)   It was already common in the 1983 accounts to use the term 'underwriting result/balance' in the manner now required for the 1984 accounts (as illustrated in Example 3) (rather than using 'technical result/ balance').

Other information sometimes given in underwriting accounts included an analysis of the manner in which the final result had been stated on Names' personal accounts.

B   Balance Sheet

The major change in presentation between the 1984 and 1983 accounts was in regard to the balance sheet layout. Less than 10% of the 1983 accounts had adopted the balance sheet layout that is now required (and illustrated in Example 3): most had kept to the more traditional presentation whereby the 1981 closed year result appeared in the same section as the open year balances.

SAB requires that accounts payable and receivable be analysed into amounts due in over and under one year from the balance sheet date. Compliance here was patchy. In the 1983 accounts it was already normal to give some analysis of creditors into those due within and after more than one year, but rare to split debtors in this way. In the sample of 1984 accounts, nearly all analysed creditors into 'under' and 'over' one year (although a quarter only analysed some elements of creditors) but less than half analysed debtors in this way (see also Example 4 and Chapter 8).

Presentation of Premiums and Claims

The effects of the requirements in SAB have been discussed above. A number of syndicates gave further analysis (often in the notes, although sometimes on the face of the account). As the figures for premiums and claims shown in the underwriting accounts are cumulative to date it is possible to show, e.g. in the case of the closed year 1982, the receipts and payments in respect of premiums and claims made:

(a)   in the first year (1982)
(b)   in the second year (1983)
(c)   in the third year (1984)

In the case of (c) (the 1984 premiums) it is further possible to show:

(i)   how much has been received or paid in 1984 in respect of the 1982 year itself ('pure');

(ii) how much has been accrued in 1984 in respect of the 1982 year itself ('pure');

(iii) how much has been received or paid in 1984 in respect of the 1981 and previous years reinsured into the 1982 underwriting account at 31 December 1983.

Further discussion of 'pure year accounting' is given in Chapter 11. With regard to calendar years, a number of syndicate reports for 1984 and 1983 gave the breakdown of premiums and claims in each underwriting account by the calendar year in which they arose (see, e.g., Example 4). Further discussion of 'calendar year' accounting is given in Chapters 9 and 13.

Accounting records are often maintained in three main currencies: sterling, US dollars and Canadian dollars. The accounting policies for translating foreign currencies to sterling for the annual accounts are considered in Chapter 10, and most syndicates just gave the sterling figures (the underwriter's report may have analysed the proportions of premium income arising in each currency). However, an example of how the underlying currency figures can be presented too is given in Example 4 below. Some reports gave the currency figures for other items, e.g. for investments (as in Example 4), bank balances or 'net assets'.

EXAMPLES

■   Example 1 explains how separate accounts have been prepared by a quasi-managing agent and for subgroups of Names participating through different members' agencies. (See also A.R. Mountain 800 in Chapter 5, Example 1.)

■   Example 2 explains how business is allocated between two syndicates and analyses the result by subgroups of Names. It departs from SAB's format.

■   Example 3 illustrates the format of accounts required by SAB, making the maximum use of notes for the detail (notes not reproduced here).

■   Example 4 gives analyses by subgroups of Names and by currencies and calendar year of underwriting ('closed' year account only reproduced here). It also gives a full analysis of debtors and creditors by maturity, and a currency breakdown by investment holdings.

■   Example 5 provides separate sets of accounts for US and other Names (extracts from only the latter being reproduced here) and adopts a presentation which includes percentages on the face of the underwriting account (compare Edwards and Payne, 304; Stenhouse Harman, 809). It departs from SAB's format in respect of the open years (1984 account not reproduced here). Managing agent: J.H.Minet Agenices Ltd.

■   Example 6 gives an explanation of syndicate allocated capacity.

Example I

E.R.H. HILL AND OTHERS
AVIATION SYNDICATE 800

NOTES TO THE ACCOUNTS 31st DECEMBER 1984 (continued)

9. GROUP ACCOUNTS

The underwriting of the syndicate is managed by E.R.H.Hill (Agencies) Ltd. Separate accounts are prepared for certain members' agents to show the participation of their Names in the syndicate. One agent also manages the sterling and United States dollars Premium Trust Funds arising from their Names' participation in this syndicate. The amounts shown as pertaining to other sections of the Group are the aggregate interests in the Group assets shown on the balance sheet of the Names underwriting through those agencies.

The figures shown in the Underwriting Accounts represent the following proportions of the Group figures:

$$1982 \ldots 89.587426\%$$
$$1983 \ldots 89.477212\%$$
$$1984 \ldots 92.022525\%$$

Example 2
Murray Lawrence & Partners

C. T. BOWRING (UNDERWRITING AGENCIES) LIMITED
T.A. BOWRING & OTHERS
MARINE SYNDICATE No. 28
Notes to the accounts – 31st December 1984

1. Basis of presentation

The accounts have been prepared in accordance with the Lloyd's Syndicate Accounting Rules, except that in two instances in each underwriting account there have been departures (without any effect on the figures concerned) from the order of presentation prescribed by the Rules. The Managing Agents consider, and the auditors agree, that the presentation adopted is more suitable to the requirements of the syndicate.

2. Principal accounting policies

The following accounting policies have been applied consistently in dealing with items which are considered material in relation to the syndicate accounts:

(a) Sharing of business

Under an agreement dated 25th June 1979, between C. T. Bowring (Underwriting Agencies) Limited and Birrell Smith Underwriting Agencies Limited, Syndicates 28 and 363 share between them all business written by the Underwriter in proportion to their respective premium income capacities. This agreement also provides that, on closing each year's Underwriting Account, each syndicate will reinsure its unsettled liabilities with the next Account of both syndicates in proportion to their respective premium income capacities for the Account assuming the reinsurance. In consequence, Syndicate 28 is due to pay £187,165 (1983: £30,782) to Syndicate 363 on closing the 1982 Account.

...

Murray Lawrence & Partners

C. T. BOWRING (UNDERWRITING AGENCIES) LIMITED

T.A. BOWRING & OTHERS

MARINE SYNDICATE No. 28

Underwriting account to 31st December 1984

1982 account as closed at end of third year

	Note	1982 Account after 3 years £	1981 Account after 3 years £
Syndicate allocated capacity		**5,105,000**	**5,030,000**
Gross premiums, less returns		5,795,606	5,871,018
Premiums in respect of reinsurance ceded		2,159,254	1,731,129
Net premiums		3,636,352	4,139,889
Net premium receivable for reinsurance to close the preceding year of account	3	2,779,797	2,344,507
		6,416,149	6,484,396
Gross claims, less refunds		5,852,990	5,366,764
Reinsurance recoveries		2,118,863	1,360,790
Net claims		3,734,127	4,005,974
Net premium payable for reinsurance to close the year of account	3	2,464,296	2,462,606
		6,198,423	6,468,580
Underwriting result		**217,726**	**15,816**
Profit/(loss) on exchange		21,387	32,368
		239,113	48,184
Syndicate expenses	5	258,230	262,928
Underwriting result, after exchange adjustments and syndicate expenses		(19,117)	(214,744)

	Note	General group £	U.S. group £	General group £	U.S. group £
Allocated capacity		**4,980,000**	**125,000**	**4,930,000**	**100,000**
Share of underwriting result		(18,649)	(468)	(210,437)	(4,307)
Investment income	4	87,053	1,822	86,154	1,544
Investment appreciation	4	189,606	4,141	191,047	4,065
Closed year of account profit/(loss), before personal expenses		**258,010**	**5,495**	**66,764**	**1,302**
Aggregate personal expenses	6	126,652	2,966	90,060	1,859
Closed year of account profit/(loss), after personal expenses		**131,358**	**2,529**	**(23,296)**	**(557)**

The notes on pages 13 to 19 form part of these accounts.

Example 3

J. E. STREET AND OTHERS
MARINE SYNDICATE No. 123/132

BALANCE SHEET AT 31st DECEMBER, 1984

	Notes	1984 £	1983 £
DEBTORS	7	2,551,728	1,191,980
INVESTMENTS	8	12,855,482	10,263,834
BALANCES AT BANKS		1,541,777	1,245,165
TOTAL ASSETS		16,948,987	12,700,979
CREDITORS	9	1,035,971	779,781
PROFIT FOR 1982 CLOSED ACCOUNT	10	1,072,548	358,590
TOTAL ASSETS LESS LIABILITIES		£14,840,468	£11,562,608

Represented by:
OPEN YEAR OF ACCOUNT BALANCES

	Notes	1984	1983
1983 Account	11	11,891,799	9,711,702
1984 Account	12	2,948,669	1,850,906
		£14,840,468	£11,562,608

This Annual Report was approved on 10th June, 1985.

D. A. POLLOCK   Active Underwriter

R. J. KILN   Director
                  Street (Underwriting Agencies) Ltd.

...

J. E. STREET AND OTHERS
MARINE SYNDICATE No. 123/132

1982 UNDERWRITING ACCOUNT CLOSED AT 31st DECEMBER, 1984

	Notes	1982 Account after 3 years £	1981 Account after 3 years £
Syndicate allocated capacity		9,053,542	8,660,000
Gross premiums		9,741,870	9,218,972
Premiums in respect of reinsurances ceded		3,030,316	2,207,970
Net premiums		6,711,554	7,011,002
Premium receivable for the reinsurance to close the 1981 (1980) account		8,783,957	6,982,681
		15,495,511	13,993,683
Gross claims		8,363,213	8,356,098
Reinsurance recoveries		2,311,428	1,886,996
Net claims		6,051,785	6,469,102
Premium payable for the reinsurance to close the year of account	3	8,631,527	7,541,847
		14,683,312	14,010,949
Underwriting result		812,199	(17,266)
Net investment income	4	300,700	278,340
Net investment appreciation	5	690,333	583,471
Profit on exchange		14,601	71,595
Syndicate expenses	6	(319,362)	(257,660)
Closed year of account profit		£1,498,471	£658,480

...

J. E. STREET AND OTHERS
MARINE SYNDICATE No. 123/132

1983 UNDERWRITING ACCOUNT AT 31st DECEMBER, 1984

	Notes	1983 Account after 2 years £	1982 Account after 2 years £
Syndicate allocated capacity		9,521,863	9,053,542
Gross premiums		9,521,964	7,756,312
Premiums in respect of reinsurances ceded		2,540,618	2,367,650
Net premiums		6,981,346	5,388,662
Premium receivable for the reinsurance to close the 1982 (1981) account	3	8,631,527	7,541,847
		15,612,873	12,930,509
Gross claims		4,638,549	3,939,450
Reinsurance recoveries		1,161,505	979,038
Net claims		3,477,044	2,960,412
Underwriting balance		12,135,829	9,970,097
Net investment income	4	79,992	77,735
Net investment appreciation	5	186,123	147,368
Profit on exchange		19,971	5,198
Syndicate expenses	6	(332,637)	(318,403)
Open year of account balance		£12,089,278	£9,881,995

...

J. E. STREET AND OTHERS
MARINE SYNDICATE No. 123/132

1984 UNDERWRITING ACCOUNT AT 31st DECEMBER, 1984

	Notes	1984 Account after 1 year £	1983 Account after 1 year £
Syndicate allocated capacity		10,502,367	9,521,863
Gross premiums		6,563,573	4,997,878
Premiums in respect of reinsurances ceded		1,707,066	1,566,552
Net premiums		4,856,507	3,431,326
Gross claims		1,494,576	1,591,380
Reinsurance recoveries		84,512	468,133
Net claims		1,410,064	1,123,247
Underwriting balance		3,446,443	2,308,079
Net investment income	4	17,860	14,100
Net investment appreciation	5	44,333	23,390
Syndicate expenses	6	(329,842)	(308,707)
Open year of account balance		£3,178,794	£2,036,862

Example 4

MERRETT MARINE SYNDICATE 418/422

Closed underwriting account 1982
at 31st December 1984

	Note	£	1982 account £	£	1981 account £
Syndicate allocated capacity			72,706,500		75,334,500
Gross premiums		78,331,662		64,719,393	
Premiums in respect of reinsurance ceded		(40,790,863)		(31,181,927)	
Net premiums	3	37,540,799		33,537,466	
Premium for the reinsurance to close the 1981 account	4	55,561,967		45,434,244	
			93,102,766		78,971,710
Gross claims		(74,088,203)		(65,976,170)	
Reinsurance recoveries		39,879,591		36,958,112	
Net claims	5	(34,208,612)		(29,018,058)	
Premium for the reinsurance to close the 1982 account		(70,706,916)		(46,352,432)	
			(104,915,528)		(75,370,490)
Underwriting result	6		(11,812,762)		3,601,220
Net investment income	6	1,804,466		1,937,228	
Net investment appreciation	6	4,654,747		4,078,505	
Profit on exchange		477,878		1,340,685	
			6,937,091		7,356,418
			(4,875,671)		10,957,638
Syndicate expenses	9		(1,499,259)		(1,400,931)
Closed year of account loss (1981-profit) .			(6,374,930)		9,556,707

...

MERRETT MARINE SYNDICATE 418 422

Notes to the annual report
continued

3   Net premiums

1982 Underwriting account at close of account
(including premiums relating to prior closed years)

	£	US$	Can$	Total 1982 account £	Total 1981 account £
Gross premiums	17,303,550	68,822,046	2,599,106	78,331,662	64,719,393
Reinsurance premiums	(9,437,895)	(35,610,409)	(1,001,140)	(40,790,863)	(31,181,927)
Net premiums	7,865,655	33,211,637	1,597,966	37,540,799	33,537,466
First year	3,205,103	27,424,595	1,937,266	28,113,182	23,738,064
Second year	3,489,962	5,894,997	(361,218)	8,335,767	8,459,572
Third year and prior	1,170,590	(107,955)	21,918	1,091,850	1,339,830

1983 Underwriting account at end of second year

	£	US$	Can$	Total 1983 account £	Total 1982 account £
Gross premiums	19,247,477	66,935,507	3,300,373	79,107,608	60,595,031
Reinsurance premiums	(10,393,213)	(33,387,039)	(1,103,887)	(39,896,639)	(30,050,191)
Net premiums	8,854,264	33,548,468	2,196,486	39,210,969	30,544,840
First year	4,267,922	28,082,920	2,611,565	30,184,242	23,188,929
Second year	4,586,342	5,465,548	(415,079)	9,026,727	7,355,911

1984 Underwriting account at end of first year

	£	US$	Can$	Total 1984 account £	Total 1983 account £
Gross premiums	13,815,569	63,467,934	2,513,491	70,172,110	51,099,246
Reinsurance premiums	(7,785,425)	(34,798,158)	(867,524)	(38,350,846)	(26,020,939)
Net premiums	6,030,144	28,669,776	1,645,967	31,821,264	25,078,307

4   Reinsurance premium received

The premium for the reinsurance to close the 1981 underwriting
account which was effected with the 1982 underwriting account at
31st December 1983 is restated in sterling in the 1982
underwriting account as follows:

	£
at rates of exchange ruling at 31st December 1984	55,561,967
at rates of exchange ruling at 31st December 1983	46,352,432
Exchange rate movement	9,209,535

...

MERRETT MARINE SYNDICATE 418/422

Notes to the annual report
continued

5   Net claims

1982 Underwriting account at close of account
(including claims relating to prior closed years)

	£	US$	Can$	Total 1982 account £	Total 1981 account £
Gross claims	13,272,924	69,895,052	858,213	74,088,203	65,976,170
Reinsurance recoveries	(5,863,931)	(39,087,415)	(489,005)	(39,879,591)	(36,958,112)
Net claims	7,408,993	30,807,637	369,208	34,208,612	29,018,058
First year	791,742	6,738,252	52,815	6,635,100	6,178,288
Second year	2,640,527	8,337,411	358,235	10,062,091	10,664,617
Third year and prior	3,976,724	15,731,974	(41,842)	17,511,421	12,175,153

1983 Underwriting account at end of second year

	£	US$	Can$	Total 1983 account £	Total 1982 account £
Gross claims	14,339,122	24,973,085	737,853	36,349,901	23,849,906
Reinsurance recoveries	(9,957,042)	(12,178,448)	(182,575)	(20,575,035)	(9,793,528)
Net claims	4,382,080	12,794,637	555,278	15,774,866	14,056,378
First year	1,677,503	4,816,431	161,919	5,935,428	5,467,992
Second year	2,704,577	7,978,206	393,359	9,839,438	8,588,386

1984 Underwriting account at end of first year

	£	US$	Can$	Total 1984 account £	Total 1983 account £
Gross claims	2,219,484	35,408,842	199,019	32,874,427	10,474,547
Reinsurance recoveries	(2,426,304)	(25,050,584)	(68,107)	(24,066,150)	(5,385,909)
Net claims	(206,820)	10,358,258	130,912	8,808,277	5,088,638

...

Notes to the annual report
continued

6   Allocation of closed underwriting account 1982

	1982 account			1981 account		
	US Names	Other Names	Total	US Names	Other Names	Total
Syndicate allocated capacity	£5,989,500	£66,717,000	£72,706,500	£6,088,500	£69,246,000	£75,334,500
Participation applicable	8.237915%	91.762085%	100%	8.081954%	91.918046%	100%
	£	£	£	£	£	£
Underwriting result	(973,125)	(10,839,637)	(11,812,762)	291,049	3,310,171	3,601,220
Untaxed investment income	14,651	163,199	177,850	23,150	263,291	286,441
Taxed (gross) investment income	154,715	2,169,023	2,323,738	161,245	2,197,023	2,358,268
Income tax on investment income	(46,415)	(650,707)	(697,122)	(48,374)	(659,107)	(707,481)
Net investment income	122,951	1,681,515	1,804,466	136,021	1,801,207	1,937,228
Investment appreciation	369,059	6,153,908	6,522,967	348,464	5,334,666	5,683,130
Capital gains tax on investment appreciation	(15,485)	(1,852,735)	(1,868,220)	(22,822)	(1,581,803)	(1,604,625)
Net investment appreciation	353,574	4,301,173	4,654,747	325,642	3,752,863	4,078,505
Profit on exchange	39,367	438,511	477,878	108,354	1,232,331	1,340,685
	(457,233)	(4,418,438)	(4,875,671)	861,066	10,096,572	10,957,638
Syndicate expenses	(123,508)	(1,375,751)	(1,499,259)	(113,222)	(1,287,709)	(1,400,931)
Closed year of account loss (1981-profit)	(580,741)	(5,794,189)	(6,374,930)	747,844	8,808,863	9,556,707

...

MERRETT MARINE SYNDICATE 418/422

Notes to the annual report
continued

10   Debtors

	1984 £	1983 £
Brokers' balances:		
Balance with Lloyd's central accounting	13,811,881	3,977,527
Other balances with brokers	189,734	(928,859)
Accruals	3,200,453	1,923,661
	17,202,068	4,972,329
Other debtors	865,360	231,264
	18,067,428	5,203,593

Debtors are realisable within 12 months, except for the following:

Balance with Lloyd's central accounting includes £37,088 *(1983—£10,578)* relating to deferred premiums which are not realisable within 12 months.

11   Investments

	£	US$	Can$	1984 total £	1983 total £
Fixed interest securities issued or guaranteed by governments and public authorities					
Realisable within one year	2,675,887	51,783,905	6,065,918	51,281,837	62,222,679
Realisable after more than one year	—	507,500	—	437,500	—
Variable interest securities issued or guaranteed by governments and public authorities					
Realisable after more than one year	930,000	—	—	930,000	—
Money market instruments					
Realisable within one year	—	37,381,603	—	32,225,520	19,337,931
Lloyd's Life Assurance Limited Ordinary Shares	921,725	—	—	921,725	761,425
	4,527,612	89,673,008	6,065,918	85,796,582	82,322,035

12   Creditors

	1984 £	1983 £
Amounts due to members' agents	14,255	1,695,917
Bank overdrafts	2,308,936	2,661,016
Other creditors and accruals	46,150	6,049
	2,369,341	4,362,982
Taxation provision (payable 1st January 1986)	2,543,844	2,231,923
Taxation provision (payable after 1986)	952,908	800,051
	5,866,093	7,394,956

Creditors are payable within 12 months, except where otherwise indicated

Example 5

G.J. BUTTS

MOTOR AND EMPLOYERS' LIABILITY SYNDICATES 887/641

Auditors' Report

1. We have audited the Annual Report set out on pages 4 and 7 to 15 and the Personal Accounts relating thereto in accordance with approved Auditing standards.

2. The Annual Report and the Personal Accounts have not been prepared to give all the information in the format required by the Lloyd's Syndicate Accounting rules. Details of these departures are set out in note 5 on page 13 of the Annual Report and in a note on page 9.

3. In our opinion:

    (a) the Annual Report has been drawn up on the basis of the Accounting policies set out in the notes on page 13 and this basis gives a true and fair view of the profit of the 1982 closed year of account

    (b) The Personal Accounts give a true and fair view of each Member's nett result

    (c) with the exception set out in paragraph 2 above, the Annual Report and Personal Accounts have been properly prepared in accordance with the Lloyd's Syndicate Accounting rules, and

    (d) the report complies with the requirements of the Disclosure of Interests Byelaw.

246 Bishopsgate
London EC2M 4PB

Neville Russell
Chartered Accountants
31st May, 1985.

...

G.J. Butts
Motor and Employers' Liability Syndicates 887/641

1982 Underwriting Account (as closed at end of third year)			1981 Account at 31 / 12 / 83	
	£	%	£	%
Syndicate allocated capacity Ex US Names	9,200,000		6,400,000	
US Names only	920,000		680,000	
	£10,120,000		£7,080,000	
Gross Premiums	4,077,941		5,350,822	
Premiums in respect of Reinsurance Ceded	333,207		499,074	
Nett Premiums	3,744,734		4,851,748	
Reinsurance Premium to close 1981 Account	3,636,366		3,381,868	
Difference on Revaluation	38,011		36,301	
	3,674,377		3,418,169	
	7,419,111		8,269,917	
Gross Claims	3,789,582		4,078,905	
Reinsurance Recoveries	243,290		298,934	
Nett Claims	3,546,292		3,779,971	
Reinsurance Premium paid to 1983 Account	3,125,921		3,636,366	
	6,672,213		7,416,337	
Underwriting Balance	746,898	19.94	853,580	17.59
Less: U.S. Names Share − 9.0909%	67,900		81,982	
	678,998	19.94	771,598	17.59
Gross Investment Income	136,726	4.02	185,774	4.23
Gross Investment Appreciation	418,513	12.29	619,939	14.14
Profit on Exchange	6,325	.19	6,000	.14
Syndicate Expenses (inc. Man. Fee)	(950,127)	(27.91)	(858,956)	(19.58)
	290,435	8.53	724,355	16.52
Deduct: Profit Commission 20%	Waived	—	144,871	3.31
	290,435	8.53	579,484	13.21
Deduct: Tax on Interest	42,547	1.25	55,679	1.27
U.S. Capital Gains Tax Reserve	120,918	3.55	174,202	3.97
Lloyd's Subscriptions	55,118	1.62	39,176	.89
Central Guarantee Fund	25,852	.76	23,707	.54
	244,435	7.18	292,764	6.67
Nett Profit	£46,000	1.35	£286,720	6.54

...

G.J. Butts
Motor and Employers' Liability Syndicates 887/641

1983 Underwriting Account (as closed at end of second year)	£	%	1982 Account at 31 / 12 / 83 £	%
Syndicate allocated capacity Ex US Names	10,275,000		9,200,000	
US Names only	975,000		920,000	
	£11,250,000		£10,120,000	
Gross Premiums	4,971,573		4,067,661	
Premiums in respect of Reinsurance Ceded	393,348		397,720	
Nett Premiums	4,578,225		3,669,941	
Gross Claims	3,086,809		2,352,251	
Reinsurance Recoveries	43,103		—	
Nett Claims	3,043,706		2,352,251	
Gross Underwriting Balance	1,534,519	33.52	1,317,690	35.90
Less: U.S. Names Share — 8.6667%	132,992		119,790	
	1,401,527	33.52	1,197,900	35.90
Gross Investment Income	59,917	1.43	63,903	1.92
Income Tax on Investment Income	(16,939)	(.41)	(19,676)	(.59)
Gross Investment Appreciation	143,065	3.42	249,254	7.47
Capital Gains Tax on Investment Appreciation	(42,761)	(1.02)	(70,244)	(2.10)
	1,544,809	36.94	1,421,137	42.60
Deduct: Syndicate Expenses (inc. Man. Fee)	1,121,049	26.81	1,012,897	30.37
	423,760	10.13	408,240	12.23
Reinsurance Premium from 1982 Account 91.3333% of £3,125,921	2,855,007		3,305,788	
Balance, 31st December, 1984	£3,278,767		£3,714,028	

Analysis of Syndicate Expenses

Staff Salaries, Bonuses etc.	482,481	460,939
Accountancy and Audit	66,771	66,488
Office Rent and Rates	85,696	93,029
Postage, Telephone, Stationery etc.	103,493	86,439
Lloyd's Association Fees	31,200	34,307
Underwriting Expenses	77,485	38,344
Sundry Expenses	48,069	43,174
Lloyd's Subscriptions	86,275	60,630
Central Guarantee Fund	19,456	28,437
	1,000,926	911,787
Management Fee	226,500	202,400
	£1,227,426	£1,114,187
Allocated: Ex US Names	1,121,049	1,012,897
US Names only	106,377	101,290
	£1,227,426	£1,114,187

...

G.J. Butts
Motor and Employers' Liability Syndicates 887/641

Notes to Balance Sheet and Underwriting Accounts

1   The Underwriting Accounts are prepared on the following bases which are, except as detailed in note 5 below, in accordance with the Syndicate Accounting Byelaw (No. 7 of 1984) and other generally accepted accounting practice at Lloyd's.

5   Schedule 4 of the Syndicate Accounting Byelaw (No. 7 of 1984) provides a standardised format for the presentation of the Underwriting Accounts: this format has been observed but for the following:

(a)   Schedule 4 of the Byelaw shows that 'Income tax on Investment Income' should be shown on the Underwriting Account immediately after 'Investment Income'. In the same respect 'Capital Gains tax on Investment Appreciation' should be stated immediately after 'Investment Appreciation'. In both instances the nett result should also be stated. Due to the terms of our Agency Agreement with the Names on the 1982 Syndicate Constitution whereby Profit Commission is calculated by reference to Gross Investment Income and Gross Appreciation it has been necessary to show 'Income tax on Investment Income' and 'Capital Gains tax on Investment Appreciation' after the deduction of Profit Commission.

(b)   With regard to the presentation of the 1983 Account, the Byelaw requires that the Reinsurance Premium from the 1982 Account be stated immediately after Nett Premiums. In order that the Accounts continue to provide meaningful percentage ratios for the purposes of useful comparison, the Reinsurance Premium continues to be shown as the final item of the Account.

In both the above instances the deviation from the prescribed format has been made, in the opinion of the Directors of the Managing Agents, in order to provide a more meaningful presentation of the Underwriting Accounts.

10   All percentages shown are percentages of the Nett Premiums of the year concerned.

Example 6

ALEXANDER SYNDICATE MANAGEMENT LIMITED

MARINE SYNDICATE 741/224 (127)
NOTES TO THE ACCOUNTS

(Continued)

15. SYNDICATE ALLOCATED CAPACITY

Syndicate allocated capacity represents the aggregation of each member's individual Premium Limit allocation to the syndicate; consequently, this figure is fixed in Sterling terms and cannot be adjusted to take account of the effect of exchange rate movements on premium income during the period for which an underwriting account remains open.

Applying the rates of exchange ruling at the commencement of each underwriting account, the gross and net premium income on the respective accounts, at 31 December 1984, is as stated below:—

Underwriting Account	1982 £'000's	1983 £'000's	1984 £'000's
Syndicate allocated capacity (gross)	£117,253	£64,129	£85,127
Gross premium income	£126,443	£52,345	£30,681
Syndicate allocated capacity	£ 90,195	£49,330	£65,482
Net premium income	£102,644	£42,147	£14,971

A 30% franchise is added to the Syndicate allocated capacity to establish the gross capacity. This franchise represents the allowance for reinsurance premiums ceded.

These notes are an integral part of the accounts.

CHAPTER 4

ACCOUNTING POLICIES AND NOTES TO THE ACCOUNTS: GENERAL

INTRODUCTION

Accounting at Lloyd's is a form of venture accounting. As a medieval merchant might keep an account for a voyage, and calculate the results to be shared by himself and his partners only when the ship returned (or was finally declared lost), so the tradition at Lloyd's (originally a marine market) has grown up of operating on a 'three year' accounting system. In the interim, the 'open' underwriting account is merely an 'on account' record of how the year's venture is developing and the items in the balance sheet represent merely the accumulating balances of assets and liabilities that have so far been recorded.

The preparation of a set of syndicate accounts therefore differs in a number of ways from that of other entities' accounts, and in particular, of an insurance company's accounts. If one refers to the 'fundamental accounting concepts' of SSAP2:

1. A syndicate is not a 'going concern' in the sense in which a company is a continuing legal entity. It is not a legal entity at all, although in practice, it is both administratively convenient to treat the syndicate as an entity, and the Names participating in one year will usually overlap extensively with those participating in later years. For accounting purposes, the practical impact of the 'going concern' concept as generally applied is that it requires long-term and other assets *not* to be valued on the basis of prompt liquidation or abandonment. This is not relevant to Lloyd's syndicates as the majority of assets are debts, investments and cash, valued at the amount receivable or current market value.
2. Consistency. This is of course applicable.
3. 'Accruals' and 'prudence'. The first of these describes how accountants attempt to bring into accounts the consequences of transactions and other

not anticipated, but all foreseeable losses are provided (and in SSAP2 it 'prevails' over the accruals concept).

In relation to Lloyd's syndicate accounting, these two concepts only apply in regard to the 'closed' year – at that stage a final settlement is made to the Names participating in the year. Because of the three year accounting, by the end of the three years most items which in a company's annual accounts would have to be accrued will have been received or paid. But some adjustments will still be necessary:

(a) to match properly premium returns, and reinsurance premiums and claims, with the premium income of the year, and

(b) to provide for remaining outstanding claims by the 'reinsurance to close'.

In relation to the open years no such accruals are generally made and consequently neither the 'accruals' nor the 'prudence' concept is applied – in particular because it would often be necessary to make a provision for outstanding claims where the balance accumulated so far on the underwriting account is insufficient. (The allowances that are made for *solvency* purposes are discussed in Chapters 2 and 6.)

It is these differences from normal company accounting principles which produce the situation that, while the audit report on the 1985 and subsequent accounts will have to refer to 'a true and fair view' (and many already do), it will only be in respect of the closed year result and its allocation to the personal accounts of Names, and not include the open year underwriting accounts or balance sheet.

SAB emphasises (in Schedule 3) that in the context of Lloyd's syndicate accounting the objective of *equity* between the Names in different years is also fundamental, particularly in regard to the 'reinsurance to close' which transfers liability from the Names on the syndicate in the closing year to those on the syndicate in a subsequent open year. It is not entirely clear how 'equity' is to be related to 'prudence' and 'accruals'. In SSAP2 (although not in SAB) prudence is said to prevail where there is a conflict with 'accruals': but in the case of a listed company the stock market can discount the prudence adopted in the accounts and reflect its anticipation of future profits in the share price. At Lloyd's, the syndicate's result for the closed year is a final settlement and 'equity' represents the need to avoid favouring one year's Names against another's. In practice the resolution of any conflicts between these principles will inevitably be a matter for professional judgement.

Another aspect of accounting practice peculiar to Lloyd's results from the use of the central policy signing and accounting office – the LPSO. It has become market practice that, although the underwriter's initialling of the broker's slip indicates acceptance of the risk, the business is allocated to the underwriting year according to when the signed policy is issued by LPSO. So if, for example, an underwriter accepted a risk in November 1982, and the policy was issued in 1983, the risk would be for the account of the

1983 syndicate participants. This practice has caused considerable argument among the auditors as some accountants take the view that, in this case, the account for the closed year 1982 cannot properly be said to be fully 'true and fair', since it does not include all risks accepted in that year. The CCAB and ICAEW have also urged Lloyd's to move as soon as is practicable towards accounting according to when the risk is assumed.

My own opinion would be that there is no question of principle here to which an accountant need object, provided the practice is clearly explained. It is the case that the syndicate of the year in which the policy is signed receives the premium and pays or provides for the claims, and it is the role of the accounts to represent, not dictate events. It means, of course, that not all business accepted up to the date of the annual report has been included (as it will be included in the account of the new open year in the next year when the policy is signed) – but as no attempt is being made to accrue all 'open' business, this is hardly a problem. One is, of couse, relying on there being a syndicate next year – but again if a syndicate ceases without business being transferred to another syndicate, special arrangements are made to 'run' the same syndicate for additional years to clear the business accepted before cessation.

The objection to the practice is therefore not that it distorts the picture given by the accounts, but that it gives scope for the allocation of risks to be manipulated by manipulating the timing of submission of policy details to LPSO for signing. Moreover, the practice would cause considerable accounting difficulties if Lloyd's ever moved to 'one year accounting' or to expecting a 'true and fair view' on the accounts as a whole. (For further discussion of this and some other difficulties arising from the use of LPSO, see Chapter 17.)

REQUIREMENTS

SAB requires that the notes to the accounts include a statement of the following accounting policies (Sch. 3, para.5):

   (a)   the number of years for which each year of account of the syndicate is normally to be kept open;

   (b)   the basis on which premiums and claims (including any related reinsurance premiums and recoveries) are allocated to a particular year of account;

   (c)   the basis on which underwriting transactions are included in a particular underwriting account;

   (d)   the basis on which premiums, claims and anticipated losses on open years of account are treated;

   (e)   the year of account into which the reinsurance to close each year of account is effected;

   (f)   the basis on which investment income and investment appreciation or

      depreciation are computed and are apportioned over different years of
      account, and the reasons for any changes in that basis;

(g) the basis of translation of foreign currency items;

(h) the basis on which UK taxation is provided; and

(i)   the basis on which US and Canadian taxation is charged in the personal
      accounts.

As regards changes of accounting policy, Sch.3, para.6 requires:

> Where there is a change in any of the principal accounting policies adopted in
> relation to a syndicate, the nature and effect of the change shall be stated in
> every subsequent annual report which includes an underwriting account in
> respect of a relevant year of account; and for the purposes of this paragraph
> 'relevant year of account' means a year of account in respect of which an
> underwriting account has previously been prepared under the principal
> accounting policies adopted before the change.

Items (a) to (d) are surveyed in the next chapter and items (e) to (i) in later
chapters.

With regard to the 1983 accounts the recommendations of PAM had been
essentially the same. In addition, it had been proposed that certain practices
be codified in 'Statements of Lloyd's Accounting Practice'. Thus SLAP2
would have dealt with the basis on which underwriting transactions are
included in accounts etc. It was, however, later decided to deal with these
recommendations by way of the explanatory notes to SAB in order to
reinforce the objective of making syndicate accounting as closely comparable
to company accounting as the nature of the business operations will allow.
Syndicate accounts are therefore subject, where relevant, to the general SSAPs
applicable to all accounts intended to show a 'true and fair view'.

In his letter of 14 February 1984 accompanying Byelaw 2 of 1984: '1983
Annual Reports of Syndicates', the Chairman of Lloyd's requested that, as far
as possible, the 1983 syndicate accounts follow the recommendations in
PAM, and that there should be a note indicating how far the accounts had
complied with them.

ANALYSIS

Fundamental Accounting Concepts

Discussion of the 'fundamental accounting concepts' is rare. In their 1983
accounts only six syndicates (all managed by the same agency group) had
specifically referred to the fact that SSAP2's 'going concern' concept does not
apply to Lloyd's syndicate accounting, and in their 1984 accounts these
references had disappeared. While it may be argued that SSAP2 was itself not
drawn up with Lloyd's syndicates in mind, nevertheless, as things now stand,
it is generally assumed that accounts are prepared on the basis of the four
'fundamental concepts' in the standard unless otherwise stated.

The application of the 'prudence' and 'accruals' concepts was generally made clear by the explanation of the three year accounting system (discussed further in the next chapter). Measurement of the impact of changes of accounting policy (relevant to 'consistency') was generally confined to cases where the basis of accounting for or of allocating investment income had been changed, with a consequent impact on the net result of the closed year (2% of the sample of 1984 reports and 4% of the 1983 reports explained and quantified such changes). Occasionally (3% of the 1984 sample; 1% of the 1983 reports) there was discussion of changes in expense allocation bases – but although this would also have had an impact on the result, there was no quantification of the effect. As discussed further in the next two chapters, although changes in the basis of accounting for underwriting transactions appeared to be fairly common, there was generally no reference to the changes, and almost no quantification of their effects. (In the 1984 sample, 2% mentioned such a change (1983: 2%), but only 1% quantified the amounts (1983: nil).) While generally these changes should not have changed the result of the closed year (but merely the classification of items in the underwriting accounts, or the amount recorded in respect of open years), nevertheless even restatement of comparative figures was very rare.

As to the fundamental concept of 'equity', stressed by SAB, direct reference to it was again rare. In the sample of 1984 accounts, only 12% (1983: 6%) mentioned 'equity' or 'fairness' – 7% (1983: 4%) with regard to the reinsurance to close an account and 5% (1983: 2%) with regard to expense allocation bases.

It may be held that *explicit* discussion of the extent to which the 'fundamental accounting concepts' apply is not needed because it is known that the accounts are prepared under Lloyd's syndicate accounting rules. Table 1 analyses the frequency with which the notes to the 1984 accounts referred to their having been prepared under the appropriate byelaws.

Even where the accounts themselves make no explicit reference it is of course now required that the auditors report on whether or not the accounts comply with the syndicate accounting rules – but in my opinion the primary responsibility for explaining the basis on which the accounts are drawn up rests with the managing agent, not with the syndicate's auditors.

In regard to the 1983 accounts, where PAM's guidance was only recommended, not mandatory, there was naturally still a greater variety of practice. As the Chairman had asked that the degree of compliance with the recommendations in PAM be stated, Tables 2 and 3 analyse the information on this that was provided in the notes to the 1983 accounts.

As regards these exceptions which had been identified in the 1983 reports, by the time the 1984 reports were prepared either they no longer applied or were now permitted (see, e.g., note 2 above) or, in most cases, the syndicates had apparently changed their practices to comply with the syndicate accounting rules. (Although changes in accounting policy were only occasionally mentioned, 8% of the 1984 sample did refer to changes in the

Table I. Stated degree of compliance with the syndicate accounting rules in the notes
to the 1984 accounts

	% of sample 1984
Full compliance stated (note 2)	
Wording 1 (or equivalent)	48
Wording 2 (or equivalent)	21
Wording 3 (or equivalent)	1
	70
Less than full compliance stated	
Wording 1 to 3, but adding 'except where otherwise stated' and departures clearly identified as such (see note 3)	6
Wording 1 to 3, but adding 'except where otherwise stated' (or equivalent), although *no* exceptions identified	2
	8
Extent of compliance not specified in notes	
Nothing said about extent of compliance	22
Total	100

Notes

1. Wordings: The following wordings were used to introduce the basis of preparation of the accounts:

   Wording 1: 'In accordance with the (Lloyd's) syndicate accounting rules (and generally accepted accounting policies at Lloyd's)'. Words in parentheses may or may not be included.

   Wording 2: 'In accordance with the Syndicate Accounting Byelaw [No. 7 of 1984] (and generally accepted accounting policies at Lloyd's)'. Words in parentheses may or may not be included.

   Wording 3: 'Comply with required Lloyd's accounting practice'.

2. In 2% of the sample, while the notes to the accounts indicated full compliance with the syndicate accounting rules, the auditors' reports were qualified on the grounds of non-compliance with regard to the classification of underwriting transactions.

3. The identified exceptions related to the format of presentation of the accounts or of comparative figures. In 2 of the 6 cases the auditors agreed with the departures and their reports were not qualified (see Example 2 to Chapter 3).

presentation of items in the accounts.) See Table 1 above and Chapter 17 for the audit qualifications that were made on the 1984 accounts on the grounds of non-compliance with the rules. The individual variations of practice are discussed in the chapters relating to the relevant account items.

Table 2. Stated degree of compliance with PAM in the 1983 reports

	1983	
	Number of reports	*%*
Full compliance (note 2)		
Wording 1 (or equivalent)	110	24
Wording 2 (or equivalent)	4	1
Wording 3 (or equivalent)	67	14
	181	39
Less than full compliance		
Wording 1 to 3, but adding 'except where otherwise stated' and departures clearly identified as such (see Table 3)	104	22
Wording 1 to 3, but adding 'except where otherwise stated' (or equivalent), although departures not clearly identified as such	50	11
	154	33
Extent of compliance not specified		
Wording 4 (or equivalent)	36	8
Wording 5 (or equivalent)	4	–
Nothing said about extent of compliance (whether or not stated policies actually complied)	93	20
	133	28
Total	468	100

Notes

1. Wordings: The following wordings were used to introduce the basis of preparation of the accounts:
   Wording 1: 'In compliance with (draft) Statements of Lloyd's Accounting Practice (and other generally accepted accounting practices at Lloyd's)'. Words in parentheses may or may not be included.

   Wording 2: 'In compliance with the Provisional Lloyd's Accounting Manual (and other generally accepted accounting practices at Lloyd's)'. Words in parentheses may or may not be included.

   Wording 3: 'In compliance with the Provisional Lloyd's Accounting Manual and (draft) Statements of Lloyd's Accounting Practice (and other generally accepted accounting practices at Lloyd's)'. Words in parentheses may or may not be included.

   Wording 4: 'In accordance with generally accepted accounting practices at Lloyd's'.

   Wording 5: 'In accordance with the 1983 Annual Reports of Syndicates Byelaw'.

2. In 88 cases of the 181, although full compliance was indicated, it appeared from the actual policies stated that the syndicates had in fact applied practices not consistent with the then proposed SLAP2.

A SURVEY OF LLOYD'S SYNDICATE ACCOUNTS

Table 3. Exceptions specifically identified in the 1983 reports as being departures
from PAM's recommended practice

	1983	
	Number of reports	%
Departures from 'SLAP2' (underwriting transactions) (note 2)		
No accruals	34	7
Closed year accruals only	11	2
Additional open year accruals	16	4
Other (including combinations of above)	8	2
	69	15
Other departures		
Capital gains tax provided on gilts held for less than 12 months	7	1
Certain significant expenses accrued for open years	6	1
Profits or losses on currency sales after year-end on open years dealt with in next closed account	5	1
Credits made directly to Names' personal reserves in respect of reinsurance recoveries arising from arrangements under investigation	7	1
Basis on which profit commission charged not shown	2	-
Foreign exchange profits or losses included in 'technical' underwriting result in format	10	2
Own format retained	21	4
No comparatives provided	4	1
Total exceptions identified (note 1)	131	

Notes:

1. Of the 104 reports (22%) specifically identifying departures (see Table 2) some identified more than one departure. Cases where these or other departures had occurred but were not specifically identified as being departures are not included here.

2. The first three types of departure in regard to accruals of underwriting transactions are equivalent to using the Methods A, B and D respectively that are described in Chapter 5. Methods B and D are now permitted under SAB.

3. There was no quantification of the effect of the departures.

4. Reasons given for departures were:
   - One syndicate said the treatment was adopted for 'prudence'.
   - Seventeen syndicates said it was to maintain comparability/continuity.
   - Six said that previous formats or procedures had been continued until the accounting rules were finalised.
   - Nineteen said that their own formats were clearer (or equivalent).
   - Two said that no appropriate comparatives were available.

EXAMPLES

■ Example 1 gives a full explanation of the basis on which the accounts are prepared in the light of the changing requirements.

■ Examples 2 and 3 refer to the fundamental concept of 'equity' in regard to the closing of the underwriting account. In Example 3 the 1981 and 1982 accounts have been kept open as 'run-off' accounts.

For exceptions to the syndicate accounting rules, see Chapter 3, Examples 2 and 5 and Chapter 5, Example 1.

For explanations of a change in accounting policy, see Chapter 5, Example 2 and Chapter 7, Example 2.

Example I

R.J.KILN & CO. LIMITED
R.F.H.WILSHAW & OTHERS, NON-MARINE SYNDICATE NO. 807

Notes to the accounts at 31st December 1984

1. Basis of preparation of accounts

These accounts have been prepared in accordance with the Lloyd's syndicate accounting rules, which are contained in a series of Lloyd's byelaws. These replace the provisional accounting manual which contained the rules in accordance with which the accounts at 31st December 1983 were prepared. The major difference between the byelaws and the manual is the requirement under the Syndicate Accounting byelaw that syndicates' annual reports should give a true and fair view of the profit or loss on a closed year of account and that a personal account should give a true and fair view of the member's net result. Although this requirement is not mandatory until 1985, these accounts have nonetheless been prepared on a true and fair basis.

Each underwriting account is kept open for three years and the profit or loss is ascertained at the end of the third year. The result of the 1982 account has now been ascertained and the share applicable to each Name has been transferred to that Name's personal account. The balances on the 1983 and 1984 accounts at 31st December 1984 are subject to further transactions up to the respective dates of closure of those accounts.

Example 2

ALEXANDER HOWDEN UNDERWRITING LIMITED
G.K. KNIGHT AND OTHERS
MARINE SYNDICATE 831/2
Notes to the Accounts

1. BASES OF PREPARATION OF SYNDICATE ACCOUNTS

    The accounts have been prepared in accordance with the bases and accounting policies set out in notes 2 to 6 which are in accordance with Lloyd's Syndicate Accounting Byelaw (No. 7 of 1984).

2. UNDERWRITING TRANSACTIONS

    (a) Each underwriting account is kept open for three years and the profit or loss is ascertained at the end of the third year when the account is closed by reinsurance into the following year of account, on a basis which is equitable between the closing and the following year.

    The balances on the open 1983 and 1984 accounts at 31 December 1984 are subject to further transactions up to the respective dates of closure of these accounts and, in particular, no provision has been made for the estimated future liability of these accounts. These balances do not purport to give any indication of the likely profit or loss that may be determined when these accounts are closed.

    (b) The accounts include:
    (i) premiums less brokerage and discount (net of return premiums), claims, including fees and settlement expenses (net of salvages), reinsurance premiums ceded and reinsurance recoveries as processed by Lloyd's Policy Signing Office, for which advice cards and tabulations have been issued with a date up to and including 31 December, 1984.
    (ii) in respect of the closed year of account, accruals of known material additional and return premiums, reinsurance premiums and recoveries.

    (c) Premiums are allocated to an underwriting account by reference to the date of signing at Lloyd's Policy Signing Office. Return premiums and claims are allocated to the year of account to which the premium was credited.

    Reinsurance premiums ceded are allocated by the Underwriter to the appropriate year of account.

    Salvages and reinsurance recoveries are allocated to the year of account to which the claim was debited.

    (d) The reinsurance to close comprises a reinsurance premium, calculated by the underwriter, based on estimated outstanding liabilities including claims incurred but not reported, net of estimated reinsurance recoveries, relating to the closing year and all previous years. Ultimate claim requirements net of reinsurance are estimated by the use of statistically based projections on previous claims history and case by case reviews of notified losses. The premium transfers the liability in respect of all claims, reinsurance premiums and return premiums in respect of the closing year and all previous years to the Names on the next open year insofar as they have not been provided for in these accounts and gives the Names on the next open year the benefit of refunds, recoveries and premiums due in respect of those years insofar as they have not been credited in these accounts.

Example 3

M.E. CHARLESWORTH (UNDERWRITING AGENTS) LIMITED
CHARLESWORTH MOTOR POLICIES AT LLOYD'S –
MOTOR SYNDICATE 678

Notes to the Annual Report at 31st December 1984

1. Accounting Policies

The accounts have been prepared in accordance with the syndicate accounting byelaw (no. 7 of 1984), and generally accepted accounting policies at Lloyd's.

(a)   Underwriting accounts
The underwriting accounts for each year, up to the 1981 account, were kept open for three years before the underwriting result was determined. The 1981 account was kept open for a fourth year and will remain open until at least 31st December 1985. The 1982 account is being kept open for at least a fourth year. No provision has been made in the 1983 open year of account for outstanding claims or estimated future liabilities, therefore there are material amounts of claims which are not reflected in these syndicate accounts.

(b)   Underwriting transactions
The underwriting accounts include gross premiums less commissions and gross claims together with fees and related costs less salvages, based on notifications received from brokers and processed up to the balance sheet date. Premiums are allocated to the appropriate underwriting accounts according to the inception date of the policy and its respective attachments.

(c)   Amount retained to meet all known and unknown liabilities
The underwriter and managing agents do not consider it equitable (due to the greatly reduced syndicate capacity) to reinsure the 1981 account into 1982 until such time as the 1981 account's ultimate outstanding liabilities have reached a significantly lower level. The 1982 account has not been reinsured into 1983 as there are still a few uncertainties to be resolved regarding the ultimate outstanding liabilities of the 1982 account. Therefore, the 1981 and 1982 accounts are being kept open for at least a further year. The amounts retained are based upon the estimated outstanding liabilities, including claims incurred but not yet reported, net of estimated reinsurance recoveries on such liabilities. Ultimate claim requirements net of reinsurance are estimated by the use of statistically based projections on previous claims history and in particular, to case by case reviews of notified losses.

CHAPTER 5

UNDERWRITING TRANSACTIONS

INTRODUCTION

With the exception of motor business, a Lloyd's policy is issued by Lloyd's Policy Signing Office (LPSO) on the basis of the information supplied by the broker about the terms on which the various underwriters have accepted 'lines' on the risk. The syndicate is on risk from the time the underwriter has initialled acceptance on the broker's slip (subject to any specified conditions having been met) but by the practice of the market the risk is allocated to the underwriting year (and thus to the Names on the syndicate in that year) in which LPSO issues the policy. LPSO also provides the central accounting system for settling balances between brokers and syndicates in the three currencies of sterling, US dollars and Canadian dollars.

Premiums are accounted for in the underwriting accounts as advice is received of the policies having been signed by LPSO. (In the case of motor business where LPSO is not used, transactions will be processed as advised, normally by the relevant brokers and premiums will normally be allocated to underwriting years according to the inception date of the policy.) As far as possible any premium adjustments, claims, and reinsurance premiums and claims relating to the same policy, are then allocated to the same year's underwriting account as they arise. One of the advantages of the three year accounting system is that, over this period of time, many of these adjustments and related transactions should have been processed, but there is no way of knowing, in principle, what will have been processed by the balance sheet date each year, so the question arises of what accruals for outstandings should be made.

There are various possibilities. With regard to the closing year the underwriter has to determine a fair amount for the 'reinsurance to close' in order to settle the result and transfer the remaining liability for that underwriting year to a succeeding year's Names. He could therefore take account of all known and estimated outstandings (both premiums and claims, and allowing for reinsurances) in arriving at the reinsurance to close, so no accounting adjustment would be needed to the figures for premiums, claims etc. processed. In respect of the open years no adjustments need be made as one of the purposes of keeping them open for three years is to allow time for the relevant transactions to be processed. I consider Method A, then, the method that makes no accounting adjustments but sweeps up all the outstandings on the closed year in the calculation of the reinsurance to close.

Alternatively it is possible to make adjustments for inwards and return premiums, and for reinsurance premiums and recoveries against claims settled, by accruing these in the accounts. Method B would do this for the closed year (in practice only for material items and sometimes only in relation to the reinsurance items) but not bother with adjusting the open years. Other things being equal any such adjustments will cancel out in the revised calculation of the reinsurance to close so that the net result is the same as by Method A.

Method C would, in addition, make accruals for certain items relating to the open years. PAM recommended (as part of its proposed SLAP2) that material outstandings on proportional reinsurance treaties should be accrued (e.g. if one knows that 20% of premiums are due to go to reinsurers, then for any inwards premiums received where the reinsurance may not have been processed one can make an accrual).

Method D would, either in addition or alternatively to the accruals under Method C, accrue certain other items (e.g. additional and return premiums, excess of loss reinsurance premiums or other reinsurance recoveries) in respect of the open years.

Where accruals are not made in regard to the open years it is important to emphasise the provisional nature of the balances to date on the underwriting accounts. Given the three year accounting system it is in any event particularly important to emphasise that no provision has been made in respect of any anticipated losses on those years. (The question of whether syndicates should move to providing for open year losses is discussed further in Chapter 17: one troubled syndicate, whose business had been terminated, did so in its 1983 accounts.)

Where accruals are made the corresponding assets and liabilities will be in 'brokers' balances'.

REQUIREMENTS

Although PAM had recommended Method C at the time of the 1983 accounts, SAB only requires that accruals be taken into account in respect of the closed year, and that the method adopted be made clear. This would appear to require the use of Methods B, C or D. However, the ICAEW (in TR 558 of October 1984) did argue that Method A should continue to be regarded as acceptable since the final effect on the result of the closed year ought to be the same (although one underwriter explained a better result for 1982 as being partly due to having changed the accounting policy to accrue additional premiums etc. – surely he ought previously to have been allowing for these outstandings in his calculation of reinsurance to close?). It is not clear why SAB should prohibit any of the traditional methods: in my opinion the choice should be left to the underwriter, whose criterion should presumably be that of providing the most useful basis for statistical analysis. The important thing is to explain clearly just what has been included (which generally was done in the notes on accounting policies) and that the use of different methods has no effect on the result (which was only rarely explained).

In relation to the requirements to explain the accounting policies adopted in regard to underwriting transactions, the explanatory notes to SAB indicate that:

52. The policy adopted by the managing agent should clearly state the basis upon which the following are determined:
    (a) gross premiums and gross claims;
    (b) accruals of material additional and return premiums for a closed year of account;
    (c) reinsurance premiums and recoveries;
    (d) accrual of material reinsurance premiums and recoveries for the closed year of account and where appropriate open years of account.

    In determining the policy which is appropriate the managing agent should have regard to the matters discussed in paragraphs 53 to 55 below.
53. In the case of business customarily accounted for through Lloyd's central accounting, the underwriting accounts will normally include all gross premiums and gross claims for which underwriters' advice cards and tabulations have been issued dated by LPSO up to and including the 31st December to which the annual report is prepared. In the case of the closed year of account, if there are material additional or return premiums which have not been included on a tabulation so dated, then the underwriting account and the brokers' balances in the balance sheet should be adjusted to reflect such items.
54. In the case of all business not customarily accounted for through Lloyd's central accounting, gross premiums should be the total premiums received or recorded in the accounting records as receivable from brokers up to and including the 31st December to which the annual report is prepared. Gross claims should be the total claims paid or recorded as payable up to and including 31st December.
55. Premiums and recoveries in respect of reinsurance ceded should generally be arrived at in a similar manner to that indicated in paragraphs 53 and 54 above. In the case of the closed year of account, where there are material reinsurance premiums and recoveries relating to gross premiums or claims already included in the underwriting accounts, those reinsurance premiums or recoveries should also be recognised in the accounts. In the

case of open years of account the managing agent may also consider it appropriate to accrue material reinsurance premiums and recoveries relating to gross premiums and claims already dealt with in the underwriting account.

SAB also requires a statement about the provisional nature of the open year balances (Schedule 3, para. 5(d)).

ANALYSIS

The information provided about the method adopted for accounting for underwriting transactions in the 1984 and 1983 accounts is analysed in Table 1.

Table I. Methods of accounting for underwriting transactions

	% of sample	
	1984	1983
Method A	9	32
Method B	39	19
Total making no open year accruals	48	51
Method C (as SLAP2)	30	28
Method D	19	15
Total making open year accruals	49	43
Other (comprising elements of more than one of above	3	5
Not stated (where business had ceased)	-	1
Total	100	100

Notes
1. For meaning of 'Method A' etc. see text. It was not always entirely clear which basis was being used, and in this case it has been classified according to the method to which it seemed to approximate most closely (i.e. what appeared to be minor deviations have been ignored).
2. In 45% (1983: 15%) of the reports in the sample there was some quantification in brokers' balances of the amount of the accruals that had been made.
3. In 25% (1983: 19%) of the reports in the sample it was stated that the underwriter 'places reliance on LPSO for the accuracy of processing of the underwriting figures' (or equivalent).

The table shows that the overall proportion of syndicates making any open year accruals has stayed about the same over the two years (although many individual syndicates had apparently changed their policy), but the majority of those not making any closed year accruals in 1983 (but rather taking them into account in the reinsurance to close) have moved to compliance with SAB in 1984. The majority of the syndicates still apparently using Method A in their 1984 accounts either had run-off accounts, or were ceasing business: however, none had received audit qualifications on the grounds of non-compliance with SAB's rules, so it may be that their accounting policy notes just failed to make clear what their policy was, and/or there were no material items to be accrued. (There were two cases in the sample where syndicates' accounts *had* been qualified for using Method A, but the accounting policy notes implied they were making accruals!) (Contrast Example 1 – this was not in the sample.)

Generally there appears to be scope for clearer explanations both of the accounting policies being adopted, and of why the closed year result is unaffected by the choice. It is presumably because there is no such effect that it was only very rarely that any changes in accounting policies were mentioned. Comparison of the policy notes given for 1984 and 1983 implied that there were in fact differences in the kinds of underwriting items accrued for the two years in 48% of the sample, but in only two cases was there specific mention of the change, and in only one instance were amounts quantified. Similarly, it only appeared that comparative figures might have been restated in two cases.

The extent to which it was made clear that the balances on the open years do not incorporate any provision for possible losses is analysed in Table 2.

Table 2. Explanation of provisional nature of open year balances

	% of sample	
	1984	1983
Categorical statement that no provision made for losses which may arise on open years (or equivalent) (note 1)	63	66
Statement that open years subject to further processing of premiums, claims etc. (or equivalent)	21	21
No statement (or merely that the open years are subject to further transactions)	10	13
Not applicable (no open years)	6	–
	100	100

Notes
1. In many cases it was also explained that the balances do not give any indication of the ultimate profit or loss for the year.

In regard to closing the underwriting account, SAB para. 3 requires a minimum period of three years and virtually all syndicates used three year accounting. The exceptions are two syndicates which provide stop-loss insurance to Names and therefore have to wait until other syndicates' results are available before closing their own accounts, normally at the end of the fourth year. In the case of short-term life syndicates, a premium transfer is made after two years, based on an actuarial valuation, but the account is closed only after three years. More accounts had been kept open beyond three years because of uncertainty in 1984 – 14% of the 1984 sample had kept all or part of the 1982 account open against 4% the previous year who had kept the 1981 account open.

EXAMPLES

For the purposes of Table 2 above, Examples 2 and 3 give a 'categorical' statement about there being no provision for any losses on open years; Examples 1 and 4 state the kinds of items for which there will be further processing on open years. (Cf. Chapter 4, Example 1 which refers only to there being further transactions.)

■ Example 1 uses Method A for some items, and explains that the choice has no effect on the result. (A further example of Method A, where the account is being kept open, is given in Chapter 4, Example 3.)

■ Example 2 quantifies a change from Method A to Method D and explains why this has no effect on the result; it also refers to reliance on LPSO. Accruals are shown in 'Brokers' balances'.

■ Example 3 uses Method B. Accruals are shown in 'Brokers' balances'. (A further example of Method B is given in Chapter 4, Example 2.)

■ Example 4 uses Method C and does not use LPSO.

Example I

A.R.MOUNTAIN & SON LIMITED
AVIATION SYNDICATE 800 (au)

Notes to the Annual Report – 31st December, 1984

1. **Syndicate Accounts**

   The syndicate accounts represent the underwriting position and the results of the section of the aviation syndicate 800, of which A.R.Mountain & Son Limited are quasi-managing agents.

   They incorporate the relevant proportion of the underwriting results of syndicate 800, as audited by firms of Chartered Accountants approved by the Council of Lloyd's, other than Arthur Young, together with investment income and appreciation of the surplus funds (sterling and United States dollars only) under the management of the quasi-managing agents.

   The joint auditors referred to above have expressed a qualified report on the syndicate 800 annual report dated 14th June, 1985 on the grounds that the reinsurance to close the 1982 account "includes certain recoveries on settled claims where the recovery has not been processed through Lloyd's Policy Signing Office up to the balance sheet date. This policy, whilst not in accordance with the accounting rules, is consistent with previous years". This qualification refers to a misclassification between reinsurance recoveries and reinsurance to close and as such has no effect on the underwriting result of the 1982 account.

2. **Accounting Policies**

   The accounts have been prepared in accordance with the Syndicate Accounting Byelaw (No. 7 of 1984) and generally accepted accounting policies at Lloyd's.

   (a) *Underwriting accounts*

   The underwriting accounts for each year are normally kept open for three years before the underwriting result is determined. Therefore, there are material amounts of premiums and claims on open underwriting accounts, which are not reflected in these syndicate accounts. No provision has been made on open years of account for outstanding claims, estimated future liabilities or premiums receivable.

   (b) *Underwriting transactions*

   The underwriting accounts include premiums, less commissions and claims together with fees and related costs, less salvages, based on notifications received from brokers and processed through Lloyd's Policy Signing Office up to the balance sheet date. Premiums and claims are allocated to the appropriate underwriting account on the basis of the date on which policies are signed through Lloyd's Policy Signing Office. However, on the closed underwriting account accruals have been made in order to match premiums payable to reinsurers and recoveries due from reinsurers with the underlying gross premiums and claims.

   ...

A.R.MOUNTAIN & SON LIMITED
AVIATION SYNDICATE 800 (au)

Notes to the Annual Report – 31st December, 1984

2. **Accounting Policies** (continued)
   (c) *Reinsurance to close*
      The closing underwriting account is closed by reinsurance into the following
      year of account. The amount of reinsurance to close comprises estimated
      outstanding liabilities including claims incurred but not reported, less
      estimated reinsurance recoveries on outstanding claims together with certain
      recoveries on settled claims where the recovery has not been processed through
      Lloyd's Policy Signing Office up to the balance sheet date. This policy, whilst
      not in accordance with the accounting rules, is consistent with previous years.
      Ultimate claims requirements, net of reinsurance, are estimated by use of
      statistically based projections on previous claims history and case by case
      reviews of notified losses.

Example 2

J.D.BOYAGIS (UNDERWRITING AGENCIES) LIMITED
NON-MARINE SYNDICATE 227

Notes to the Accounts – 31st December 1984

1. **Accounting Policies**
   (a) Underwriting transactions
   (i)   The underwriting accounts for each year are kept open for three years before the underwriting result is determined. This allows account to be taken of claims and adjustments of premiums arising after the end of the first year. The underwriting account is closed by reinsurance into the following year of account, normally at the end of the third year. No provision is made on open years of account for underwriting losses, if any, which may arise.

   (ii) The underwriting accounts include transactions as processed through Lloyd's Policy Signing Office up to the balance sheet date. The underwriter places reliance upon the Lloyd's Policy Signing Office for the accuracy of processing the underwriting figures. Premiums are allocated to the appropriate years of account on the basis of the date on which policies are signed through Lloyd's Policy Signing Office. Gross premiums and claims represent transactions net of returns and refunds. For the open, closing and closed underwriting accounts certain additional premium adjustments, and recoveries due from reinsurers are recorded in order to match the related gross premium and claim amounts. This represents a change in accounting policy as in previous years no adjustments were made to transactions included in the underwriting accounts. The effect of this change has been to increase the reported open year balances by £974,130 for 1983 and £12,890 for 1984. There is no effect on the closed year profit as previously the Underwriter, when calculating the reinsurance to close, took into account any reinsurance premiums ceded or reinsurance recoveries not processed through the Lloyd's Policy Signing Office at the balance sheet date.

   (iii) The reinsurance to close comprises a reinsurance premium, calculated by the Underwriter based on estimated outstanding liabilities including claims incurred but not reported, net of estimated reinsurance recoveries, relating to the closing year and all previous years. The contract transfers the liability in respect of all claims, reinsurance premiums and return premiums in respect of the closing year and all previous years to the Names on the next open year insofar as they have not been provided for in these accounts and gives the Names on the next open year the benefit of refunds, recoveries and premiums due in respect of those years insofar as they have not been credited in these accounts.

5. **Brokers' Balances**
   Brokers' balances comprise the following:–

	1984	1983
	£	£
Realisable within twelve months		
Net Lloyd's central accounting balance	372,343	938,916
Reinsurance Accruals	1,290,892	
	£1,663,235	£938,916

Example 3

S.A.MEACOCK AND COMPANY
NON MARINE SYNDICATE NO. 727

Notes to the Annual Report – 31 December 1984

1. **Accounting Policies**

   The accounts have been prepared in accordance with the accounting policies set out below which are in accordance with the Lloyd's Syndicate Accounting Rules.

   (a) **Underwriting transactions**

      (i)   Each underwriting account is kept open for three years and the result is ascertained at the end of the third year when the account is closed by reinsurance into the following year of account.

           The balances on the open 1983 and 1984 Accounts at the Balance Sheet date are subject to further transactions up to the respective dates of closure of these accounts and in particular no provision has been made for the estimated future liability of these accounts. These balances do not purport to give any indication of the likely result that may be determined when these accounts are closed.

     (ii) The underwriting accounts include:–

          (1) Premiums less brokerage and discount (net of return premiums), claims, including fees and settlement expenses (net of salvages), reinsurance premiums ceded and reinsurance recoveries as processed by Lloyd's Policy Signing Office for which advice cards and tabulations have been issued with a date up to and including the Balance Sheet date.

          (2) In respect of the closing 1982 Account, accruals of known material additional and return premiums, reinsurance premiums and reinsurance recoveries.

           Premiums are allocated to an underwriting account by reference to the date of signing at Lloyd's Policy Signing Office. Return premiums and claims are allocated to the year of account to which the premium was credited.

           Reinsurance premiums ceded are allocated by the Underwriter to the appropriate year of account.

           Salvages and reinsurance recoveries are allocated to the year of account to which the claim was charged.

    (iii) The 1982 Account has been closed by reinsurance with the 1983 Account. The reinsurance to close comprises a reinsurance premium, calculated by the Underwriter, based on estimated outstanding liabilities relating to the closing year and all previous years reinsured therein, including claims incurred but not reported, net of estimated reinsurance recoveries. The premium transfers the liability for all underwriting transactions settled on or after 1 January 1985 in respect of the closed year and all previous years reinsured therein insofar as they have not been included in the closed account.

           ...

S.A.MEACOCK AND COMPANY
NON MARINE SYNDICATE NO. 727

Notes to the Annual Report – 31 December 1984 (Continued)

3.   **Debtors**

	1984 £000's	1983 £000's
Brokers' Balances:		
Net Lloyd's Central Accounting Balance	1431	3377
Accruals	637	–
Other Debtors	331	118
	£2399	£3495

Example 4

DUGDALE (UNDERWRITING) LIMITED
HERMES MOTOR SYNDICATE NO. 508

Notes on the accounts – 31 December 1984

1. **Accounting Policies**

   The accounts have been prepared in accordance with the Syndicate Accounting Byelaw (No. 7 of 1984) and generally accepted accounting policies at Lloyd's.

   Underwriting transactions

   (a) The underwriting accounts for each year are normally kept open for three years before the underwriting result is determined. This allows account to be taken of claims and adjustments of premiums arising after the end of the first year. The underwriting account is closed by reinsurance into the following year of account, normally at the end of the third year. No provision is made on open years of account for outstanding claims, estimated future liabilities or premiums receivable.

   (b) The underwriting accounts include transactions processed up to the balance sheet date. Premiums are allocated to the appropriate underwriting accounts on the basis of the date of inception of each policy. Gross premiums and claims represent transactions net of returns and refunds. For closing and closed underwriting accounts, premium adjustments, return premiums payable to reinsurers and recoveries due from reinsurers are recorded in order to match the related gross premium and claim amounts. For open years, material outstanding balances on outwards proportional reinsurance treaties have been accrued. However, no further adjustments are made to other transactions and accordingly there are material amounts of premiums and claims on open underwriting accounts which are not reflected in these syndicate accounts.

   (c) The closing underwriting account is closed by reinsurance into the following year of account. The amount of the reinsurance to close is based upon the estimated outstanding liabilities including claims incurred but not yet reported, net of estimated reinsurance recoveries on such liabilities, relating to the closing year and all previous years. Ultimate claim requirements net of reinsurance are estimated by the use of statistically based projections on previous claims history and case by case reviews of notified losses.

CHAPTER 6

REINSURANCE TO CLOSE

INTRODUCTION

The reinsurance to close is the most significant item in the preparation of the syndicate accounts. The traditional wisdom behind Lloyd's three year accounting has been that by the end of the third year all the material items in respect of a year's underwriting will have been settled or determined, so the account can be closed and any profit distributed to Names, without any impact on later years' results. In many areas of insurance activity, however, this no longer holds – the longer the 'tail' of the business (the longer it takes to work out the final details of premiums due, or to discover the incidence and extent of liability for loss) the smaller the proportion of the final result of a year's underwriting that will be known about by the end of the third year. Thus third-party liability insurance will have a much longer tail than insurance for damage to property; and reinsurance will tend to have a longer tail than direct insurance because of the need for information about the ceding insurer's exposure (particularly where the reinsurance is non-proportional, e.g. where the ceding insurer is covered for losses in excess of some stated amount, or if his whole account exceeds some stated loss ratio).

It is this outstanding liability (and, to a much lesser extent, income) that gives rise to the need for the 'reinsurance to close' an underwriting account, i.e. the need to determine what funds need to be passed over to the succeeding Names on the syndicate if they are to take over the burden of settling the outstandings on the closed year. This is no longer a minor adjustment as can be seen from the Lloyd's 'global' figures for the 1982 accounting year. Even if one takes the figures for all classes of business combined (i.e. aggregating 'long' and 'short' tail classes of business) the reinsurance to close is the largest of the underwriting items, which comprised (see Appendix V):

	£ m
Net premium income	2892
Reinsurance to close received from 1981 account	3216
Net claims	2517
Reinsurance to close the 1982 account	3780

The length of the 'tail' is illustrated by the frequent discussion in underwriters' reports on Non-Marine syndicates of the problems of the claims now arriving for latent diseases, in particular asbestosis, under policies stretching back many years.

In SAB the reinsurance to close receives a particular mention in the context of the fundamental accounting principles set out in Sch.3, para.4 and the statement there of the need for equity between Names in different years of account '... in particular the amount charged by way of premium in respect of reinsurance to close shall, where the reinsuring members and the reinsured members are members of the same syndicate for different years of account, be equitable as between them, having regard to the nature and amount of the liabilities reinsured'.

Estimates of outstanding liabilities are required for two purposes:

1. to calculate the reinsurance to close in order to settle the result of the closed year;
2. to estimate whether the balances on the open years are likely to be sufficient to cover the future development of those years' premiums and claims.

Point 2 is only carried out for the purposes of the 'solvency audit' (see Chapter 2). Point 1 is also necessary for the purpose of the solvency audit, but in addition determines finally the result for the closed year. While the assessment of whether a Name has adequate deposits and reserves at Lloyd's, and adequate other means, depends on both 1 and 2, 2 is only an 'on account' estimate while 1 is final and later adjustment is not possible.

In testing the adequacy of the reserves for the solvency audit the following factors are taken into account:

(a) The minimum percentages of premium income laid down for each class of business by the Council of Lloyd's each year in the audit *Instructions*. These percentages are determined for the whole of the market on the basis of 'run-off' statistics supplied by all the syndicates, and have to be approved by the DTI.
(b) The underwriter's own calculation of known and estimated outstandings. This will take into account both known outstanding claims and a loading for claims incurred but not reported (IBNR), and estimate the likely final outcome in the light of inflation, trends in court judgements, statistics on past experience and all other relevant factors,

with allowance for any further premium adjustments and for reinsurance recoveries.

(c) If for any reason the auditors consider that the greater of (a) and (b) is inadequate, a larger amount will be reserved.

The primary concern in the solvency audit is of course that the reserves available should not be *less* than the amount likely to be needed, so the largest of (a), (b) and (c) is normally reserved. To ensure equity between Names in different underwriting years it is also important that the 'reinsurance to close' relating to the closing year should not be *greater* than the amount needed (or Names in later years may benefit at the expense of Names in earlier years). Finding the right balance will always be a difficult matter of judgement but one impact of the new 'true and fair view' requirement has been a shift in emphasis more towards getting the provision in the right range, rather than concentrating primarily on making sure it is at least the minimum needed.

This changing emphasis is reflected in the new accounting rules. Whereas PAM had recommended that if the reinsurance to close was less than the minimum audit reserves prescribed by the Council of Lloyd's this should be disclosed in the accounts, together with the financial effect and the reasons for it, SAB does not require any such disclosure as this is now regarded as of relevance only for the solvency audit. One may therefore expect the notes to the accounts to concentrate on explaining the way in which the reinsurance to close has been built up from a review of the available evidence (whereas many of the notes in the 1983 accounts, and some in the 1984 accounts, still referred to it in solvency terms such as 'not less than the minimum requirements laid down by the Council of Lloyd's and approved by the DTI' (see Table 1 below)). From a 'true and fair' point of view it is not the 'minimum requirements' of the solvency guidelines that should be the prime consideration, but whether or not the provision represents the 'best estimate' in the light of the information available.

Some audit firms have also considered taking the view that where the reinsurance to close has always been very conservatively measured by the underwriter, continuation of consistently conservative calculation will still produce an equitable 'true and fair' *result* year by year (at least until the syndicate significantly alters the scale of business). However, it is now generally agreed that the objection to this view must be that there would remain a kind of 'secret reserve' hidden in the provision, which might at some future time be used to bolster results in a bad year. The spirit of the requirement for a 'true and fair' result must be that the 'reinsurance to close' must itself be 'true and fair'. Further pressure not to overestimate the reinsurance to close has been coming from the Inland Revenue which has been investigating whether provisions are excessive and may be disallowable for tax purposes.

Whether the change in emphasis has in fact produced material differences in the amounts provided is impossible to tell. None of the syndicate accounts examined mentioned the effect of any change in basis of calculation, apart from in regard to certain specific items (see Table 1 below).

There is dispute amongst accountants as to what items should enter into the calculation of the reinsurance to close. Two important items are:

(a) whether future expenses should be allowed for, and
(b) whether the provision should be discounted for the future investment income that will be earned by the funds retained.

With regard to (b), the traditional practice of the insurance industry has been to make provision for outstanding claims without any discounting, although some companies do now discount for future investment income in respect of certain categories of business (see Peat, Marwick, Mitchell & Co., 1984, pp. 11–12). There is, in my opinion, need for a systematic study of the issues involved on an industry-wide basis, given that protection obtained by buying 'time and distance' reinsurance policies has essentially the same impact as discounting (cf. Example 2).

Where the underwriter feels that the uncertainties are too great to be able to estimate the reinsurance to close, he may leave the account open (a 'run-off account') but is required to include his estimate of the necessary 'amount retained to meet all known and unknown outstanding liabilities' at the end of each year until the account is finally closed (see Example 3 to Chapter 4).

As regards the transfer of the reinsurance to close to a later year, this could in principle be to any later year for which the syndicate has been constituted, e.g. 1982 could be closed to 1983 ('even to odd' and 'odd to even'), 1984 ('even to even' and 'odd to odd') or 1985. However, although practice has varied in the past, it is now almost universal to transfer the reinsurance to close to the following year (i.e. 1982 was closed to 1983). (Only one syndicate (1983: one) still uses 'even to even' and 'odd to odd' (i.e. 1982 was closed to 1984), although in the previous year three other syndicates had referred to having formerly used this policy.)

REQUIREMENTS

With regard to the syndicate accounts, the only requirements relating to the reinsurance to close in SAB are:

(a) that any item included in an underwriting account for a closed year of account shall be determined on a prudent basis (Sch.3, para.2.);
(b) the emphasis on the fundamental need for equity between Names in Sch.3, para.4;
(c) that the notes to the accounts shall state the year of account into which the reinsurance to close each year of account is effected (Sch.3, para.5).

In addition, the format in Schedule 4 requires disclosure of any quota share element.

ANALYSIS

The factors that were mentioned in explaining the calculation of the reinsurance to close (or the provision for outstanding liabilities where accounts were kept open) are analysed in Table 1 (normally several factors were mentioned). In the sample, only 7% of the 1984 reports (1983: 4%) referred to the fundamental consideration of 'equity' between Names in regard to the reinsurance to close: four reports (all managed by the same agency group) used the word 'equitable' (see Example 2 to Chapter 4); two (managed by another agency group) made clear that the amount needed to be both 'adequate for the assuming year to charge' and 'reasonable ... for the closing year to pay' (see Example 1 below), and 1 other explained that the account had been kept open because of the difficulty of computing a 'fair' figure (see also Chapter 4, Example 3 (not in the sample)). As regards future expenses, in 4% of the 1984 sample (all cases where the business of the syndicate was being terminated) a provision had been included (1983: 1% in respect of a run-off account). As regards future investment income, while there was no explicit reference to 'discounting', 3% of the 1984 and 1983 sample (all managed by the same agent) referred to 'delay in settlement' as a factor in the calculation. While these words themselves might be interpreted as referring either to discounting or, by contrast, to allowance for future inflation (or indeed to both these time related factors) it was clear from other notes in the accounts and the underwriters' comments that some assumptions had been made about the interest to be earned on these funds.

Generally it appeared that Lloyd's syndicates follow the normal insurance industry practice in not discounting for future investment income. In 6% of the 1984 sample (1983: nil) it was emphatically stated that no allowances for either future investment income or future expenses had been made in arriving at the amount of the reinsurance to close (see Examples 2 and 3).

Table 1 illustrates the change in emphasis from solvency related requirements (factors (f) and (g)) to the building up of a best estimate on the information available (factors (a) to (d)). However, although a marked change as between the 1983 and 1984 accounts is apparent, in a significant proportion of cases the notes to the accounts still refer to the solvency related factors, so in these cases change is still needed. Moreover, in a number of instances, underwriters in their reports are still making comments such as 'an increase in the Lloyd's minimum requirements means that the reserve for these years has had to be increased'.

Table I. Factors in reinsurance to close commonly referred to

	% (Note 1)	
	1984	1983
(a) Review of individual notified claims	47	36
(b) IBNR claims	89	69
(c) Projections from past claims history (note 3)	40	25
(d) Deduction for reinsurance (note 4)	89	70
(e) 'Calculated by Underwriter'	65	67
(f) Requirements of Council of Lloyd's (note 5)	17	36
(g) Basis approved by Department of Trade	7	29
(h) 'Approved by Managing Agent' (or equivalent)	11	16
(i) Stated to cover outstandings of latest and all prior closed years (note 6)	89	90
Reinsurance to close not described (as only open years of account or all liabilities settled)	4	9
Provision for outstanding liabilities on run-off account made, but basis not described.	1	–

Notes

1. The percentages for items (a) – (i) relate to those reports (95% of the 1984 sample and 91% of the 1983 sample) which included a description of the basis of calculation.
2. Where accounts were kept open (1984: 14%; 1983: 4% of the sample) the elements refer to the provision for outstanding liabilities. In the case of short-term life syndicates reference was also made to the actuarial valuation.
3. With regard to item (c), 3% of the sample in 1983 (all in the same agency group) referred to the past statistics that were available being unreliable as a basis for estimation of IBNR.
4. With regard to item (d), 6% of the sample (1983: 2%) quantified the amount allowed for various reinsurance protections e.g. excess of loss, stop-loss or rollover reinsurance. Nine per cent (1983: 5%) quantified the deduction for quota-share reinsurance and 3% (1983: 1%) said there was no quota share reinsurance.
5. With regard to item (f) 3% of the sample (1983: 10%) said the provision was 'not less than' Lloyd's requirements and 4% (1983: 3%) made reference to the 'minimum percentages'. None identified differences between the solvency requirements and the provision made, whereas in 1983 3% indicated that the amount provided was greater than the minimum required by the Council of Lloyd's and 1% that it was less. One per cent (1983: 2%) mentioned the *Instructions* to Lloyd's auditors.
6. In regard to item (i), 1% of the sample (1983: 1%) quantified the amount provided to cover liability for asbestosis and other latent diseases. 3% (1983: 1%) identified the amount of the reinsurance to close relating to other syndicates with which they had been merged.
7. Except as already noted, there was no quantification in the accounts or notes of the factors comprising the reinsurance to close.

Several factors entering into the calculation would normally be mentioned. 2% (1984 and 1983) of the sample mentioned all the factors (a) – (i) (see Example 1). The most common combinations of factors used to describe the reinsurance to close were as set out in Table 2 (coded as in Table 1).

Table 2. Common descriptions of reinsurance to close

| | % of sample | |
	1984	1983
b, d, e, i (note 2)	39	36
a, b, c, d, i (note 3)	26	19

Notes

1. The percentages relate to those reports (95% of the sample in 1984, and 91% in 1983) which included a description of the basis of calculation.
2. As in Chapter 5, Example 2 (at note 1. (a) (iii)) and Example 3 (at note 1. (a) (iii))
3. As in Chapter 5, Example 4 (at note 1. (c))

EXAMPLES

■ Example 1 gives an unusually full description of all the factors (a – i in Table 1) entering into the calculation of the reinsurance to close.

■ Example 2 discusses future investment income and indicates the extent to which external reinsurance of liabilities has been purchased.

■ Example 3 explains that neither future investment income or expenses have been included, and illustrates the analysis of quota share reinsurance.

Managing Agent: Edwards & Payne (Underwriting Agencies) Ltd.

See also Richard Beckett, 810 and 918; R.H.M.Outhwaite, 317.

Example I

R.J. KILN & CO. LIMITED

R.F.H. WILSHAW & OTHERS, NON-MARINE SYNDICATE NO. 807

Notes to the accounts at 31st December 1984

8. **Premium Payable for the Reinsurance to Close the 1982 Year of Account**

    The reinsurance to close the 1982 account has been effected with the 1983 account which has taken over the liability for further claims. The reinsurance premium has been calculated by the underwriter and approved by the managing agent, and is not less than the requirements laid down by the Council of Lloyd's and approved by the Department of Trade and Industry.

    The quantum of the reinsurance to close is based upon an assessment of the following items:

    – The cash movement during the most recent calendar year on all closed years.
    – Changes in noted outstandings in respect of all closed years.
    – Comparison of cash movements and changes in noted outstandings, looked at in conjunction with similar comparisons at previous year-ends.
    – Consideration of special factors which should be taken into account on individual risks, or alternatively groups of risks, in respect of the previously closed years.
    – Consideration of the settlements and noted outstandings on the year to be closed, and comparison of these with the equivalent figures at recent year-ends.
    – Consideration of the protection afforded by reinsurers in respect of the previously closed years and the year to be closed, which would include an assessment of the likely effect of any insolvencies.
    – Assessment of an appropriate reinsurance premium to take care of specific losses incurred but not reported (IBNR) and any other IBNR that could be predicted by the use of statistical techniques.
    – Assessment of an appropriate reinsurance premium to take care of the unknown and unknowable liabilities which might fall to the years already closed and the year about to be closed.

    The reinsurance premium takes into account the appropriate figures from each of the above items. The total reinsurance premium charged to the closing year is therefore that figure which in the opinion of the underwriter is adequate for the assuming year to charge in order to write the reinsurance giving the protection to the year to be closed and all prior years, which figure must also appear to be a reasonable amount for the closing year to pay.

Example 2

MERRETT NON-MARINE SYNDICATE 421

Notes to the Annual Report

6.   **Net Premium Payable for Reinsurance to Close the 1982 Account**

Full provision has been made for all known outstanding claims and additionally a substantial sum has been included to cover incurred but not reported losses (IBNR). The figures include a significant reserve in respect of "special risks" or "run-off" contracts which are described in the Underwriter's Report.

In assessing the provision for the special risks, information has been received from each reinsured of the losses outstanding at 31st December 1984 to which has been added a substantial further provision for IBNR. In arriving at the IBNR provision, the Underwriter of Syndicate 421 has made his estimate on the basis of the non-marine classes of business known to have been written by the reinsureds and his knowledge and experience of such syndicates in the market. Consideration has also been given to the effect of variations in amount and timing of payment of claims. Whilst there will inevitably be divergences between the ultimate losses and the amounts provided it is the view of the Underwriter that such variations will not have a material effect on the adequacy of the overall reinsurance premium. No account has been taken of the fact that as the losses will be paid over a number of years the balance of the fund carried forward after payment of the premium for the special reinsurance policy referred to below will earn significant amounts of interest.

Since many of the outstanding losses will not be settled for some years, it has been possible to purchase specific excess of loss reinsurance protection (sometimes described as "time and distance" reinsurance) in US dollars for the 1982 account. In calculating the net premium for the reinsurance to close the account, credit has been taken in full for anticipated recoveries under this policy which are collectable in the period 1990 to 1995.

The resultant effect is as follows:

	£
Outstanding claims and IBNR:	
Run-off contracts	7,821,548
Other business	3,171,150
	10,992,698
Less: Credit taken for recoveries under the specific excess of loss reinsurance policy	6,250.000
Premium payable to the 1983 underwriting account	4,742,698
Add: Premium payable for the specific excess of loss reinsurance policy	2,823,276
Net premiums for the reinsurance to close the 1982 account	7,565,974

Example 3

C.D.RAYNOR

MARINE SYNDICATE NO. 304/303

Accounting Policies and Notes to the Accounts at 31st December 1984

1. **Accounting Policies**

   (d) *Reinsurance to close*

   The reinsurance to close is calculated by the Underwriter based on estimated outstanding liabilities, including claims incurred but not reported, net of estimated reinsurance recoveries relating to the closing year and all previous years. Ultimate claim settlements, net of reinsurance, are estimated by use of statistically based projections on previous claims history and reviews of notified losses. The reinsurance to close has had the benefit of full credit for reinsurance recoveries on long-term excess of loss contracts. No allowance has been made for the investment income which will be earned on the reinsurance premium in future years nor has provision been made for the Syndicate's cost of administering the settlement of the outstanding losses.

   The premium transfers the liability for all underwriting transactions settled on or after 1st January 1985 in respect of the closed year and all previous years reinsured therein in so far as they have not been included in the closed account.

2. **Net Premium Receivable for Reinsurance to Close**

	1982 account after 3 years £000's	1981 account after 3 years £000's
Closed year of account:		
Gross premium	5965	4315
Proportion due to whole account quota share reinsurers	206	163
Net premium	5759	4152

	1983 account after 2 years £000's	1982 account after 2 years £000's
Open year of account:		
Gross premium	6713	5083
Proportion due to whole account quota share reinsurers	230	181
Net premium	6483	4902

...

3.   **Net Premium Payable for Reinsurance to Close**

	1982 account £000's	1981 account £000's
Gross premium	6713	5083
Proportion due from whole account quota share reinsurers	230	181
Net premium	6483	4902

CHAPTER 7

INVESTMENTS

INTRODUCTION

Premiums are invested pending payment of claims, expenses and distribution of profit, and the main objective is that of securing ready realisability. Under the rules of Lloyd's, as approved by the Department of Trade, for admissibility in regard to solvency purposes the range of investments is limited to certain specified classes. The investments also need to be of a kind whose value is not likely to be disputed as, at the end of each year, some of them will have to be notionally sold by the closing year to the open years. Listed investments are therefore stated at market value in the balance sheet. Unlisted investments are rare – the exception having been shares in Lloyd's Life Assurance Ltd (for which the Council of Lloyd's provided a year-end valuation) until the company was sold in 1985.

Unrealised as well as realised appreciation and depreciation in value are included in the underwriting accounts. This departure from 'historical cost' accounting is the only sensible accounting procedure if one is to obtain equity between the Names underwriting in different years (e.g. MacNeal, 1939). It is also the basis for UK, US and Canadian tax purposes in respect of Lloyd's. Because the investments of all three open years of account in each currency are usually managed as a single fund it is necessary to apportion the interest, dividends and capital appreciation or depreciation between the three years of account. This apportionment is known (after its inventor) as *riesco*.

Where a separate fund is managed for US Names, or other subgroups, there will be a separate apportionment of the returns in their funds.

Where the investments for several syndicates are pooled and managed on a group basis, similar apportionment is needed to each underwriting year of each syndicate.

REQUIREMENTS

SAB requires that the basis on which investment returns are computed and apportioned be disclosed, together with the reasons for any change in that basis.

In the balance sheet, it is required that investments are stated at market value and analysed between:

(a) fixed interest securities issued or guaranteed by any government or public authority
(b) other listed fixed interest securities
(c) variable interest securities issued or guaranteed by any government or public authority
(d) other listed variable interest securities
(e) listed equity shares
(f) other (specifying their nature).

Similar provisions were recommended in PAM in regard to the 1983 accounts. In addition, where investments are pooled, allocation to the balance sheets of individual syndicates is now explicitly required.

ANALYSIS

In the 1984 accounts all the syndicates in the sample that had investments stated that they were valued at 'mid-market' value, or 'market' value at 31 December 1984 (20% mentioning that this included accrued interest and 1% that it did not). Thirty-six per cent showed (in the notes or in an investment schedule appended to the accounts) that they had shares in Lloyd's Life: 22% noted that in this case the valuation was that provided by the Council of Lloyd's, and 14% did not.

With regard to the analysis of classes of investments held, required by SAB to be given in the notes to the accounts, Table 1 gives the percentage of the 1984 accounts in which each class of investment was shown for 1984 or 1983 (coded as above).

Table I. Classes of investments analysed

	1984 sample %
(a)	99
(b)	21
(c)	18
(d)	1
(e)	18
(f) – specified (note 2)	54
(f) – unspecified	11

Notes
1. One syndicate (1%) had no investments in either 1984 or 1983. Another 1 had investments in 1983 only.

2. The other investments specified comprised:

	%
Lloyd's Life shares	29
Short-term deposits	7
Unlisted equity shares	5
Sundry others	13

Many syndicates went beyond the basic requirement to give an analysis of the classes of investments held. Some gave currency totals of investments or totals by country and a few made reference to realisability within and over one year (see Example 4 to Chapter 3). Twenty-eight per cent of the sample gave full investment schedules listing all the individual securities held. In twenty cases these schedules were covered by the auditors' opinion, but in the case of the remaining eight they were outside the scope of the auditors' opinion. As the auditors will have had to check such listings in order to complete their audit work, it would seem more sensible that where this extra information is given it is presented as part of the audited accounts.

Table 2 analyses the statements made as to the basis on which investment returns were allocated to underwriting accounts.

Table 2. Method of allocation of investment returns

		% of sample	
		1984	1983
(a)	Allocated according to average balances of underwriting accounts	89	90
(b)	Allocated on some quantified basis	3	3
(c)	Allocated 'according to basis set out in agency agreement' (or equivalent)	4	5
(d)	All allocated to one year (because syndicate commenced in 1984 (1983) or ceased in 1982 (1981) (or earlier))	4	2
		100	100

Notes
1. Many syndicates also mentioned that (a) or (b) was the basis set out in the agency agreement (as in Example 1 below).
2. In some cases it was also mentioned that, where separate funds were managed for US Names, the income on the relevant funds had been allocated to them; or where funds were held in more than one currency, that the allocation had been made separately for each currency. One agent's syndicates stated that while the allocation had been made by method (a) for their US and Canadian dollar funds, in respect of sterling investments each underwriting year held its own securities.
3. With regard to method (a), some syndicates further specified that the calculations were made by reference to average quarterly balances, some by reference to monthly balances and some by reference to balances at 30 June.

Two per cent of the 1984 sample (1983: nil) had changed the basis of allocation. In one case this was said to be in order to comply with SAB, but as the byelaw specifies no particular method the intention must have been to achieve more equitable allocation (see Example 2).

EXAMPLES

- Example 1 gives a full explanation of *riesco*.
- Example 2 deals with a change in the basis of allocation from method (b) to (a) (see Table 2 above).

Example I

R.J.KILN & CO. LIMITED

R.F.H.WILSHAW & OTHERS, NON-MARINE SYNDICATE NO. 807

Notes to the accounts at 31st December 1984

2. **Accounting Policies**
   (c) Investments
   Investments are included in the balance sheet at market value on 31st December 1984.

   Investment income receivable and investment appreciation for the year are apportioned between underwriting accounts in proportion to the mean balances on those accounts during the year. Mean balances represent the average funds available for investment throughout the year, including the balances brought forward from the previous year on the then open years of account and the cash flows during the current year in respect of premiums and claims. This apportionment, known as the Riesco calculation, is applied on a basis which is consistent with previous years and is in accordance with the agency agreement.

Example 2

TROJAN UNDERWRITING AGENCY LTD
TROJAN MOTOR POLICIES SYNDICATE 378

Notes to the Accounts – 31st December, 1984

1. **Basis of Preparation of Syndicate Accounts**
   The Syndicate Accounts have been prepared in accordance with the Syndicate Accounting Byelaw (No. 7 of 1984).

2. **Accounting Policies**

   Investments
   (a) *Funds*
      The Syndicate has not maintained separate investment portfolios for Names who are resident in the United States for taxation purposes.

   (b) *Valuation*
      Investments are stated at their mid-market values at the balance sheet date.

   (c) *Income and appreciation*
      In order to comply with the Syndicate Accounting Byelaw (No. 7 of 1984), the Syndicate has changed its accounting policy for allocating investment income and realised and unrealised investment appreciation arising in a calendar year.

      Under the new accounting policy, investment income and realised and unrealised investment appreciation arising in each calendar year are allocated to underwriting accounts in proportion to average balances on each underwriting account for the calendar year.

      Under the previous accounting policy, investment income and realised and unrealised investment appreciation arising in each calendar year were allocated to underwriting accounts in the following proportions:-

      30% First year of account
      40% Second year of account
      30% Third year of account

      The effect of this change in accounting policy is shown in Note 7.

                                                                                          . . .

TROJAN UNDERWRITING AGENCY LTD
TROJAN MOTOR POLICIES SYNDICATE 378

Notes to the Accounts – 31st December, 1984 (cont)

6. **Exceptional Items**

    As stated in Note 2, the Syndicate has changed its accounting policy for allocating investment income and realised and unrealised investment appreciation. This has resulted in exceptional debits to the 1982 closed underwriting account, as set out below.

	1982 Account after 3 years
Net investment income under new accounting policy	20,339
Exceptional debit arising from change in accounting policy	2,113
Net investment income	£18,226
Net investment appreciation under new accounting policy	34,516
Exceptional debit arising from change in accounting policy	3,409
Net investment appreciation	£31,107

7. **Change of Accounting Policy**

    As stated in note 2, the Syndicate has changed its accounting policy for allocating investment income and realised and unrealised investment appreciation arising in a calendar year. If the 1981 Account after 3 years had been prepared under the new accounting policy, net investment income and net investment appreciation would have been £17,124 and £19,794 respectively.

CHAPTER 8

OTHER ASSETS, LIABILITIES AND CONTINGENCIES

INTRODUCTION

Apart from investments and cash balances the other assets of a syndicate normally comprise:

- Overseas deposits (required by the insurance laws of some countries or states before they permit the conduct of insurance business there).
- Debtors (amounts due from brokers; managing agent; members' agents; and others (e.g. amounts due from Names in regard to closed year losses)).

Because of the 'one year life' of each syndicate it is regarded as inappropriate for syndicates to hold long-term assets. The managing agents therefore normally acquire the computers, office equipment, cars etc. that are needed and either lease them to the syndicates they manage, or charge for their use. Because of the need for an 'exit value' at which the closing year hands over assets to the open years of account, the accounting basis required is that all assets other than investments are stated at net realisable value.

The creditors of a syndicate normally comprise:

(a) amounts due to those parties listed under debtors above
(b) taxation
(c) bank loans and overdrafts
(d) other borrowings
(e) other creditors and accruals.

With regard to contingencies and post balance sheet events, the division between 'closed' and 'open' years, and the closing of an underwriting account only after a minimum of three years, is designed to reduce uncertainty by allowing time for the consequences of underwriting to emerge and be reflected in premium adjustments, claims settlements and reinsurance recoveries. When an underwriting account is closed, the calculation of the 'reinsurance to close' should take account of all available knowledge, at the date the accounts are prepared and audited, in respect of outstanding contingencies.

As the nature of insurance is to cover contingencies, and to make this manageable by ensuring an adequate spread of risks, there are unlikely to be significant outstanding contingencies that cannot be taken account of. Where there are (e.g. a major legal dispute with a reinsurer about whether a loss on the whole account is recoverable under the terms of the stop-loss protection) the underwriter will normally choose instead to keep the account open beyond three years and run it off until the uncertainty is sufficiently resolved before calculating the final reinsurance to close the account and distributing the result to Names.

REQUIREMENTS

SAB (Sch.4, para.2) requires:

(a) an analysis of brokers' balances as appropriate for the class of business;
(b) that a distinction is made between amounts payable or realisable within the next twelve months and amounts payable or realisable thereafter;
(c) that all assets other than investments be included in the balance sheet at net realisable value;
(d) that if any of a syndicate's assets have been mortgaged or charged this fact should be stated;
(e) details of any borrowings of material amount (i.e. over 5% of the latest year's syndicate allocated capacity) and for a material period (i.e. over 14 days) during the year.

PAM gave similar recommendations for the 1983 accounts.

With regard to post balance sheet events and contingencies, the explanatory notes to SAB indicate that SSAP17 and SSAP18 should be applied, but that the criteria for determining adjusting and non-adjusting entries may differ from ordinary company accounting because: (a) in respect of the closed year post balance sheet events will generally be taken into account in determining the reinsurance to close, while (b) in respect of open years the fact that they are open may be held to obviate any need to adjust, rather than disclose.

Similar considerations apply to contingencies; and in deciding on appropriate disclosure, the manner of disclosure needs to be considered to avoid prejudicing the interests of syndicate members.

For the 1983 accounts, PAM had made generally similar recommendations in its proposed SLAP7.

ANALYSIS

Assets
In spite of the requirement to show all assets at net realisable value, 8% (1983: 4%) of the syndicates in the sample showed that they had assets

such as motor vehicles, fixtures and fittings, and computers described as 'fixed assets' and stated at cost less depreciation. Three per cent included these in debtors in the balance sheet, and another 2% stated that their balance sheet value was considered to be equal to net realisable value. In the previous year, a number of syndicates had changed their arrangements regarding such fixed assets since the preceding year: one had disposed of its fixed assets; one had arranged for a service company to own the assets, financed by a loan from the syndicate and hire charges; and one had eliminated the computer development costs that were in its balance sheet at 31 December 1982. Two per cent of the 1984 sample included a note explaining why the syndicates had no fixed assets (see Example 1 in Chapter 9).

Apart from some of these cases of 'fixed assets' there was generally no mention of assets being valued at net realisable value except that, in the sample of 1984 accounts, 3% referred to debtors being stated after a provision for bad and doubtful debts, and 1% to no such provision having been made.

In the 1983 accounts, only 3% of syndicates' reports had referred to the classification of debtors into amounts receivable in over and under twelve months, all but one of these showing all (material) debtors as due in less than twelve months. In the sample of 1984 accounts, there was a considerable increase – 40% giving a full analysis of debtors into over and under twelve months, and a further 2% analysing some of the debtors this way – but still only 42% in total gave any classification. (See Example 1 (not in the sample) and Example 4 in Chapter 3.)

A new requirement for the 1984 accounts (SAB Sch.4, para.2.14) was to give a breakdown of any overseas deposits: 47% (1983: 8%) of the sample explained that they had a deposit in the State of Illinois as a condition of transacting business there or in the State of Kentucky, and 5% (1983: 1%) referred to a 'claims payable abroad loan' (see Example 2).

No syndicate in the sample indicated that any assets were charged, while just one syndicate gave a definite statement that an overdraft in 1984 was unsecured (see also Example 1 – not in the sample).

In the 1983 accounts 6% of the syndicates had referred to the fact that considerable amounts of the assets supporting Names' underwriting were 'off balance sheet', or stated that details about personal reserves etc. were given only to the individual Names concerned. Such references were very rare in the 1984 accounts, although 5% of the sample (1983: 5%) referred to the interest on personal reserves having been credited to Names' personal accounts.

In the case of some troubled groups of syndicates there were references to indemnities that had been made available to certain Names which were not reflected in the accounts; to certain reinsurance recoveries having been credited to Names' personal reserves under the terms of an offer made by the agency; and to the availability of Lloyd's Central Fund if Names defaulted on the calls being made on them.

Liabilities

With regard to liabilities, it was already normal in the 1983 reports to show a split in the balance sheet between amounts payable within one year and amounts payable after one year. Of the 1984 sample, 72% gave a full analysis of creditors in this way, while 26% just split out the amount of taxation due after more than one year. No loans over five years were shown in the sample for either year.

Borrowings during the year were described by 8% of the syndicates in the sample (1983: 4%), while 2% (1983: 4%) said they had had no material loans (see also Example 1 – not in the sample). However, several syndicates had overdrafts in the balance sheet without further explanation, although in some cases an explanation was given that an 'overdraft' represented the result of deducting unpresented cheques at the year-end from a credit balance on the bank statement.

Contingencies and Post Balance Sheet Events

There were no disclosures under these headings in the notes to the accounts. However there were some references, e.g. to litigation outstanding; to the solvency position on the open years (as in Example 3); to adjustments to the deposits required in Illinois; or to the subsequent purchase of reinsurance protection for an account.

Generally, discussion of any litigation or of any major uncertainties was dealt with in the managing agents' and underwriters' reports (especially where an account had been kept open beyond three years) (see Chapters 15 and 16).

EXAMPLES

■   Examples 1 (non-marine syndicate 190) and 2 give information about several aspects of assets and liabilities.

■   Example 3 refers to the open years' solvency position (see Chapters 2 and 6) (Managing agent: K.P.H. Underwriting Agencies Ltd.).

Example I

THREE QUAYS UNDERWRITING
MANAGEMENT LIMITED

9.   **Debtors and Creditors**
No material amounts are payable or realisable outside twelve months. As at
May 1985 the amounts owed by brokers shown on the Balance Sheet, at
31.12.84, have been substantially paid to the syndicate.

At 31st December 1984 there were no material amounts due to the managing
agent and there were no amounts due from the managing agent.

Creditors include an amount of £1,453,202 due to members' agents.

Taxation is analysed as follows:–

Payable within twelve months	£2,492,788
Payable outside twelve months	£4,841,907
	£7,334,695

10. **Syndicate Assets**
None of the Syndicate's assets are subject to any charge or lien.

11. **Syndicate Borrowings**
There were no amounts borrowed by the syndicate during the year.

Example 2

STENHOUSE EPPS (UNDERWRITING AGENCIES) LTD.

N. F. EPPS & OTHERS LIVESTOCK SYNDICATE 454

Notes to the Accounts 31st December 1984

4. **Overseas Deposits**
    These amounts were deposited with the State of Illinois, USA, as a condition of carrying on business there.

5. **Debtors**
    All debtors are due within one year.

6. **Creditors**
    All creditors are due within one year, except the taxation provisions in respect of the 1983 and 1984 years of account amounting to £1,805 (1983 – £5,041 in respect of 1982 and 1983 accounts).

7. **Loan from Stenhouse Syndicates Ltd**
    During the year the syndicate required a loan from Stenhouse Syndicates Ltd. and at the year end the balance was £256,000, the maximum amount owing. The rate of interest charged was 1% over bank base rate. The syndicate writes only a small sterling account and has therefore required the loan to meet sterling liabilities, in particular sterling claims and syndicate expenses.

Example 3

D. G. KING AND OTHERS

MARINE SYNDICATE NO. 745/748

Notes to the Accounts

12. **Open Year Audit Position**
    As at 31st December 1984, the open years' solvency position calculated in accordance with the Instructions for the Guidance of Lloyd's Auditors was as follows:

1983 Account	£103,156 Surplus
1984 Account	£185,934 Surplus

    It should be understood that an open year surplus in any year of account would not necessarily lead to a closed year profit. Similarly, an open year deficiency would not necessarily lead to a closed year loss.

CHAPTER 9

EXPENSES

INTRODUCTION

The expenses incurred in underwriting on behalf of Names are divided into two groups: 'Syndicate' expenses and 'Personal' expenses. The former appear in the underwriting accounts and are thus charged in arriving at an individual Name's share of the result (usually in the same proportion as his proportion of the syndicate's allocated premium capacity, although there may be different bases of allocation to different subgroups of Names) while the latter are charged or apportioned directly to Names' personal accounts (and different individual Names or different groups of Names on a syndicate may be charged on different bases, according to the terms of their own underwriting agency agreements).

Syndicate Expenses

Syndicate expenses normally comprise, according to the classifications that are required by SAB to be shown in the notes to the accounts (and were recommended by PAM for the 1983 accounts):

salaries and related costs
accommodation costs
interest payable
Lloyd's charges (e.g. for use of LPSO)
auditor's remuneration
other expenses

The expenses are often incurred by a managing agent on behalf of one or more syndicates, and passed on in an inclusive management fee. In turn the expenses passed on by the agent may originally have been incurred by the holding company or fellow subsidiaries in a larger group. One feature of the new audit arrangements introduced under Byelaw 10 of 1984 is that (with effect from the 1985 annual reports) the same auditors will not be able to audit both the managing agent and the managed syndicates. While this should help generally to reinforce syndicate auditors' independence, one may question whether it will improve or detract from their ability to be satisfied about the propriety and proper, consistent allocation of expenses between other group companies, the managing agent and the syndicates. While syndicate auditors do have a right of access to the accounting and other records kept by the managing agent in respect of the syndicate, and to require such information and explanations as they consider necessary, it is not, for example, entirely clear to how much information they would have a right of access where the agent is part of a larger group.

Personal Expenses

Personal expenses normally comprise:

> profit commission (to the managing agent)
> Lloyd's subscription
> contribution to Lloyd's Central Fund
> agent's salary
> other expenses
> overseas taxation

Personal expenses are deducted from the Name's share of the net result of the closed underwriting account in arriving at the cheque to be paid to him, or the amount of the deficiency to be covered. They are shown in the 'personal account' (which is not filed on the public file). In the syndicate accounts they appear as yearly totals in the balance sheet, where they are deducted from the balance due to Names in regard to the closed year, and from the balances accumulated in regard to the open years. An average of them also appears in the 'Seven Year Summary' (see Chapter 12).

REQUIREMENTS

In addition to the requirement (recommendation for the 1983 accounts) that syndicate expenses be analysed under the headings given above (the breakdown being estimated if necessary where the agent charges an inclusive management fee) SAB requires that the notes to the underwriting accounts state:

(a) the basis on which expenses have been charged to the syndicate, including details of apportionment between the syndicate, other syndicates and the managing agent;

(b) the basis on which expenses charged to the syndicate have been allocated to different groups of Names within the syndicate;

(c) the basis of the allocation or apportionment to a particular underwriting account.

With regard to the 1983 accounts PAM had recommended (a) and (c), and also that the notes to the underwriting accounts disclose the basis on which profit commission had been charged (SAB does not require this disclosure).

There is no requirement that parallels the Companies Act requirement for details to be disclosed about the remuneration of directors and senior executives (such as the Underwriter).

ANALYSIS

Syndicate expenses
The expense breakdowns disclosed in the 1984 accounts are analysed in Table 1.

Table I. Expense classifications

	% of sample 1984
Salaries and related costs (note 1)	97
Cost of accommodation (note 1)	95
Interest payable	25
Lloyd's charges	99
Syndicate auditor's remuneration	99
Other expenses (note 2)	99
No analysis of total	1

Notes
1. One per cent stated that it was not practicable to allocate the amount of the management fee between salaries etc. and accommodation.
2. Forty-nine per cent gave individual amounts for certain other expenses, such as accounting, data processing and investment services.
3. Sixteen per cent included a statement of the amount of a management fee or of the total amount charged by the agent or related companies which had, in all but four cases, been analysed over the various expense categories.

The expenses are allocated over the three years' underwriting accounts and it is normally only possible to calculate the expenses charged in the calendar year by comparing the cumulative amounts in each underwriting account from one year to the next. However, 5% of the sample of 1984 accounts (1983: 7%) included a statement of the total expenses charged in the calendar year. As regards the various classifications analysed in Table 1, practice was evenly divided between giving full comparative figures (e.g. as in Example 1) or only a comparative for the previously closed year (as e.g. in Example 6). The variety apparently arose because of an ambiguity in the scope of SAB's requirement that comparative figures be stated for all items in the accounts (Sch.4, para.1.5(a)), and because the specimen layout in PAM had not given the full comparative figures (most notes in the 1983 accounts had followed PAM in this respect). Without the cumulative amount under each heading that had been charged to each underwriting year by the previous year-end it is not possible to calculate how much has been charged during the calendar year for each item (although the total calendar year expenses charged can be deduced from the comparatives in the underwriting accounts). It would of course be more straightforward if an analysis of the calendar year expenses were given (see also Chapter 13.)

As to bases of allocation:

(a) In the sample of 1984 accounts 40% gave some explanation of how expenses had been allocated between managing agent and syndicates, and sometimes there was mention of certain specific items having been borne by the agency. Seventy per cent gave some explanation of how expenses were allocated between syndicates and in another 13% the syndicate was the only one managed by the agent: the most common basis was 'according to volume of business' (often with some expenses being specifically charged to the appropriate syndicate).

This was an improvement on the 1983 accounts when it was rare to have any explanations of the first kind and 51% gave explanations of the second kind.

(b) In the reports of two syndicates in the sample (both managed by the same agent) (1983: two) the note explained that expenses were allocated to individual Names according to their share in the syndicate. The most common case of allocation between groups of Names is where separate investment funds are managed, e.g. for UK and US Names.

(c) Syndicate reports usually included a note giving some explanation of the basis of the allocation or apportionment to each underwriting account (see Table 2). However, the wordings used were often ambiguous. 'Charged to the year in which incurred' probably refers to the year in which the expense arose (a wording that was sometimes used). This probably implies that, for example, electricity for the last quarter of 1984 not billed until 1985 would be charged to the 1984 underwriting account when the 1985 accounts are prepared, but it might be taken to refer to the year in which the expense is invoiced (e.g. this electricity bill would be charged to the 1985 underwriting account) or even to the year in which it is paid. It presumably implies that the charge is not allocated over the three underwriting years that have benefitted from it.

Some wordings described expenses as charged 'to the relevant year', 'to the appropriate year', or 'to the year to which they relate', and I assume these include allocation over the three years.

Again it was generally not entirely clear whether expenses were only included in the accounts if they had been invoiced by 31 December 1984, or whether some accruals were made. It would seem that, where material, any outstanding expenses chargeable to the closed year would have to be accrued, but that expenses for open years would not normally be accrued. Most expenses relating to the closed year will have been paid by the third year but, for example, the audit fees will not normally be paid until the following year, so that if they are to be allocated over the three underwriting years some accrual ought to be made.

The main alternatives that were described are set out in Table 2. Some further details about the basis charging were sometimes given in the Managing Agent's report (see Chapter 15).

Table 2. Basis of expense allocation over underwriting years

		% of sample 1984	1983
(a)	Specific expenses charged to each underwriting account and the remainder to the latest underwriting account (or equivalent) (note 1)	29	20
(b)	All expenses charged to the latest year or 'to the year in which incurred' (or equivalent)	62	70
(c)	Allocated 'in accordance with a consistent formula' (or equivalent) (e.g. 'equally')	3	3
(d)	Specific expenses charged to each underwriting account and the remainder according to a formula (e.g. by premium income)	–	1
		94	94
(e)	No mention of allocation basis (note 5)	6	6
		100	100

Notes
1. In 1983, 4% of the reports (none of which is included in the sample) used wordings such as 'to the relevant year', 'to the appropriate year' or 'to the year to which they relate'.
2. While the descriptions of the bases given in the sampled reports differed as between 1983 and 1984 in 10% of the cases, there was no reference made in the 1984 reports to there having been any change in the basis used, although there was one reference to a change between 1982 and later years.
3. In no case (1983: 2%) was it stated that expenses had been accrued for the open years and in 7% (1983: 5%) of cases it was clearly stated that they had not. In 1% (1983: 1%) it was stated that there were no outstanding closed year expenses to be accrued.
4. In 79% (1983: 83%) of the sample the notes included a statement that expenses to date on open years were only provisional and further expenses would be charged in future years.
5. Of the reports not stating any allocation basis, half (i.e. 3%) (1983: 2%) had an underwriting account for only one year.

Personal Expenses

In the case of 3% of the sampled syndicates (1983: 2%) the notes stated that the audit fees were charged to personal accounts, and in a further 2% (1983: nil) it was noted that audit fees had been charged in this way in previous years but were now charged in syndicate expenses.

In the 1983 accounts, 67% of syndicates' reports had followed PAM's recommendation and had given a note about profit commission. Forty-one per cent stated that the basis was shown in the personal account; 3% merely that profit commission was charged in accordance with the agency agreement (or equivalent); while 16% gave some indication of the computation (e.g. 20% of the net result, less agent's salary, where this is a profit); and 7% showed that no commission was payable (either because business started after 1981; or because 1981 was still open; or because the 1981 result was a loss or was not a large enough profit to cover previous losses; or because the commission had been waived).

These disclosures about profit commission are not required by SAB, and in the sample of 1984 accounts only 27% gave a note in their published accounts (4% stating that the basis was shown in the personal accounts; 1% that it was according to the agency agreement; 20% giving details of the computation; and 2% showing the amount charged to personal accounts). However, all syndicate reports now have to include a seven year summary of past results (see Chapter 12) and a further 58% (as well as several of those who had given a note) showed the amount of profit commission as a separate item there, in some cases also explaining the basis of calculation.

Some reports also gave the basis on which other personal items were charged, and some gave the amounts of these charges. Four per cent of the sampled syndicates (1983: 4%) charged personal expenses (including profit commission) in the underwriting accounts.

Five per cent of the sampled reports (1983: 5%) also explained that Names' personal accounts had been credited with interest and appreciation on the investments in their personal reserves.

EXAMPLES

■ Example 1 discusses the equitable allocation of expenses to syndicates and to years of account; explains its policy on accruals and how the cost of equipment etc. is dealt with (cf. Chapter 8). Full comparatives for the analysed expense items are given and there is some discussion of profit commission.

■ Example 2 gives a 'standard' note about expense allocation and the provisional nature of open year expenses. It gives full comparatives for the analysed expense items and also a considerable amount of detail about personal expenses.

■ Examples 3 and 4 give above average detail about the bases of charging expenses to the syndicate. They also give full comparatives for analysed items (not reproduced). (Example 3 ceased business at the end of 1983 and is running off the 1981 and 1982 accounts.)

■ Example 5 gives inter alia the total calendar year expenses; full comparatives for analysed items; a depreciation charge; explanation of profit commission; and explanation of the restatement of past results for a change in basis of presentation. (Managing agent: Norman Frizzell Underwriting Ltd.)

■ Example 6 shows inter alia the amount of expenses charged by the managing agent. It does not give full comparatives for the analysed expense items. The policy on accruals is explained.

See also, Cassidy, Davis, 582; Eamonn Murphy, 242; Merrett, 799; S.A. Meacock, 727; Sedgwick Forbes, 48.

Example I

PULBROOK UNDERWRITNG MANAGEMENT LIMITED
BRITISH STANDARD MOTOR SYNDICATE 533

Accounting Policies and Notes to the Accounts 31st December 1984

2. **Syndicate Expenses**
    The major part of syndicate expenses relating to syndicates managed by Pulbrook
    Underwriting Management Ltd are specific to individual syndicates. Where
    allocation of non-specific expenses is necessary the apportionment is made by
    the managing agency on an equitable basis. Pulbrook Underwriting Management
    Ltd follows the general Lloyd's practice of allocating expenses which are specific
    to a year of account to that account and allocating non-specific expenses to the
    year of account in which they were incurred. Outstanding expenses are not
    reserved for the open accounts but are reserved for the closed account.

    The syndicate's managing agency Pulbrook Underwriting Management Ltd was
    until January 1985 a member of the Stewart Wrightson Group. The Group's
    personnel department and systems department made 'at cost' charges to the
    syndicate for personnel and computer bureau services.

    The Underwriter's remuneration is charged to the syndicate. The syndicate also
    pays an equitable proportion of the expenses of the agency's management office
    in St. Mary Axe where Pulbrook Underwriting Management Ltd's managed
    syndicates' accounting and taxation affairs are dealt with.

    It is not usual for syndicates to own fixed assets. The agency purchases syndicate
    motor cars, office equipment and the like from its own resources charging the
    syndicate over the useful life of the asset with fees in lieu of depreciation and
    accounting to the syndicate for any profit or loss made from disposal of the
    asset. A charge was made to compensate the agency for interest lost in financing
    the purchase of these assets. Similarly, syndicate employees' season ticket loans
    were made by the agency which charged the syndicate for interest lost.

    The cumulative expenses charged to the syndicate for each underwriting account
    were as follows:-

	1982 account £	1981 account £
Closed year of account after three years		
Salaries and related costs	426,315	419,349
Costs of accommodation	110,367	94,703
Lloyd's charges	2,259	2,110
Syndicate auditors' remuneration	8,157	7,683
Other expenses	125,300	138,491
	672,398	662,336

...

	1983 account £	*1982 account* £
Open year of account after two years		
Salaries and related costs	490,281	431,231
Costs of accommodation	110,787	106,482
Lloyd's charges	2,555	2,259
Syndicate auditors' remuneration	9,367	8,157
Other expenses	149,569	132,451
	762,559	680,580

	1984 account £	*1983 account* £
Open year of account after one year		
Salaries and related costs	552,075	484,849
Costs of accommodation	101,938	99,117
Lloyd's charges	3,070	2,555
Other expenses	167,649	129,868
	824,732	716,389

3. **Profit Commission**
    Profit commission is calculated on the sub-total immediately preceding profit
    commission on the member's personal account.

Example 2

PETER PEPPER (UNDERWRITING AGENCIES) LIMITED

MARINE SYNDICATE 228/229

Notes to the Accounts – 31st December 1984

1. **Accounting Policies** (continued)

(e) Syndicate expenses

Expenses incurred in the administration of the syndicates managed by the agency company, where they do not relate solely to this syndicate, are allocated between the syndicates according to the volumes of business transacted and are charged to the underwriting account for the year in which they are incurred. Expenses for the open underwriting accounts are included on a provisional basis and are not finalised until the accounts are closed.

3. **Syndicate Expenses**

1982 Account	£	1981 Account at 31.12.83 £
Salaries and related staff costs	158,199	99,479
Professional, computer and accounting charges	37,662	26,070
Cost of accommodation	9,123	7,952
Interest payable	2,599	2,298
Lloyd's charges	62,992	41,844
Auditors' remuneration	13,000	7,750
Investment management fees	16,449	–
Other expenses	57,761	21,576
Total Expenses	£357,785	£206,969

1983 Account	£	1982 Account at 31.12.83 £
Salaries and related staff costs	184,057	158,199
Professional, computer and accounting charges	50,265	37,662
Cost of accommodation	22,405	9,123
Interest payable	3,403	2,599
Lloyd's charges	90,600	60,435
Auditors' remuneration	16,000	13,000
Investment management fees	24,463	16,449
Other expenses	101,615	54,175
Total Expenses	£492,808	£351,642

...

PETER PEPPER (UNDERWRITING AGENCIES) LIMITED

MARINE SYNDICATE 228/229

Notes to the Accounts (continued) – 31st December 1984

		1983 Account at 31.12.83
1984 Account	£	£
Salaries and related staff costs	300,581	184,057
Professional, computer and accounting charges	59,770	45,954
Cost of accommodation	40,429	22,405
Interest payable	1,859	3,403
Lloyd's charges	84,230	69,024
Auditors' remuneration	–	1,900
Investment management fees	21,113	18,019
Other expenses	67,552	68,399
Total Expenses	£575,534	£413,161

4. **Personal Expenses**

Certain payments were made during the year on behalf of the Names of the Syndicate including the underwriting salary due to members' agents and the managing agency and the Name's proportion of the annual subscription due to Lloyd's.

The underwriting salary was calculated in accordance with clause 8 of the Underwriting Agreement at a rate of 1% of allocated premium limit subject to a minimum of £200 per annum.

Profit commission has been charged at a rate of 20% of the profit as defined in clause 10 of the Underwriting Agreement.

The Name's proportion of the annual subscription is paid by the Syndicate at a rate of 0.6% of allocated premium limit for 1982 year of account, at a rate of 0.75% for 1983 year of account, and at a rate of 0.85% for 1984 year of account.

Example 3

M.E.CHARLESWORTH (UNDERWRITING AGENTS) LIMITED

CHARLESWORTH MOTOR POLICIES AT LLOYD'S – MOTOR SYNDICATE 678

Notes to the Annual Report

4.   **Syndicate expenses**

Expenses incurred in the administration of the syndicate by the managing agency are recharged relative to the total premiums received and claims paid during the year. Expenses for open underwriting accounts are included on a provisional basis and are not finalised until the accounts are closed.

Expenses incurred by the managing agency are allocated among all the syndicates it administers on the following basis:-

Computer costs – Syndicate 678 ran on a bureau basis for its 1980 and previous years of account, thereafter an in-house system was developed for the 1981/2/3 years of account. Syndicates 734 and the agency and its subsidiary do not run programmes on the above system.

Box expenses – Syndicate 734 except for 1983 and prior when the cost of one seat, as charged by Lloyd's, was recharged to syndicate 678 and one seat to syndicate 24.

Underwriters remuneration – Specific to 31st December 1983, 100% to syndicate 734 thereafter.

Other salaries and related costs – Time expended.

Syndicate auditors' remuneration – Syndicates bear their own specific audit costs.

Costs of accommodation – Specific, except for shared accommodation which is divided on a time expended basis.

Interest payable – Based on balances with managing agency at each month end and calculated at the National Westminster Bank PLC deposit account rate.

Other expenses – Specific expenses are allocated to the syndicates concerned. Other general expenses are charged to syndicates based on time expended.

The managing agency and its subsidiary bear their own audit, occupancy and other relevant costs.

[Expenses not reproduced]

Example 4

CRESCENT UNDERWRITING AGENCIES LIMITED
MARINE SYNDICATE NO. 936/NON-MARINE SYNDICATE NO. 279

Notes to the Annual Report at 31st December 1984

2. **Syndicate Expenses**
    The expenses incurred by the managing agent in relation to services provided
    to all the syndicates it administers are allocated on the following bases:

Computer department and computer depreciation	−net premium income
Box expenses and underwriters' remuneration	−net premium income
Other payroll and related costs	−net premium income
Auditors' remuneration	−average underwriting balance
Occupancy costs	−net premium income
Interest payable	−net premium income
Equipment hire charge	−net premium income
Investment advisory fees	−average underwriting balance
Other expenses	−net premium income

    The managing agent bears its own audit costs and its proportion of occupancy
    costs.
    [Expenses not reproduced]

3. **Lloyd's Central Fund and Lloyd's Subscriptions**
    From 1982 these costs were charged direct to the Names' personal accounts.

Example 5

THE SERVICE MOTOR POLICIES
SYNDICATE NUMBER 979

Notes to the Accounts — 31st December 1984

6. **Syndicate Expenses**

Expenses incurred in the administration of the Syndicate are allocated to the year of Account in which the expenditure was incurred, with the exception of investment management expenses, which are allocated equally between the three Underwriting Accounts.

Expenses directly relating to claims settlements are included as claims.

Expenses for the open Underwriting Accounts are included on a provisional basis and are not finalised until the Accounts are closed.

Total expenses charged to the Syndicate during the calendar year 1984 amounted to £4,714,498 (1983 – £4,170,197). The accumulative expenses charged to the Syndicate for each year of Account as at 31st December 1984 are shown in the analysis below.

The Scheme Administration Fee referred to in the analysis of expenses reflects the fact that, in addition to normal brokerage, Norman Frizzell Motor & General receive a handling fee in order to defray the costs incurred by them of running the Syndicate's Scheme business under the terms of the relevant binding authority.

	1982 £	1981 £
1982 Account after three years		
Scheme Administration Fee	3,279,924	3,397,662
Salaries and related costs	555,175	569,502
Auditors' remuneration	30,380	20,734
Occupancy costs	76,216	67,413
Lloyd's charges	800	750
Interest payable	1,346	—
Other expenses	296,454	169,102
Quota-Share reinsurers contribution	(346,777)	(448,314)
	£3,893,518	£3,776,849

...

THE SERVICE MOTOR POLICIES
SYNDICATE NUMBER 979

Notes to the Accounts — 31st December 1984

	1983	1982
1983 Account after two years	£	£
Scheme Administration Fee	3,135,197	3,280,024
Salaries and related costs	711,020	417,286
Auditors' remuneration	19,190	7,368
Occupancy costs	109,025	76,216
Lloyd's charges	850	800
Interest payable	1,013	1,346
Other expenses	314,158	267,905
Quota-Share reinsurers contribution	(245,120)	(346,751)
	£4,045,333	£3,704,194

	1984	1983
1984 Account after one year	£	£
Scheme Administration Fee	3,176,106	3,082,753
Salaries and related costs	783,606	681,937
Auditors' remuneration	17,500	—
Occupancy costs	108,652	104,211
Lloyd's charges	950	850
Interest payable	979	1,013
Other expenses	266,861	241,862
Quota-Share reinsurers contribution	—	(237,813)
	£4,354,654	£3,874,813

7.   Fixed Assets

	Motor Vehicles	Fixtures, fittings & equipment	Total
Cost —	£	£	£
At 1st January 1984	92,258	9,777	102,035
Additions	30,690	13,121	43,811
Disposals	(32,598)	—	(32,598)
At 31st December 1984	90,350	22,898	113,248
Depreciation —			
At 1st January 1984	33,458	2,988	36,446
On disposals	(14,705)	—	(14,705)
Charge for the year	22,555	4,580	27,135
At 31st December 1984	41,308	7,568	48,876
Net Book Amount			
At 31st December 1984	£49,042	£15,330	£64,372
At 31st December 1983	£58,800	£6,789	£65,589

In the opinion of Norman Frizzell Underwriting Ltd., the net book amount of fixed assets is not materially different from their net realisable value.

...

THE SERVICE MOTOR POLICIES
SYNDICATE NUMBER 979

Notes to the Accounts — 31st December 1984

13.   Profit Commission

Profit Commission has been charged, as shown in the Personal Account, at 20% of the figure arrived at on the following basis:

Underwriting Profit (after deduction of Syndicate Expenses) plus Sterling Untaxed Interest, Gross Dividends and Interest and Capital Appreciation,

Less:

Names Expenses;

Less:

Income Tax on Dividends and Interest, and Capital Gains Tax;

Less:

Notional Income Tax at 30% on Sterling Untaxed Interest.

In addition, in arriving at the profit for the purposes of profit commission, a deduction has been made in respect of the loss arising on The T. Norman Frizzell Syndicate (Non Marine), Syndicate Number 975, for those Names underwriting on that syndicate, whose Names agreements allow such a deduction to be made.

14.   Seven Year Summary of Results of Closed Years

The seven year summary has been prepared from the audited accounts of the syndicate, adjusted to comply with the current accounting policies adopted in respect of the treatment of the Scheme Administration Fee. Prior to the 1979 account, this fee was treated as a deduction from Premium Income, but has since been accounted for as a Syndicate Expense. The change in policy does not affect the reported final result. The adjustments to Net Premium Income and Syndicate Expenses for the 1976, 1977 and 1978 account in respect of a Name with a standard £40,000 share are as follows:-

	1976 Account £	1977 Account £	1978 Account £
Old Accounting Policy			
Net Premium Income	31,330	34,938	30,656
Syndicate Expenses	972	907	820
Current Accounting Policy			
Net Premium Income	36,209	40,025	34,929
Syndicate Expenses	5,851	5,994	5,093

Example 6

R.J.KILN & CO. LIMITED

R.F.H.WILSHAW & OTHERS, NON-MARINE SYNDICATE NO. 807

Notes to the accounts at 31st December 1984

11. **Syndicate Expenses**

Expenses are charged to the underwriting account for the year in which they are incurred. Expenses for the open underwriting accounts are included on a provisional basis and are not finalised until the accounts are closed.

Expenses charged to the syndicate during the year by the managing agent totalled £106,938. This figure is derived from an apportionment between the managing agent and its managed syndicates on a time basis for salaries and a costed basis for joint services, the syndicates' individual charges then being an allocation according to volumes of business transacted.

The cumulative expenses charged to the syndicate for each year of account were as follows:

	Open years		Closed years	
	1984	1983	1982	1981
	£	£	£	£
Salaries and related costs	88,870	95,609	55,856	48,472
Costs of accommodation	10,114	6,067	2,000	1,900
Lloyd's charges	12,814	27,321	26,213	19,977
Auditors' remuneration	–	6,105	5,263	5,000
Other expenses	26,037	49,614	52,650	34,808
Total expenses	137,835	184,716	141,982	110,157

In accordance with the syndicate accounting rules, the above figures exclude any provisions for outstanding unpaid expenses except within the charge by the managing agent.

CHAPTER 10

FOREIGN CURRENCY
TRANSLATION AND TAXATION

I. FOREIGN CURRENCY TRANSLATION

INTRODUCTION

As part of the arrangements required by insurance regulations in the USA and Canada the premiums in respect of US and Canadian dollar policies are held in specified trust funds in those countries, to be used only for the payment of claims and legitimate expenses, until such time as the result for the underwriting year is determined, when the profit may be distributed to Names. These arrangements parallel the requirements in the UK for all premiums to be paid into the premiums trust fund, and not distributed to Names until the result for the year has been determined (i.e. after the end of at least the third year).

Syndicates writing business in the USA and Canada therefore have to have funds in three currencies. Syndicates may also have assets, liabilities and transactions in other currencies; while syndicates writing, say, only UK motor business, will not have any foreign currency transactions.

REQUIREMENTS

While SAB does not specify any particular accounting treatment, the explanatory notes set out the appropriate treatment (in line with the earlier recommendations in PAM) and in practice treatment is almost completely standard. This 'standard' practice is as illustrated in Example 1 below.

The explanatory notes recommend:

57. *Translation of foreign currency items for the preparation of the annual report*
   Transactions and assets and liabilities denominated in US or Canadian dollars for which separate accounting records are required to be maintained by virtue of Schedule 2 paragraph 2 should be translated into

sterling at the rates ruling at the reference date to which an annual report is made up.

The rates of exchange for this purpose will be advised to managing agents by Lloyd's. Where assets denominated in other currencies are held at the reference date a similar treatment will be appropriate (e.g. in the case of a Deutsche Mark deposit account).

58. *Exchange differences on convertible currency items processed through Lloyd's central accounting*
Exchange differences on convertible currency transactions processed through Lloyd's central accounting arising between the dates of signing and of settlement should be treated as a restatement of the relevant underwriting transaction and included under the appropriate underwriting account format heading.

59. *Purchase and sale of currency*
Where it is necessary to purchase or sell a currency to liquidate a closed year of account and the purchase or sale takes place after the reference date and at a rate different from that then ruling the profit or loss arising should be attributed to the year of account into which the liabilities of the closed year of account have been reinsured. Where the closed year of account has been reinsured outside the syndicate, then the profit or loss arising on the sale or purchase of a currency should be allocated to the members participating in the closed year of account and should be separately disclosed in the personal account. Where it is necessary to purchase or sell a currency in respect of an open year of account then any profit or loss arising from a movement in the exchange rate since the previous 31st December should be reflected in the next underwriting account prepared for that open year of account.

ANALYSIS

The prescribed format for the 1984 and subsequent accounts (and as recommended for the 1983 accounts) requires profit or loss on exchange to be shown in the underwriting account after the 'technical' underwriting result and in the section dealing with investment returns and expenses. Most syndicates were already doing this in their 1983 accounts, but, as noted in Chapter 3, the positions of items within this section of the account frequently varied that year. By the 1984 accounts the presentation was standardised. The underwriting accounts are presented in sterling: but some agents' syndicates also gave the underlying currency figures and some gave figures for investments, cash or the balance of net assets held in each currency (see also Example 4 to Chapter 3).

In both years the majority of reports gave a 'standard' note like that illustrated in Example 1. They commonly included the explanation (not included in PAM's specimen) that the comparative figures were stated at the rates ruling at the previous year-end; several syndicates pointed out that the figure for the 'reinsurance to close' that had been transferred into the closing underwriting account from the preceding year differed from that shown in the preceding year's account as transferred out, because of restatement at the new rates of exchange; some gave the rates used (see also

Appendix V); and several referred to having translated transactions at 'rates advised by Lloyd's Central Accounting Bureau'. On the other hand, some syndicates omitted the general explanation that brought-forward figures had been retranslated.

2. TAXATION

INTRODUCTION

It is not the purpose of this section to explain the (extremely complex) bases on which Names' income from Lloyd's underwriting and investment activities is taxed in the UK, the USA, Canada and other countries, but merely to try and explain its impact on the accounts. It is easiest to start from the basic position that each Name is assessed individually by the relevant Revenue services according to the type of income he derives from the syndicate, the country in which that income arises, his own resident status, the effect of any double tax treaties and the remainder of his personal tax situation. If it was this simple there would, of course, be no need for any accounting for tax in the syndicate accounts. It would be left entirely to Names to deal with on their personal tax returns.

It is, however, not that simple. Subject to certain concessions, the managing agent is normally responsible for withholding and paying over to the UK Inland Revenue basic rate income tax on investment income, and capital gains tax at the basic rate on investment appreciation (both realised and unrealised) on account of Names' final liability. This withholding is shown in the underwriting account in arriving at the net profit or loss for the closed year or net balance for the open years. Individual Names will then be liable for settling any tax due at higher rates (or be able to claim repayments, e.g. under capital gains tax minimum level exemption rules) as part of their own tax return.

Where a separate fund of US and Canadian dollar securities has been established for the investments attributable to US Names, usually no UK capital gains tax will be withheld. Similarly UK government securities held for more than one year are exempt from capital gains tax. In no case is any tax withheld or otherwise dealt with in respect of the underwriting profit or loss (including exchange profits and losses).

In the case of income taxable in the USA or Canada, arrangements are normally made for the filing of tax returns on behalf of UK Names by the managing agent through Lloyd's and nominated attorneys. Tax liabilities are settled by the agent on Names' behalf and charged to their personal accounts. Practice varies as to whether agents charge payments on account to Names' personal accounts before the year in which the liability is finally settled. Where no such filing arrangements apply, individual Names are responsible for their own tax returns and settlements.

US, Canadian and other overseas residents are responsible for their own domestic tax returns and no amounts are charged by the managing agent to their personal accounts.

There is thus no general systematic relationship between the before-tax earnings of a syndicate and the amounts of tax deducted in arriving at the net cheque payable to a Name, other than for the normal withholding of UK basic rate income tax and capital gains tax on the investment returns shown in the underwriting accounts. Correspondingly this is the only taxation included in the seven year summaries of past results (see Chapter 12).

REQUIREMENTS

In regard to Schedule 3, para. 5(h) (requirement to disclose the basis on which UK taxation is provided) the explanatory notes to SAB suggest:

60. This paragraph requires the basis on which UK taxation has been provided to be disclosed as an accounting policy. In addition the underwriting account format set out in Schedule 4 paragraph 1.1 includes, as items to be disclosed, income tax on investment income and capital gains tax on investment appreciation. In arriving at the amounts to be included in the underwriting account the practices set out in paragraphs 61 to 63 of these explanatory notes will normally be appropriate.

61. Where arrangements exist for the agent to pay to the Inland Revenue:
    (i)   basic rate income tax on investment income from which tax has not been deducted at source; and
    (ii) capital gains tax on realised or unrealised investment appreciation; the tax payable should be charged in the underwriting account and included in the balance sheet as a liability at the same time as the related income or appreciation is recognised. Interest, dividends and capital appreciation included in the underwriting account should therefore be stated before deduction of any taxation (or grossed up to reflect any tax credit) with the deduction for taxation being disclosed separately as indicated in the underwriting account format.

62. Where at any reference date gilt-edged securities have been held for less than 12 months the agent may assume that they will not be disposed of until at least 12 months have elapsed and that capital gains tax therefore will not be payable, *provided* that at the time the annual report is prepared disposal has not taken place and there is not at that time an intention to dispose of the securities within 12 months of the date of purchase.

63. A note to the annual report should state that it is the personal responsibility of each member of the syndicate to agree final taxation liabilities with the Inland Revenue and to settle any higher rate liability or investment income surcharge.

In regard to para.5(i) (disclosure of the basis on which US and Canadian taxation is charged in the personal accounts) the explanatory notes suggest:

64. The basis upon which the managing agent charges to the personal accounts of members of the syndicate amounts in relation to US and Canadian taxation is to be disclosed as an accounting policy. The policy should indicate the treatment of payments on account as well as that relating to

the final tax charge or recovery. Where arrangements do not exist for the filing of tax returns in respect of the US or Canadian taxation affairs of certain members of the syndicate the annual report should state that it is the personal responsibility of each such member to settle any tax due. A similar policy should apply to the treatment of overseas taxation charged to members of the syndicate in relation to countries other than the United States or Canada.

ANALYSIS

Notes to the accounts that cover the items recommended to be disclosed in the 1984 and subsequent accounts by the explanatory notes to SAB (essentially the same as were earlier recommended by PAM) are illustrated in the Examples.

The notes about Names' personal responsibilities and about double tax relief sometimes referred generally to all overseas countries, rather than just the USA or Canada.

One agent's accounts for its US Names included a 25% reserve for US taxation on unrealised capital gains, to equalise charges between Names on the syndicates in different years.

EXAMPLES

■   Example 1 gives a fairly standard note about foreign currencies and tax, of the kind recommended by PAM, with the addition of discussion about double taxation relief.

■   Examples 2 and 3 cover the essential elements about tax in a briefer form.

■   Example 3 – Managing Agent: R.K.Harrison & Graves Ltd.

See also J.H.Minet, 887.

Example 1

STENHOUSE EPPS (UNDERWRITING AGENCIES) LTD
N.F.EPPS & OTHERS LIVESTOCK SYNDICATE 454

Notes to the Accounts 31st December 1984

1. **Accounting Policies**

    Basis of currency translation and conversion
    The syndicate operates in three separate currency funds of sterling, United States
    dollars and Canadian dollars. Items expressed in United States and Canadian
    dollars are translated to sterling at the rates of exchange ruling at the balance
    sheet date. Items brought forward from the previous year are therefore revalued
    at those rates. Transactions during the year in other overseas currencies are
    recorded at the rates ruling at the transaction date. Where United States or
    Canadian dollars are sold or bought relating to the profit or loss of a closed
    underwriting account after 31st December, any profit or loss arising is reflected
    in the underwriting account into which the liabilities of that year have been
    reinsured. Where United States or Canadian dollars are bought or sold in respect
    of any open underwriting account after 31st December then any profit or loss
    arising is reflected in the next underwriting account prepared for that open
    account. The comparative figures are translated into sterling at the exchange
    rates ruling at 31st December 1983.

    Taxation
    (a) Amounts are deducted on Names' behalf to provide for tax on both realised
         and unrealised chargeable gains and investment income at basic rates of
         United Kingdom capital gains tax and income tax respectively. No provision
         has been made in these accounts for United Kingdom income tax on the
         underwriting result or for higher rate income tax on investment income
         the agreement and settlement of which with the Inland Revenue are the
         personal responsibility of each Name. For United States Names, no capital
         gains tax on appreciation has been provided on United States and Canadian
         dollar investments.
    (b) Names resident outside the United Kingdom should be aware that no
         provision has been made for taxation liabilities arising in the country of
         residence. Whilst double taxation relief is usually available, substantial
         additional tax liabilities can sometimes arise as a result of the differing
         bases of taxation in other countries. This is particularly relevant to invest-
         ment appreciation which, in some countries, is reclassified as investment
         income.
    (c) Amounts reflected in personal underwriting accounts for United States
         Federal Income Tax relate to the final 1983 assessment of US source under-
         writing results of the 1980 account and US source investment earnings for
         calendar year 1983, and the provisional 1984 assessment relating to the
         1981 US source underwriting result and 1984 US source investment earn-
         ings. No provision has been made for any tax payable on United States
         underwriting results of 1982 and later years. It is the personal responsibility
         of Names resident in the United States for taxation purposes to agree and
         settle their taxation direct with the Internal Revenue Service.
                                                                              ...

STENHOUSE EPPS (UNDERWRITING AGENCIES) LTD
N.F.EPPS & OTHERS LIVESTOCK SYNDICATE 454

Notes to the Accounts 31st December 1984 (continued)

Taxation (continued)

(d) Amounts reflected in personal underwriting accounts for Canadian Federal Income Tax relate to the Canadian source underwriting results, including investment earnings, of the 1980 account. No provision has been made for any tax payable on Canadian underwriting results of 1981 and later years. It is the personal responsibility of Names who are resident in Canada for taxation purposes to agree and settle their Canadian Federal tax liabilities.

Example 2

MURRAY LAWRENCE & PARTNERS

C.T.BOWRING (UNDERWRITING AGENCIES) LIMITED
T.A.BOWRING & OTHERS
MARINE SYNDICATE No. 28

Notes to the accounts – 31st December 1984 (continued)

(f) Taxation
The taxation charged in the underwriting accounts represents United Kingdom taxation payable by the syndicate trustees on behalf of members, and comprises basic rate Income Tax on investment income and capital gains tax on chargeable gains included in investment appreciation.

Overseas taxation charged in each personal account represents United States Federal Income Tax and Canadian Federal Income Tax as paid by the syndicate trustees on behalf of the member concerned, and generally relates to United States tax for the 1983 US tax year, based on the underwriting result for the 1980 Account and investment yield realised during 1983, and Canadian tax based on the overall result of the 1980 Account.

No other provision has been made for taxation based on the results of the syndicate, and it is the personal responsibility of each member to agree and settle any taxation liability arising from participation in the syndicate.

Example 3

J. B. O. CARLETON PAGET AND OTHERS AVIATION SYNDICATE No. 451

NOTES TO THE ACCOUNTS AT 31st DECEMBER, 1984

(d) Taxation

Amounts are deducted on Names' behalf to provide for tax on both investment income and realised and unrealised chargeable gains at basic rate of United Kingdom tax. No provision has been made in these accounts for United Kingdom tax on the underwriting result or for higher rate tax on investment income which are the personal responsibility of each Name.

The amount of United States or Canadian Federal Income Tax as shown on the final tax assessment relative to each Name is charged to the earliest available personal account.

No provision is made for any tax that may be payable on subsequent assessments.

Payments on account of United States and Canadian Federal Income Tax, pending receipt of final tax assessments, have been included in personal expenses for 1983.

It is the personal responsibility of Names, resident in the United States or Canada for taxation purposes, to agree and settle their United States or Canadian taxation liabilities.

CHAPTER 11

EXTRAORDINARY AND EXCEPTIONAL ITEMS AND 'PURE YEAR' ACCOUNTING

INTRODUCTION AND REQUIREMENTS

As the purpose of insurance is to cover risks which, individually, are unexpected and often abnormal, it is difficult to suggest what it would be appropriate to treat as extraordinary or exceptional. The examples in SSAP6 itself (or in ED36, *Accountancy*, February 1985, pp. 106–116) are mostly inapplicable to the circumstances of a Lloyd's syndicate. Nevertheless, the explanatory notes to SAB indicate that SSAP6 should be treated as applying to Lloyd's accounting (including the open years even though a 'true and fair view' is not required); and there is a line in the underwriting account format for 'extraordinary items'.

It is pointed out that the provisions in SSAP6 relating to restatement of prior year profits will not be applicable because once the closed year result is determined and distributed the year of account is liquidated (although there are special provisions with regard to the gains or losses on the purchase or sale of foreign currencies to liquidate an account that has been reinsured outside the syndicate (see Chapter 10)).

Pure Year Accounting
Under 'exceptional items' PAM recommended for the 1983 accounts that that part of the 'technical' (i.e. underwriting) result of the closed year attributable to profits or losses relating to prior years reinsured into it should be disclosed in the notes, if material, but following market opposition this is not now a requirement. However, some syndicates are still giving this information (see Examples 2 and 3) and the amounts disclosed are often very substantial. In some cases, either an overall profit can be the result of a

'pure' 1982 year loss offset by a favourable adjustment of prior years' reserves, or an overall loss can result from a pure 1982 profit eliminated by the adverse development of the prior years. The trend shown for the pure figures can therefore be the reverse of that shown for the overall underwriting result. In the case of one agency group which provided this figure in both years (in 1984 for nine out of fifteen syndicates managed and in 1983 for fourteen out of sixteen), the average amount in the 1982 closed account was only 11% of the reinsurance to close brought forward from 1981 but was 148% of the 1982 closed year underwriting result (1981 underwriting account: 4% and 63% respectively). As information is rarely provided in other ways about the run-off of prior years, it is, in my opinion, regrettable that this recommended disclosure has not been incorporated into the requirements of SAB for the 1984 and subsequent years' accounts. It would at least aid understanding of the kind of margin of error within which the estimates have to be made. Although fewer syndicates gave this information in their 1984 accounts than in their 1983 accounts, I hope that the syndicates which have been giving this information will continue to do so and that others will choose to follow them.

   To give a full analysis of how the prior years had affected the syndicate's results for the underwriting year being closed in the 1984 accounts (i.e. 1982), would require the premiums and claims in respect of those years to be segregated and matched against the 'reinsurance to close' received. In addition, the 'reinsurance to close' transferred out to the succeeding year of account (1983) would need to be analysed into the 'pure' amount relating to the outstandings of 1982 underwriting, and the amount now carried forward for 1981 and prior years. This would show to what extent the underwriter considered that his reserves for prior years needed strengthening, were adequate, or were proving over-conservative. The most complete analysis would further analyse the 'prior years' into each individual underwriting year, and ultimately show how each had finally run off. (See Examples 4 and 5 below).

   Whether pure year accounting should become the norm at Lloyd's is ultimately a question of the objectives and uses of the accounts, and of Names' rights to information. (It would, for example, be a more stringent requirement than that for industrial long-term contractors, but no more onerous than the present requirements for insurance companies to file returns with the DTI [SI1983 No.1811, Sch. 2].) As can be seen from the analysis below, in general information is not currently given to show pure year results for the year being closed, let alone full run-off statistics to show how the individual past years have finally turned out.

ANALYSIS

In the sample, no syndicate reported any extraordinary items in the under-writing accounts. However, of the sample, 5% (1983: 5%) included a note about exceptional items and another 5% (1983: 6%) gave similar informa-tion even though it was not labelled as 'exceptional'. Two reports (1983: seven) showed the effect on the closed year result of the previous year's reinsurance to close, as in Examples 2 and 3 below; six reports (1983: four) gave the amount of recovery on a whole account stop loss policy in respect of the 1982 (1981) underwriting account (one of these also gave in 1983 an amount relating to reinsurance premiums paid); one (1983: nil) gave other amounts relating to reinsurance recoveries; and one (1983: nil) explained the impact of a change in its policy of allocating investment income (see Chapter 7, Example 2).

Apart from the statements of the net effect of prior years on the underwrit-ing result, some syndicates included some other information in their 1984 accounts about the way the pure years had developed, as follows:

(a) Some syndicates included information about the 'settlement ratio' for each year (percentage of claims to premiums) and in the case of closed years gave this 'excluding prior years'. However, this ratio appears only to cover claims settled (without provision for claims incurred but not settled, or not reported) so that with just this information one cannot disentangle the composition of the reinsurance to close.

(b) Some syndicates included in addition to their seven year summary of past results both the settled ratio and the incurred ratio for the past closed years (see Example 3 in Chapter 12.) If the premium income was pure this should enable a reader to work out: (i) how much of the settled claims appearing in the underwriting account were pure, and how much related to prior years (although in fact this information was provided – see Example 1); and (ii) how much of the reinsurance to close each year had been the provision for outstanding claims of that pure year (and therefore how much related to prior years). So if one could assume that premiums after the third year were insignificant, these ratios would effectively give the same information for each year in the summary as that given, more obviously, in the 'total' line of Example 4 below.

(c) One agent's syndicates gave a full analysis of how the underwriting items might be analysed between the current closed year and prior years. The analysis was also given by class of business, but it was not broken down by the *individual* prior years (see Example 4 below).

(d) In one case (in both 1984 and 1983) a full analysis was given for each prior year (back as far as 1958) (Example 5).

(e) The underwriters also frequently commented in their reports on how the old years were behaving (see Chapter 16).

EXAMPLES

■ Example 1 (the same syndicate as Example 3 to Chapter 12) gives some information about the claims etc. relating to prior years. See also C.J.W., 553 and Gardner Mountain & Capel-Cure, 2.

■ Examples 2 and 3 show the effect of the prior years' on the current year's result. (Example 3 – managing agent: Edwards & Payne (Underwriting Agencies) Ltd.)

■ Example 4 gives a full analysis of the development of the reinsurance to close brought forward (managing agent: Lambert Brothers (Underwriting Agencies) Ltd.)

■ Example 5 gives an analysis of the individual prior years' development.

Example I

SEDGWICK FORBES (LLOYD'S UNDERWRITING AGENTS) LIMITED

W.E.SIMMS & OTHERS AVIATION SYNDICATE NO. 48

Notes to the Accounts

2. **Net Premium for Reinsurance to Close the 1982 (1981) Underwriting Account**

	1982 Account After 3 Years	1981 Account After 3 Years
Reinsurance Premium from previous closed year revalued at exchange rates ruling at 31 December 1984 (1983)	20,857,629	16,400,506
Reduced by settlements made on 1981 (1980) and previous Years of Account made during 1984 (1983)	4,578,022	3,138,002
	16,279,607	13,262,504
Increased by additional fund required to cover estimated liabilities on 1982 (1981) and previous Years of Account at 31 December 1984 (1983)	6,324,800	3,763,600
	£22,604,407	£17,026,104

Example 2

STENHOUSE EPPS (UNDERWRITING AGENCIES) LTD.
N.F.EPPS & OTHERS LIVESTOCK SYNDICATE 454

Notes to the Accounts 31st December 1984

2. Underwriting result

The 1982 account underwriting result of £132,999 includes a profit of £23,866 in respect of the incoming premium for the reinsurance to close of the 1981 account.

Example 3

C.D.RAYNOR MARINE SYNDICATE NO.304/303
Accounting Policies and Notes to the Accounts at 31st December 1984

4.   Underwriting Result of the Closed Year

	1982 account £000's	1981 account £000's
Pure account	410	(78)
Surplus/(Deficit) on previous accounts	(451)	229
	(41)	151

Example 4

NOTE 10

MARINE SYNDICATE 434,437/438

ANALYSIS OF PREMIUM FOR REINSURANCE OF OUTSTANDING LIABILITIES ON 1981 ACCOUNT AND PREVIOUS YEARS INTO 1982 ACCOUNT AT 31ST DECEMBER 1983, DURING 1984.

	Reinsurance Premium on 1981 Account & Previous at 31.12.83 Syndicate 352,353/354	Reinsurance Premium on 1981 Account & Previous at 31.12.83 Syndicate 434,437/438	Reinsurance Premium on 1981 Account & Previous at 31.12.83 (Total)	(Settlements) /Recoveries during 1984	(Surplus) /Deficit	Balance on 1981 Account & Previous at 31.12.84	Outstanding Liabilities on 1982 Account at 31.12.84	Reinsurance to Close 1982 Account & Previous at 31.12.84
	£	£	£	£	£	£	£	£
Time All Risks	1,479,380	5,509,560	6,988,940	(996,530)	(276,667)	5,715,743	1,400,231	7,115,974
Total Loss Only	-	-	-	(20,370)	20,370	-	-	-
Liabilities	148,475	826,574	975,049	(743,249)	255,080	486,880	155,589	642,469
Voyage	342,992	1,743,995	2,086,987	(55,535)	(857,979)	1,173,473	424,150	1,597,623
War	2,721	32,036	34,757	5,690	(10,958)	29,489	33,000	62,489
Yachts	-	-	-	(5,416)	5,416	-	-	-
Non Marine	11,932	1,511,431	1,523,363	(4,090)	(407,441)	1,111,832	-	1,111,832
Aviation	1,617	10,587	12,204	(632)	(465)	11,107	87	11,194
TOTAL £	1,987,117	9,634,183	11,621,300	(1,820,132)	(1,272,644)	8,528,524	2,013,057	10,541,581

Example 5

PIERI (UNDERWRITING AGENCIES) LIMITED

MARINE SYNDICATE 872/873

RE-INSURANCE TO CLOSE 1982 ACCOUNT

		Lloyd's Audit Requirements 31.12.84	Additional Requirements	Re-insurance to close 31.12.84
		£	£	£
MARINE				
Voyage	10%	54,292	50,000	104,292
Voyage - Livestock	5%	2,024	–	2,024
Time	30%	287,932	100,000	387,932
Time - TLO	15%	47,613	–	47,613
Time - Liability	75%	34,788	–	34,788
Time - Yacht	12%	5,666	–	5,666
War	5%	7,237	–	7,237
Aviation - ST	10%	5,476	–	5,476
OB	60%	–	–	–
		445,028	150,000	595,028
NON-MARINE				
Short	7½%	1,677	–	1,677
Other - US$ Business	85%	1,261	6,237	7,498
All other Business	58%	598	2,957	3,555
		3,536	9,194	12,730
TOTAL		£448,564	£159,194	£607,758

...

PIERI (UNDERWRITING AGENCIES) LIMITED

MARINE SYNDICATE 872/873

SETTLEMENTS ON YEARS REINSURED INTO 1982 ACCOUNT – MARINE

Year		R.I. Premiums at 31.12.83	Net Premiums during 1984	Net Settlement during 1984	Net Claims during 1984	Balance of R.I. Premium 31.12.84	Lloyd's Audit Requirements 31.12.84	Additional requirements	Re-insurance to close 31.12.84
1981	V	166,069	12,223		20,658	157,634	51,939	80,695	132,634
	T	839,349	153,346		247,135	745,560	394,131	291,429	685,560
	W	12,473	(2,096)		(434)	10,811	–	5,811	5,811
	AV	11,776	6,289		(19)	18,084	166	2,918	3,084
1980	V	54,309	2,405		11,515	45,199	32,616	12,583	45,199
	T	512,571	1,778		83,697	430,652	199,631	191,021	390,652
	W	51,400	(173)		26,073	25,154	–	25,154	25,154
	AV	5,231	143		(382)	5,756	353	15,403	15,756
1979	V	35,287	510		(74,520)	110,317	–	73,201	73,201
	T	383,292	(1,282)		71,969	310,041	96,035	155,422	251,457
	W	845	252		(20,818)	21,915	–	1,915	1,915
	AV	4,810	–		2	4,808	231	4,577	4,808
1978	V	15,490	(492)		6,227	8,771	–	8,771	8,771
	T	278,283	1,959		51,997	228,245	70,314	123,946	194,260
	W	5,080	(54)		(3,030)	8,056	–	3,056	3,056
	AV	11,166	15		619	10,562	550	5,012	5,562
1977	V	5,048	(198)		(40)	4,890	–	4,890	4,890
	T	184,371	(2,356)		12,029	169,986	42,190	58,637	100,827
	W	2,412	(76)		2,274	62	–	62	62
	AV	12,513	53		1,602	10,964	1,529	9,435	10,964
1976	V	15,625	(119)		(2,108)	17,614	–	17,614	17,614
	T	82,102	(876)		17,372	63,854	35,141	18,827	53,968
	W	81	2		–	83	–	83	83
	AV	25,240	17		837	24,420	2,118	12,302	14,420
1975	V	20,305	(44)		(1,034)	21,295	–	5,404	5,404
	T	61,408	(676)		16,266	44,466	2,201	42,265	44,466
	W	315	23		–	338	–	18,525	18,525
	AV	17,310	37		(84)	17,431	2,476	7,455	9,931
1974	V	9,089	2		(1,186)	10,277	–	10,277	10,277
	T	63,752	(529)		942	62,281	1,598	17,566	19,164
	W	19,015	–		–	19,015	–	11,173	11,173
	AV	15,329	15		675	14,669	–	12,169	12,169
1973	V	6,439	8		(29)	6,476	–	3,476	3,476
	T	28,992	(45)		(3,161)	32,108	–	7,108	7,108
	W	(122)	–		–	(122)	–	(122)	(122)
	AV	11,957	(64)		589	11,304	–	6,304	6,304
1972	V	7,604	(82)		85	7,437	–	–	–
	T	22,282	(312)		896	21,074	–	6,074	6,074
	W	(405)	–		–	(405)	–	(405)	(405)
	AV	3,896	(37)		291	3,568	–	3,568	3,568
1971	V	4,710	(2)		46	4,662	–	–	–
	T	5,533	(11)		363	5,159	–	5,159	5,159
	W	(211)	–		–	(211)	–	(211)	(211)
	AV	9,480	(25)		133	9,322	–	17,493	17,493
1970+	V	12,852	–		(186)	13,038	–	3,038	3,038
Previous	T	49,890	(6)		5,087	44,797	–	24,797	24,797
	W	362	–		–	362	–	362	362
	AV	23,215	3		(174)	23,392	–	15,892	15,892
TOTAL		£3,107,820	£169,525	£(302,649)	£472,174	£2,805,171	£933,219	£1,340,131	£2,273,350

Notes

1. With effect from 1st January 1984 Syndicate 872 assumed responsibility for 53% of the net outstanding liabilities on the 1981 account and years reinsured therein of Syndicate 232 group, which ceased underwriting on 31st December 1981. The abovementioned table, represents the 100 percent figures, of which 53 per cent relates to Syndicate 872.

2. The figures stated for the reinsurance to close at 31.12.84 are shown gross before quota share reinsurance recoveries (note 2(b) to the accounts refers).

...

PIERI (UNDERWRITING AGENCIES) LIMITED

MARINE SYNDICATE 872/873

SETTLEMENTS ON YEARS REINSURED INTO 1982 ACCOUNT – NON-MARINE

		R.I. Premiums at 31.12.83	Net Premiums during 1984	Net Settlement during 1984	Net Claims during 1984	Balance of R.I. Premium 31.12.84	Lloyd's Audit Re-quirements 31.12.84	Additional re-quirements	Re-insurance to close 31.12.84
1981	ST/OB	46,111	(177)		954	44,980	7,237	19,869	27,106
1980	ST/OB	30,043	(212)		(698)	30,529	2,084	8,907	10,991
1979	ST/OB	15,551	(1,116)		789	13,646	7,072	17,314	24,386
1978	OB	8,260	141		14	8,387	1,520	4,748	6,268
1977	OB	15,085	82		–	15,167	601	12,312	12,913
1976	OB	30,717	(271)		(367)	30,813	704	12,226	12,930
1975	OB	35,859	–		–	35,859	588	17,771	18,359
1974	OB	31,187	–		–	31,187	1,277	11,370	12,647
1973	OB	29,612	21		–	29,633	354	12,176	12,530
1972	OB	28,154	–		40	28,114	582	19,917	20,499
1971	OB	34,226	–		67	34,159	5,429	14,974	20,403
1970	OB	32,107	–		84	32,023	459	35,726	36,185
1969	OB	44,685	–		31	44,654	1,033	54,891	55,924
1968	OB	55,640	5		12	55,633	–	67,922	67,922
1967	OB	23,855	–		4	23,851	–	50,344	50,344
1966	OB	14,836	–		2	14,834	–	30,778	30,778
1965	OB	17,511	–		7	17,504	–	25,256	25,256
1964	OB	39,100	–		4,914	34,186	–	59,240	59,240
1963	OB	17,780	–		2	17,778	–	41,069	41,069
1962	OB	48,906	–		64	48,842	–	72,066	72,066
1961	OB	61,588	–		130	61,458	...	44,524	44,524
1960	OB	86,237	–		9,709	76,528	–	58,729	58,729
1959	OB	66,745	–		–	66,745	–	64,440	64,440
1958+ Previous	OB	249,029	–		28,543	220,486	–	295,087	295,087
TOTAL		£1,062,824	£(1,527)	£(45,828)	£44,301	£1,016,996	£28,940	£1,051,656	£1,080,596

Notes

1. With effect from 1st January 1984 Syndicate 872 assumed responsibility for 53% of the net outstanding liabiliies on the 1981 account and years reinsured therein of Syndicate 232 group, which ceased underwriting on 31st December 1981. The abovementioned table represents the 100 per cent figures, of which 53 per cent relates to Syndicate 872.

2. The figures stated for the reinsurance to close at 31.12.84 are shown gross before quota share reinsurance recoveries (note 2(b) to the accounts refers).

CHAPTER 12

THE SEVEN YEAR SUMMARY AND THE EFFECTS OF INFLATION

INTRODUCTION

SAB requires (Para.5) that the audited annual reports include a statement showing the results of the closed year and the six preceding years. Because the size of a syndicate's business may vary from year to year (due to changes in the number of Names, and/or its premium capacity, as well as in the proportion of capacity actually used by the underwriter), much of the information is to be expressed in terms of results for a 'standard share', i.e. how much of the underwriting and investment results would be attributable to a Name whose capacity on the syndicate was, say, £10,000 net premium income for the year. The objective is similar to that of calculating 'earnings per share' in a company's accounts.

The size of the standard share is for the managing agent to choose in the light of the actual premium limits of members of the syndicate, but the most commonly used amounts are £10,000 and £20,000 (see Table 1). The 'League Tables' (Rew & Sturge, 1985) use a £10,000 share for making comparisons between syndicates. The argument for not requiring all syndicates to use the same amount in their accounts is probably based on the fact that such a seven year summary is part of the information that a new Name is required to be given in respect of the syndicates he is joining [CII (1981) 3 B1J] so that it is convenient for it to be prepared by reference to the 'normal' share for each syndicate. However, for comparison between syndicates a uniform share would be the most useful.

The Effects of Inflation

There are no requirements in SAB (and there were no recommendations in PAM) for any form of supplementary statements to show the effect of changing prices; nor did any syndicate provide them with their 1984 or 1983 accounts. However, syndicates hold no long-term productive assets; their investments are already stated at market value in the balance sheet; and all other assets should appear at net realisable value. The three year accounting system precludes the need for most accruals. Syndicates have little or no borrowing, so no question of gearing adjustments would arise. Current cost accounting would therefore generally add nothing to the information provided. (Insurance companies too were exempted from SSAP16, as they were from ED35 – though their case may be less strong (Macve, 1977).)

Inflation, however, has a serious impact on insurers' operations in at least two ways: first the need to cover escalation in cost of claims as prices rise and second the need to increase premium capacity.

With regard to claims, there is the need to provide for the estimated escalation in costs (particularly severe in long-tail business) in estimating the reinsurance to close, the size of which thus partly depends on the underwriter's estimate of future cost levels – but no indication of the kinds of assumption being made about inflation was given. Insurance companies too give no indication of the levels they are assuming (see Peat, Marwick, Mitchell & Co., 1984, section 3.13).

Premium capacity also needs to be raised to keep up with rising price levels (and over the seven years from the beginning of 1976 to the end of 1982 UK prices, as measured by the Index of Retail Prices, more than doubled). In the case of an insurance company, this requires increasing assets to provide the necessary solvency margin (so some 'solvency margin adjustment' might be appropriate). In the case of a Lloyd's syndicate, either individual Names must increase their 'shares' (and correspondingly must have increased wealth to support their underwriting) or new Names must be found.

The need for increased personal asset backing to support the level of Names' underwriting (see also Appendix VI) is, of course, an off balance sheet item in regard to the syndicate accounts. So there is little scope for the accounts to reveal the effects of inflation.

I believe (and have argued elsewhere (1977)) that further consideration needs to be given to the possibility of re-expressing all the figures in the underwriting accounts in terms of a constant price level; but it would be unreasonable to expect this of Lloyd's when the problems have not yet been researched by the insurance companies, and when CPP adjustments are politically out of favour in the inflation accounting debate.

The Sandilands report, in arguing for current cost accounting, nevertheless saw a role for the use of CPP adjustments in historical tables of dividend levels, and for the use of ratios in indicating real trends in profitability over time (paras. 625–627). Lloyd's syndicates' historical tables of results are the seven year summaries. Should these include inflation adjustments?

In fact, the presentation by a 'standard share' seems an effective way of meeting this need. If, for example, a Name had a £10,000 share for 1976 and a £20,000 share for 1982, and his cheque was £1,500 for 1976 and £2,500 for 1982 (and he was in line with the 'average' for his syndicate), the seven year summary, which might give results for a standard share of

£20,000, would show net results of £3000 for 1976 and £2500 for 1982 indicating that the real result for the amount of assets he was required to show was worse. It would, of course, be necessary for the Name to make his own calculations of how far he had been increasing his 'real' capacity at Lloyd's after adjusting for inflation.

A further useful feature of a number of the seven year summaries provided in the 1983 reports was the expression of the various outgoings as a percentage of the net premium income for the standard share, which again helps to reveal real trends. Given the fluctuation in the level to which capacity is used, such ratios can also help significantly in identifying real changes in the level of variable costs, and the impact of premium fluctuations on the absorption of fixed costs. In my opinion, these additional calculations should be more widely presented; but unfortunately, the tendency to uniformity seems to have led some agents to stop giving them in their 1984 reports (although to do so would in no way conflict with SAB) (cf. Examples 2, 3 and 4 below).

REQUIREMENTS

Under SAB the seven year summary has to show for each year the following information about the syndicate:

(a) the syndicate allocated capacity
(b) the number of members of the syndicate
(c) the aggregate net premium income (i.e. gross premiums less reinsurance premiums).

It then shows (but computed for the 'standard share'):

(a) all the information that will have appeared in the underwriting account for each closed year (apart from any 'extraordinary items') – arriving at the 'profit or loss before personal expenses'
(b) standard personal expenses
(c) profit or loss after standard personal expenses.

The figures in (a) are to be taken from the audited accounts, adjusted where necessary for changes in accounting policy since the accounts for a year were originally prepared. Where the underwriting accounts may be analysed or split between different subgroups of Names to reflect the results of the different administration of their investments, the figures in the seven year summary will be split also. Where an account has not been closed, this is to be made clear in the summary.

The figures in (b) are essentially an average of the various actual personal expenses incurred by the Names on the syndicate (apart from overseas tax) and enable a Name to compare 'the average' with the charges appearing in his own personal account (by relating it to his own capacity in the syndicate).

There are some technical difficulties about computing the results for a 'standard share'. For example, where Names die during a year the final participation of the remaining Names will be a slightly higher percentage of the total than originally envisaged. While the Byelaw requires computation of the standard share by reference to the year-end situation, the ALM considers comparisons would be easier by reference to the opening position. It may also be argued that as keeping a year open means that the investment earnings, expenses and re-estimates of outstanding liabilities that would normally affect the results of later years are thereby segregated into the run-off year, comparisons between earlier and later years' results are thereby inevitably distorted.

For the 1983 reports, the summary was only a recommended attachment to the accounts, and it was not required that it be audited. The information recommended in PAM was generally similar to that now required by SAB for the 1984 and subsequent accounts, except that it only showed net premium income for the standard share (not gross and net) and did not include any tax charges.

It may be noted that PAM's recommendations and SAB's requirements only relate to the information to be disclosed, and do not specify any particular order or format beyond requiring a tabular layout for the seven years' figures (although PAM also gave a specimen).

ANALYSIS

In no case in either year were specific comments made about the incidence of inflation on the growth of the figures over the years; but, as discussed above, the use of the standard share calculation acts as a deflator, and in some cases items expressed as a percentage of the net premium income were also given (see Examples 2, 3 and 4 below).

Table 1 analyses the sizes of standard share used for the summaries in the 1984 and 1983 reports (one 1984 summary omitted the share and in a few cases the size varied during the seven years).

1984 Reports
Of the 457 reports filed, 422 (92%) included a seven year summary. The following data relate to the random sample of one hundred syndicate reports. Three syndicates had started business after 1982 and so had no past results. Of the remaining 97 all provided the summaries except for one which was due to merge with another syndicate and where the agents considered the information would serve no useful purpose (the auditors reporting that, subject to this, the annual report complied with the syndicate accounting rules).

Summaries for shorter periods were given in forty-two cases (presumably where syndicates had less than seven years' past results although only half

Table I. Size of standard share

£000	1984 reports Number of summaries	%	1983 reports Number of summaries	%
1	1	—	1	1
2	2	—	1	1
3	1	—	—	—
4	2	1	—	—
5	13	3	10	6
6 (see note)	2	1	2	1
8 (see note)	1	—	1	1
10	130	31	47	29
12 (see note)	1	—	1	1
14 (see note)	1	—	2	1
15	21	5	3	2
16	1	—	—	—
20	119	29	46	28
25	23	6	10	6
30	26	6	13	8
35	—	—	1	1
36	1	—	—	—
40	43	10	15	9
45	5	1	2	1
50	23	6	3	2
60	4	1	3	2
135	—	—	1	1
190	1	—	—	—
	421	100	162	100

Note   Four of these shares are divisions of £20,000 shares where there are two syndicates on both of which Names participate.

stated the commencement date). None of the sample provided summaries for more than seven years (but three other 1984 reports did give figures for longer periods: one for eight years and two for ten years). SAB requires a tabular presentation: of the sample 72 set out the table with 1982 in the right hand column; nineteen with 1982 in the left-hand column: and five only had one year's result.

Although the order of items in SAB is not mandatory, it reflects the order in the underwriting accounts (except for profit/loss on exchange and syndicate expenses) and so it is not surprising that nearly all syndicates used this order. Of the sample, 65 itemised the personal expenses, while 31 just gave the total (which is all that SAB requires). Nine had given a split between results for UK and US Names in their underwriting accounts but only eight gave separate figures in their seven year summaries (six giving separate summary tables for each subgroup). Where separate accounts had been provided for funds managed by different quasi-managing agents or for 'mirror' syndicates, separate summaries were provided too.

SAB requires that if an account has been left open this must be made clear in the seven year summary. Of the sample, fourteen had left open all or part of the year that would usually close at 31 December 1984 and one which had closed 1982 still had 1981 running off. This was indicated in various ways. Eleven used the label 'amount returned to next net outstanding liabilities' in the table, of whom six in addition gave a note explaining that the relevant year had not been closed and three others headed the column for that year 'unclosed'. The remaining four used the label 'reinsurance to close' in the table, three of these gave an explanatory note and the other headed the column for that year 'run-off'.

SAB (Sch. 4 paras 5.4 and 5.5) requires the information in the seven year summary to be derived from the audited underwriting accounts, but where accounting policies have been charged, the preceding years' figures are to be adjusted, as far as reasonably possible, to comply with the latest policies, and a note is to be given explaining the adjustments or how far and why any figure has not been fully adjusted. Recognising that the syndicate accounting rules are a new requirement, transitional provisions, in SAB para. 18, allow for certain dispensations in respect of information for years prior to the 1981 underwriting account.

It was usual in the 1984 summaries to include some notes about the basis on which they had been prepared. Of the sample, only nine had no notes, while 41 included a 'standard' note that the summary had been prepared from the audited accounts of the syndicate, often accompanied by a note explaining the basis on which personal expenses had been included and that foreign tax had been excluded (as in Examples 3 and 5 below).

A common variation (in about another third of the summaries) was to state that the figures for 1982 had been prepared in accordance with SAB, while the 1981 and all prior years' figures had been derived from the annual accounts originally presented to Names, usually without restatement. However, in nineteen cases it was stated that where necessary the results had been adjusted to comply with current accounting policies, although in most of these cases no details were given. In some other cases there were specific references to items which had been restated (although generally without quantification); eight cases related to the basis on which the agent charged profit commission or a management fee, and four to the presentation of expenses. (See also Example 5 to Chapter 9.) In some cases it was specifically stated that it was not possible to restate prior years for certain changes in the basis of accounting: in five cases this related to underwriting transactions (where results were unaffected) and in two cases to the apportionment of investment returns. (See also Chapter 4.)

In five cases there was reference to certain information about earlier prior years not being available (in two of these mentioning that specific dispensation had been obtained from the Committee of Lloyd's), and in one case to information having been included even though it was not considered comparable.

SAB requires the summaries to be part of the audited annual report, but for three of the sample, the seven year summaries provided (and in one further case, the notes to the summary) were not within the stated scope of the auditors' report.

As regards additional information, three of the sample gave tables both for total syndicate figures and for the standard share; one gave an analysis by constituent 'mirror' syndicates; two gave an additional table of information about 'pure year' elements of the past results (see Example 3 below); one included an average, and an average percentage, of items over the seven years (Example 2); and one included an abbreviated table and a graphical presentation (see Example 1 below for another syndicate managed by the same agent).

1983 Reports

In the previous year, of the 468 reports filed, 162 (35%) voluntarily included a summary of past closed year results. Of those not providing summaries, 38 had started business in or after 1981. In the main the summaries were for seven years, but of course where syndicates had not been in existence that long the period was shorter. Three syndicates produced summaries covering more than seven years (ten, eleven and twenty years respectively).

The format adopted was generally that of PAM's specimen though there were often some alternative orderings of items in the table, and different levels of detail. All but fifteen summaries gave the syndicate allocated capacity; and fifteen did not give the number of Names.

Twenty-three of the syndicates had given separate results in their underwriting accounts for different subgroups of Names, of whom fourteen also gave separate seven year summaries for each subgroup.

In 71 cases the notes to the summary did not include a statement that the figures had been taken from the audited accounts. In only three cases did the auditors include the summary in the stated scope of their report.

No syndicate's summary for 1983 included the information now required by SAB as to the standard share of gross premiums.

SAB also treats UK tax differently from PAM's recommendations, requiring the statement of investment returns gross and net of tax. In 83 cases in the 1983 summaries (i.e. just over half of those filed) no specific amounts were stated for UK income or capital gains tax on investment returns, and of these 58 (like PAM) gave gross figures and did not deduct tax in arriving at the net result. The remaining 25 deducted UK tax, but gave merely the figures for net investment income and appreciation.

Of those syndicates that did show the amount of UK tax, some gave a combined figure for income and capital gains tax, but others split them.

The six syndicates of one agent gave an additional table showing the 'impact of estimated personal UK tax' assuming various levels of Names' other taxable income (see Example 5 for a similar presentation in 1984).

(It should be noted that foreign tax is always excluded from the summaries.)

EXAMPLES

■ Example 1 gives separate summaries for different groups of Names as well as tables for the 'main' and 'incidental' syndicates and a graphical presentation of the information (managing agent: Merrett Syndicates Ltd).

■ Examples 1 and 2 (managing agent: J.H.Minet Agencies Ltd) give very full explanatory notes (see also M.W.E., 275).

■ Examples 2, 3 and 4 give some useful ratios (although Example 3 is from the 1983 report).

■ Example 3 gives some supplementary 'pure year' information.

■ Example 5 gives a helpful presentation of UK personal tax estimates.

Example 1

MERRETT MARINE AND INCIDENTAL NON-MARINE SYNDICATES 418/422/417

Syndicate past closed year results

Merrett Marine Syndicate 418/422

	1976 £000	1977 £000	1978 £000	1979 £000	1980 £000	1981 £000	1982 £000
Underwriting result	6,281	7,717	7,842	4,856	4,992	3,601	(11,813)
Profit or (loss) on exchange	85	(1,020)	(1,233)	2,555	1,708	1,341	478
Net investment income	1,059	1,065	984	1,614	2,017	1,937	1,804
Net investment appreciation	1,474	2,546	2,832	3,583	4,991	4,079	4,655
Syndicate expenses	(454)	(613)	(699)	(901)	(1,239)	(1,401)	(1,499)
Syndicate profit or (loss)	8,445	9,695	9,726	11,707	12,469	9,557	(6,375)

Merrett Incidental Non-Marine Syndicate 417

	1976 £000	1977 £000	1978 £000	1979 £000	1980 £000	1981 £000	1982 £000
Underwriting result	156	1,450	(532)	290	(3,442)	(3,838)	(9,293)
Profit or (loss) on exchange	(66)	(312)	(323)	919	535	197	(68)
Net investment income	386	413	416	812	945	862	1,375
Net investment appreciation	581	995	1,219	1,673	2,438	2,053	3,567
Syndicate expenses	(107)	(145)	(181)	(149)	(147)	(158)	(203)
Syndicate profit or (loss)	950	2,401	599	3,545	329	(884)	(4,622)

...

MERRETT MARINE AND INCIDENTAL NON-MARINE SYNDICATES 418/422/417

1979	1980	1981	1982
£80,890,000	£83,510,000	£83,705,000	£80,785,000
2,233	2,300	2,296	2,200
£27,042,121	£35,243,376	£39,567,933	£46,056,623
£	£	£	£
50,000	50,000	50,000	50,000
32,044	40,200	46,908	61,434
16,715	21,101	23,635	28,506
26,330	32,019	43,161	59,432
(10,852)	(12,759)	(19,578)	(27,595)
(29,011)	(39,433)	(47,359)	(73,405)
3,182	928	(141)	(13,062)
2,106	2,497	2,303	2,734
(584)	(711)	(613)	(735)
1,522	1,786	1,690	1,999
4,592	6,254	5,202	7,292
(1,366)	(1,817)	(1,529)	(2,157)
3,226	4,437	3,673	5,135
(676)	(831)	(932)	(1,053)
2,147	1,343	919	254
9,401	7,663	5,209	(6,727)
(500)	(500)	(500)	(500)
(1,776)	(1,424)	(927)	—
●	(279)	(538)	(403)
(2,276)	(2,203)	(1,965)	(903)
7,125	5,460	3,244	(7,630)

1979	1980	1981	1982
£80,890,000	£83,510,000	£83,705,000	80,785,000
2,233	2,300	2,296	2,200
£27,042,121	£35,243,376	£39,567,933	£46,056,623
£	£	£	£
50,000	50,000	50,000	50,000
32,044	40,200	46,908	61,434
16,715	21,101	23,635	28,506
26,330	32,019	43,161	59,432
(10,852)	(12,759)	(19,578)	(27,595)
(29,011)	(39,433)	(47,359)	(73,405)
3,182	928	(141)	(13,062)
1,686	2,277	1,962	2,196
(459)	(646)	(510)	(574)
1,228	1,631	1,452	1,622
3,873	4,949	3,789	4,801
(338)	(384)	(250)	(232)
3,535	4,565	3,539	4,569
(654)	(830)	(932)	(1,053)
2,147	1,343	919	254
9,438	7,637	4,837	(7,670)
(500)	(500)	(500)	(500)
(1,779)	(1,419)	(852)	—
●	(279)	(538)	(403)
(2,279)	(2,198)	(1,890)	(903)
7,159	5,439	2,947	(8,573)

Notes on past underwriting results

(i) The agent requires all names to make such transfers to personal reserve as the agent shall deem prudent. These figures are shown before any such transfer.

(ii) Profit commission is charged in accordance with the basis stated in the underwriting agency agreement.

(iii) Neither the income nor the appreciation of the name's personal investments is included in the above.

(iv) No provision has been made for taxation liability on underwriting profits.

(v) Other Lloyd's expenses have been excluded from the analysis of past underwriting results for 1979 account and prior for the following reasons:

  (a) Lloyd's annual subscriptions

    (i) Prior to the 1979 account, Lloyd's annual subscriptions were charged to individuals and not on a syndicate participation basis.

    (ii) For 1979 account a charge was made of 0.45% of syndicate stamp allocation. A minimum charge of £400 and a maximum charge of £800 applied to each underwriting member irrespective of syndicate participation.

    (iii) For 1980 account and later years the ratio of charges were as follows:

Year of account	Syndicate stamp allocation
1980	0.55%
1981	0.60%
1982	0.60%

  (b) Central fund
Contributions are charged at a rate of 0.45% on the previous calendar year's premium income. There was no charge in 1980 but the Lloyd's subscription was increased by 0.30% in 1981 to include a contribution to the "Sasse" syndicate and applied to names who participated in the 1980 underwriting account.

(vi) Names who are US citizens or are resident in the United States may elect to participate in the special investment fund which invests mainly in US tax exempt bonds.

(vii) The allocated premium and number of names in the open years are:

	1983	1984
Allocated premium	£84,445,000	£100,955,000
Number of names	2,274	2,758

...

Seven year summary of past underwriting results

Main account

	1976	1977	1978
Syndicate allocated capacity	£36,280,500	£56,505,000	£72,685,000
Number of members of the syndicate	926	1,440	1,972
Aggregate net premiums	£25,338,297	£28,879,131	£21,803,047
	£	£	£
Standard share	50,000	50,000	50,000
Gross premiums	62,063	43,026	28,503
Net premiums	34,501	25,554	14,998
Premium for the reinsurance to close an earlier year	45,239	30,981	25,386
Net claims	(20,284)	(14,048)	(10,544)
Premium for the reinsurance to close the account	(50,677)	(34,376)	(24,811)
Underwriting result	8,779	8,111	5,029
Gross investment income	2,842	1,921	1,396
Income tax on investment income	(876)	(589)	(429)
Investment income net of taxation	1,966	1,332	967
Gross investment appreciation	4,017	4,530	3,978
Capital gains tax on investment appreciation	(1,222)	(1,358)	(1,193)
Investment appreciation net of taxation	2,795	3,172	2,785
Syndicate expenses	(788)	(671)	(606)
Profit or (loss) on exchange	28	(1,179)	(1,070)
Profit or (loss) before personal expenses	12,780	10,765	7,105
Standard personal expenses:			
Agent's salary	(500)	(500)	(500)
Profit commission	(2,437)	(2,040)	(1,314)
Other expenses (see note (v))	●	●	●
	(2,937)	(2,540)	(1,814)
Profit or (loss) after standard personal expenses	9,843	8,225	5,291

US Names' account

	1976	1977	1978
Syndicate allocated capacity	£36,280,500	£56,505,000	£72,685,000
Number of members of the syndicate	926	1,440	1,972
Aggregate net premiums	£25,338,297	£28,879,131	£21,803,047
	£	£	£
Standard share	50,000	50,000	50,000
Gross premiums	62,063	43,026	28,503
Net premiums	34,501	25,554	14,998
Premium for the reinsurance to close an earlier year	45,239	30,981	25,386
Net claims	(20,284)	(14,048)	(10,544)
Premium for the reinsurance to close the account	(50,677)	(34,376)	(24,811)
Underwriting result	8,779	8,111	5,029
Gross investment income	2,842	1,166	1,284
Income tax on investment income	(876)	(332)	(391)
Investment income net of taxation	1,966	834	893
Gross investment appreciation	4,017	2,690	3,146
Capital gains tax on investment appreciation	(1,222)	(330)	(321)
Investment appreciation net of taxation	2,795	2,360	2,825
Syndicate expenses	(788)	(671)	(606)
Profit or (loss) on exchange	28	(1,179)	(1,070)
Profit or (loss) before personal expenses	12,780	9,455	7,071
Standard personal expenses:			
Agent's salary	(500)	(500)	(500)
Profit commission	(2,437)	(1,779)	(1,308)
Other expenses (see note (v))	●	●	●
	(2,937)	(2,279)	(1,808)
Profit or (loss) after standard personal expenses	9,843	7,176	5,263

...

MERRETT MARINE AND INCIDENTAL NON-MARINE SYNDICATES 418/422/417

Past underwriting results chart

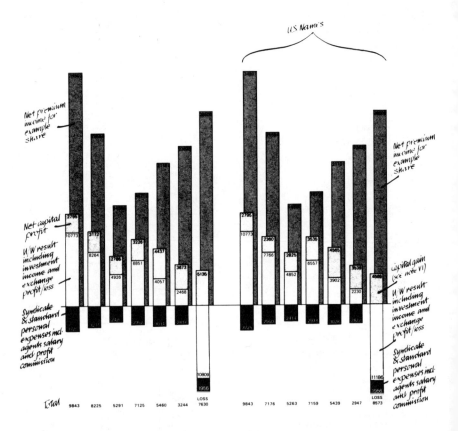

(i)   The agent requires all names to make such transfers to personal reserve as the agent shall deem prudent. These figures are shown before any such transfer or retention.
(ii)   Profit commission is charged in accordance with the basis stated in the underwriting agency agreement.
(iii) Investment appreciation is shown after provision for UK capital gains tax.
(iv)   Neither the income not the appreciation of the name's personal investments is included in the above.
(v)   No provision has been made for taxation liability on underwriting profits.
(vi)   Names who are US citizens or are resident in the United States may elect to participate in the special investment fund. The gain on the sterling fund is included net of UK capital gains tax. The U.S. dollar element, which is mainly invested in US tax exempt bonds, and the Canadian dollar fund are exempt from UK capital gains tax.

G.J. Butts
Motor and Employers' Liability Syndicates 887/641

Example 2

Notes to Past Underwriting Results

The seven year record of the Syndicate is shown on Page 15. These figures should be read in conjunction with the following explanatory notes.

1 Gross premiums less returns, and cost of reinsurance protection.

2 Reinsurance Premium received from previous year in return for accepting the liability for all previous years unsettled claims.

3 Gross claims less refunds and reinsurance recoveries.

4 Reinsurance Premium paid to following year in return for transferring all outstanding liabilities to that account.

5 The result of $(1 + 2) - (3 + 4)$.

6 Nett Dividends and Interest earned on Syndicate funds after deduction of 30% UK basic rate tax.

7 Nett Capital Gains earned on Syndicate funds after deduction of 30% UK Capital Gains tax (where applicable).

8 Syndicate Expenses including Box Expenses, Accountancy, Audit, LPSO charges.

9 Profit/Loss on Exchange arising from the sale of surplus US and Canadian Dollars.

10 Agent's Remuneration — all years have been adjusted to reflect the current Management Fee.

11 Agent's Profit Commission — all years have been adjusted to reflect the current Management Fee.

12 Lloyd's Subscriptions — Annual charge per Syndicate split over Members pro rata. Prior to the 1980 Account these were charged per Member (not per Syndicate) and therefore the 1980 Account charge of .55% of Premium Limit has been used in respect of 1979 Account and previous in order to make all years strictly comparable.

13 Central Guarantee Fund — Annual levy per Syndicate split over Members to a fund designed to protect Policy holders in the event of default by any Member. Prior to the 1979 Account, Central Guarantee Fund contributions were charged per Member (not per Syndicate) and therefore the 1978 Account and previous has been debited with an average figure (the actual charge is based on written income) in order to make all years strictly comparable. No Central Guarantee Fund contribution was made in 1980 but Lloyd's Subscriptions were increased to include a contribution to the Sasse Syndicate.

14 Amount due to Members but before deduction of Personal Reserve retention, Personal Stop Loss Premium, Accountants Fees and other sundry expenses which would all be deducted from a Member's Consolidated Personal Statement.

...

G.J. Butts
Motor and Employers' Liability Syndicates 887/641

Past Underwriting Results

	1982	1981	1980	1979	1978	1977	1976
Number of Members	522	397	324	260	204	154	119
Syndicate allocated capacity (in 000's)	10,120	7,080	4,960	3,475	2,595	1,765	1,365
Written nett premiums (in 000's)	3,745	4,852	4,557	2,937	1,780	2,051	2,154
% of Written to Allocated	37.0	68.5	91.9	84.5	68.6	116.2	157.8

Results per £25,000 Share	1982	1981	1980	1979	1978	1977	1976	Seven Year Average	% of Allocated Share
Gross Premiums	10,074	18,894	25,020	24,032	23,006	32,681	43,218	25,275	101.10
1) Nett Premiums	9,251	17,130	22,965	21,127	17,146	29,045	39,445	22,301	89.20
2) Reinsurance In	9,077	11,942	12,788	15,526	19,638	27,019	27,403	17,627	70.51
3) Nett Claims	(8,761)	(13,218)	(14,045)	(12,920)	(11,644)	(19,916)	(28,323)	(15,546)	(62.18)
4) Reinsurance Out	(7,722)	(12,840)	(17,046)	(18,253)	(20,790)	(28,874)	(34,937)	(20,066)	(80.26)
5) Underwriting Result	1,845	3,014	4,662	5,480	4,350	7,274	3,588	4,316	17.27
Gross Investment Income	370	725	1,025	1,080	1,100	1,680	1,810	1,113	4.45
Income Tax on Investment Income	115	218	304	325	361	570	633	361	1.44
6) Nett Investment Income	255	507	721	755	739	1,110	1,177	752	3.01
Gross Investment Appreciation	1,137	2,423	3,935	2,170	3,250	4,474	4,524	3,130	12.52
Capital Gains Tax	328	680	1,148	625	984	1,322	1,291	911	3.64
7) Nett Investment Appreciation	809	1,743	2,787	1,545	2,266	3,152	3,233	2,219	8.88
8) Syndicate Expenses	(2,082)	(2,855)	(3,083)	(2,905)	(3,085)	(4,199)	(4,312)	(3,217)	(12.87)
9) Profit/Loss on Exchange	18	23	—	50	(78)	11	(11)	2	—
Profit Before Personal Expenses	845	2,432	5,087	4,925	4,192	7,348	3,675	4,072	16.29
10) Agency Salary	(500)	(500)	(500)	(500)	(500)	(500)	(500)	(500)	(2.00)
11) Profit Commission	—	(567)	(1,208)	(1,075)	(1,007)	(1,749)	(1,020)	(947)	(3.79)
12) Lloyd's Subscriptions	(150)	(153)	(219)	(137)	(137)	(137)	(137)	(153)	(.61)
13) Central Guarantee Fund	(70)	(92)	—	(95)	(100)	(100)	(100)	(79)	(.32)
Personal Expenses	(720)	(1,312)	(1,927)	(1,807)	(1,744)	(2,486)	(1,757)	(1,679)	(6.72)
14) Profit After Personal Expenses	125	1,120	3,160	3,118	2,448	4,862	1,918	2,393	9.57

Example 3

SEDGWICK FORBES (LLOYD'S UNDERWRITING AGENTS) LIMITED

W.E. SIMMS & OTHERS
AVIATION SYNDICATE NO. 48

Notes to Seven Year Summary of Results

1.   The seven year summary has been prepared from the audited Accounts of the Syndicate.

2.   Personal expenses have been stated at the normal amount incurred by Names writing
     the stated premium income in the Syndicate. Foreign Taxes, which may be treated as a
     credit for personal tax purposes, have been excluded.

W. E. SIMMS & OTHERS
AVIATION SYNDICATE NO. 48

Seven Year Summary of Results of Closed Years

Year of Account	1976	1977	1978	1979	1980	1981	1982
Syndicate allocated capacity	£2,990,000	£4,005,000	£6,335,000	£7,225,000	£8,175,000	£13,650,000	£16,905,000
Number of underwriting members	221	268	402	452	522	838	975
Aggregate net premiums	£3,688,833	£3,414,144	£4,886,614	£8,529,107	£11,089,267	£16,691,664	£23,562,462
Results for a standard share (£20,000)							
Gross Premiums	73,824	52,409	45,166	72,563	74,279	49,316	41,547
Net Premiums	24,591	17,624	15,427	23,670	27,132	24,467	27,889
Premium for reinsurance to close an earlier year of account	23,946	21,778	16,201	23,429	33,315	24,040	24,687
Net Claims	12,152	14,529	10,642	20,942	26,309	22,361	18,073
Reinsurance to close the year of account	31,522	27,319	21,998	32,686	36,361	24,957	26,754
Underwriting result	4,863	(2,446)	(1,012)	(6,529)	(2,223)	1,189	7,749
Gross investment income	1,390	846	720	1,022	1,969	1,307	1,732
Income tax on investment income	487	288	238	306	591	392	507
Investment income net of taxation	903	558	482	716	1,378	915	1,225
Gross investment appreciation	1,972	1,786	1,956	3,493	4,269	2,830	3,031
Capital gains tax on investment appreciation	635	499	562	1,046	1,280	830	894
Investment appreciation net of taxation	1,337	1,287	1,394	2,447	2,989	2,000	2,137
Syndicate expenses	1,174	1,198	944	1,075	1,296	905	899
Profit or (loss) on exchange	76	(418)	(308)	1,102	574	104	54
Profit or (loss) before personal expenses	6,005	(2,217)	(388)	(3,339)	1,422	3,303	10,266
Standard personal expenses	1,803	488	409	424	395	1,248	2,657
Profit or (loss) after standard personal expenses	£ 4,202	£ (2,705)	£ (797)	£ (3,763)	£ 1,027	£ 2,055	£ 7,609

W.E. SIMMS & OTHERS
AVIATION SYNDICATE NO. 48

Syndicate Whole Account Summary

Year of Account	Net Premium Income after Reinsurance	Paid Loss Ratio %	Incurred Loss Ratio %	Expense Ratio %	Combined Ratio %	Reinsurance* Premium to close Account
1972	1,681,545	50.4	92.1	5.2	97.3	2,260,829
1973	1,884,435	43.1	73.1	6.1	79.2	2,843,039
1974	2,791,850	43.7	81.3	5.0	86.3	3,982,828
1975	2,231,673	42.5	74.8	8.3	83.1	3,767,520
1976	3,676,376	36.5	64.1	6.6	70.7	4,695,701
1977	3,414,144	70.5	105.0	7.7	112.7	5,470,735
1978	4,886,614	56.5	92.2	6.4	98.6	6,967,963
1979	8,529,106	77.3	111.5	4.5	116.0	11,778,185
1980	11,089,267	64.6	96.8	4.8	101.6	14,861,553
1981	16,691,664	72.6	84.5	3.7	88.2	17,026,104
1982	23,562,462	45.6	59.8	3.2	63.0	22,604,407

	1982	1983	1984
Syndicate allocated capacity	16,905,000	16,465,000	15,850,000
Number of Underwriting Members	975	1,005	961

Settlement Loss Ratios (Pure Years Only) at 31st December 1984

	1982	1983	1984
12 months	14.7%	33.3%	10.1%
24 months	30.0%	40.8%	
36 months	45.6%		

Pure Year figures represent results for only the year of account concerned in isolation from any other account year.

*   The Reinsurance premium to close an account is the fund carried forward to the following open year to cover outstanding claims on the closing year and all previous years and contains a loading to cover unknown claims which may arise. The U.S. and Canadian Dollar amounts included in these figures have not been revalued for subsequent conversion rate changes.

Example 4

MANAGING AGENT: STEWART & HUGHMAN LTD
B.A.STEWART & OTHERS MARINE SYNDICATE 16/17/18

Summary of Underwriting Results

Year of Account	1975 £	1976 £	1977 £	1978 £	1979 £	1980 £	1981 £
Premiums	10,294,326	11,011,381	11,468,797	10,893,858	12,824,782	16,231,526	19,050,089
Reinsurance premium received from previous account	7,712,061	7,886,674	8,333,292	9,001,531	10,582,980	12,246,225	13,382,766
	18,006,387	18,898,055	19,802,089	19,895,389	23,407,762	28,477,751	32,432,855
Claims	8,815,231	8,948,044	8,947,965	9,565,253	12,940,985	16,187,932	18,832,142
Reinsurance premium paid to following account	8,200,000	8,750,000	9,400,000	9,250,000	11,000,000	12,500,000	15,000,000
Reinsurance premium paid to third parties						339,506	
	17,015,231	17,698,044	18,347,965	18,815,253	23,940,985	29,027,438	33,382,142
Pure underwriting	991,156	1,200,011	1,454,124	1,080,136	(533,223)	(549,687)	(1,399,287)
Profit/(loss) on exchange	(15,033)	13,547	(50,877)	(28,359)	410,455	341,094	213,013
Gross underwriting profit/(loss)	976,123	1,213,558	1,403,247	1,051,777	(122,778)	(208,593)	(1,186,274)
Gross investment appreciation	1,145,091	804,520	756,786	1,061,210	1,711,611	2,224,970	2,112,119
Gross investment income	494,823	555,355	570,085	562,107	607,558	690,539	759,108
	2,616,037	2,573,433	2,730,118	2,675,094	2,196,391	2,706,916	1,684,953
Syndicate expenses	(369,337)	(407,781)	(497,887)	(619,521)	(670,816)	(767,804)	(824,592)
Balance	2,246,700	2,165,652	2,232,231	- 2,055,573	1,525,575	1,939,112	860,361
Capital gains tax	(199,804)	(164,713)	(178,238)	(289,892)	(426,099)	(573,343)	(590,802)
Income tax	(160,778)	(184,554)	(182,549)	(170,008)	(165,704)	(189,400)	(193,274)
Net profit	1,886,118	1,816,385	1,871,444	1,595,673	933,772	1,176,369	76,285

MANAGING AGENT: STEWART & HUGHMAN LTD
B.A.STEWART & OTHERS
MARINE SYNDICATE 16/17/18

Summary of Underwriting Results

Year of Account	1975	1976	1977	1978	1979	1980	1981
Premiums	£10,294,326	£11,011,381	£11,468,797	£10,893,858	£12,824,782	£16,231,526	£19,050,089
	%	%	%	%	%	%	%
	100.00	100.00	100.00	100.00	100.00	100.00	100.00
Reinsurance premium received from previous account	74.92	71.62	72.66	82.63	82.52	75.45	70.25
	174.92	171.62	172.66	182.63	182.52	175.45	170.25
Claims	85.63	81.26	78.02	87.80	100.91	99.73	98.86
Reinsurance premium paid to following account	79.66	79.46	81.96	84.91	85.77	77.01	78.74
Reinsurance premium paid to third parties						2.09	
	165.29	160.72	159.98	172.71	186.68	178.83	177.60
Pure underwriting profit/(loss)	9.63	10.90	12.68	9.92	(4.16)	(3.38)	(7.35)
Profit/(loss) on exchange	(0.15)	0.12	(0.44)	(0.26)	3.20	2.10	1.12
Gross underwriting profit/(loss)	9.48	11.02	12.24	9.66	(0.96)	(1.28)	(6.23)
Gross investment appreciation	11.12	7.31	6.59	9.74	13.34	13.71	11.09
Gross investment income	4.80	5.04	4.97	5.16	4.74	4.25	3.98
Syndicate expenses	25.40	23.37	23.80	24.56	17.12	16.68	8.84
	(3.59)	(3.70)	(4.34)	(5.69)	(5.23)	(4.73)	(4.32)
Balance	21.81	19.67	19.46	18.87	11.89	11.95	4.52
Capital gains tax	(1.94)	(1.50)	(1.55)	(2.66)	(3.32)	(3.53)	(3.10)
Income tax	(1.56)	(1.67)	(1.59)	(1.56)	(1.29)	(1.17)	(1.02)
Net profit	18.31	16.50	16.32	14.65	7.28	7.25	0.40

Example 5

Lloyd's underwriting syndicates managed by
C E Heath & Co (Underwriting) Limited
404 NON-MARINE SYNDICATE — No. 1

Seven Year Summary 1976–1982

	1976	1977	1978
Syndicate allocated capacity	£15,475,000	£16,585,000	£15,340,000
Number of members of the syndicate (note 5)	377	400	370
Aggregate net premiums (note 2)	£14,248,311	£11,797,797	£8,186,400
Results for a standard share of £50,000	£	£	£
Gross premiums	75,246	57,172	48,086
Net premiums	46,036	35,568	26,683
Premium for the reinsurance to close an earlier year of account	77,775	66,244	68,161
	123,811	101,812	94,844
Net claims	47,750	39,373	35,340
Reinsurance to close the year of account	75,483	67,539	58,617
Underwriting result	578	(5,100)	887
Gross investment income	3,731	2,913	3,754
Income tax on investment income	1,306	990	1,239
Investment income net of taxation	2,425	1,923	2,515
Gross investment appreciation			
Subject to capital gains tax	4,141	5,463	6,635
Not subject to capital gains tax	29	164	712
	4,170	5,627	7,347
Capital gains tax on investment appreciation	1,255	1,646	2,012
Investment appreciation net of taxation	2,915	3,981	5,335
	5,918	804	8,737
(Profit)/loss on exchange	(112)	(71)	(336)
Syndicate expenses	1,923	1,946	2,034
Profit/(loss) before personal expenses	4,107	(1,071)	7,039
Standard personal expenses (note 3)			
Commission	774	—	1,358
Agent's salary	250	250	250
Lloyd's Central fund	222	241	244
Annual subscription to Lloyd's	330	365	403
Other (approximate)	50	50	50
	1,626	906	2,305
Profit/(loss) after standard personal expenses	£2,481	£(1,977)	£4,734

Above Results After Impact of Estimated Personal U.K. Tax

Approximate net profit/(loss) after all personal tax (note 4)

assuming other taxable income of:	1976	1977	1978
£25,000	3,070	3,920	6,040
£20,000	3,070	3,550	6,090
£15,000	3,140	3,040	6,150
£10,000	3,230	2,070	6,250

...

31st December 1984

1979	1980	1981	1982
£20,240,000	£32,435,000	£30,290,000	£35,755,000
518	908	890	1,091
£12,705,685	£23,691,912	£26,640,035	£35,740,593
£	£	£	£
45,918	51,458	61,812	67,288
31,388	36,522	43,975	49,980
70,645	63,315	67,854	62,647
102,033	99,837	111,829	112,627
43,644	46,376	53,387	60,114
59,740	53,703	57,946	52,798
(1,351)	(242)	496	(285)
4,041	3,721	3,862	3,382
1,211	1,116	1,159	1.015
2,830	2,605	2,703	2,367
3,981	7,752	4,663	5,839
350	1,088	593	394
4,331	8,840	5,256	6,233
1,228	2,330	1,417	1,757
3,103	6,510	3,839	4,476
4,582	8,873	7,038	6,558
(165)	392	485	1,261
2,132	2,195	2,702	2,797
2,615	6,286	3,851	2,500
476	1,752	1,090	863
250	500	500	500
215	183	158	142
225	279	305	305
30	20	12	12
1,196	2,734	2,065	1,822
£1,419	£3,552	£1,786	£678
3,670	6,580	4,350	4,590
3,650	6,490	4,310	4,500
3,620	6,390	4,260	4,250
3,550	6,120	4,130	4,030
			...

Lloyd's underwriting syndicates managed by

C E Heath & Co (Underwriting) Limited

404 NON-MARINE SYNDICATE — No. 1   31st December 1984

Notes to the Seven Year Summary

1. The summary has been prepared from the audited accounts of the syndicate.

2. The premium income written has been translated to sterling at the United States and Canadian dollar rates of exchange ruling at the end of the third year of each year of account. The exchange rates used for premium income control against allocated limits are those ruling at the beginning of each calendar year.

3. Personal expenses have been stated at the normal amount incurred by Names writing the stated premium income in the syndicate. Foreign tax, which may be treated as a credit for personal tax purposes, has been excluded.

4. In estimating the net profit/(loss) of a resident of the United Kingdom, no account has been taken of foreign taxes, double tax relief or special reserve fund transfers. Any underwriting losses of the syndicate have been set off firstly against investment income of the syndicate, then against the member's other income subject to United Kingdom tax. The member's estimated other income is presumed to be earned income net of all allowances and other deductions.

5. The apparent increase in the size of the syndicate between 1979 and 1980 was caused by the consolidation of the separate members' agencies into the No. 1 Syndicate.

CHAPTER 13

SOURCE AND APPLICATION OF FUNDS STATEMENTS AND CALENDAR YEAR ACCOUNTING

There is no requirement in SAB for a source and application of funds statement to be included with the accounts, and PAM had only suggested it as optional (and gave no specimen). However, the report of the Fisher Task Group 4 (1982) on Lloyd's financial reporting did recommend its inclusion and gave a specimen (see Example 1 below). Four syndicates (all managed by the same agent) included such a statement with their 1983 and 1984 accounts, although these followed a somewhat different format (see Example 2 below).

Insurance companies are not exempt from SSAP10 (although in regard to their long-term business they normally provide equivalent information in other ways). The main arguments against the need for such a statement for Lloyd's syndicates might include:

(a) If one takes a 'cash and readily realisable assets' view of funds, then the asset changes that occur between balance sheet dates are largely in these funds because syndicates have few, or no, long-term assets, and only fairly short-term liabilities (other than their insurance liabilities). Assets are valued at current value. So a simple reading of the balance sheet and comparative figures tells most of the story.

(b) Like other insurance enterprises, syndicates provide detailed underwriting accounts which show the flows of premiums and claims, but unlike insurance companies they do not give a separate profit and loss account. While provisions for outstanding claims etc. may result in a loss even though there has been a net increase of cash and investments from operations in a period, these flows can be fairly readily identified from the underwriting accounts.

(c) Syndicates have no capital (in the form of shares, retained profits or debentures) so there are no capital flows (apart from distributions to Names) to be confused with operating flows. (Any increases in capital

– apart from covering deficits – are a personal matter for each Name in deciding the amounts to be placed in his off balance sheet reserves, Special Reserve Funds etc. or as required to be added to his Lloyd's deposit.)

The balance of opinion at Lloyd's seems to be that a source and application of funds statement would not help to reveal much that is not already apparent to a reader of the balance sheets and underwriting accounts.

On the other hand, the underwriting accounts are expressed in a cumulative form (see Chapter 3, on 'Formats') which makes it harder to disentangle the current year's flows (except where the accounts volunteer a breakdown over the calendar year of receipt or payment). There is, therefore, an argument for a calendar year underwriting account to be included in lieu of a flow of funds statement to show how funds have moved during the year.

The formats in the examples do not fully meet this objective. Understanding of the change in underwriting account balances may be confused by the transfer of the reinsurance to close from one year to another (which in itself involves no movement of syndicate funds), although this does cancel out in Example 2's overall 'increase in insurance funds'. It would be clearer to show the calendar year premiums, claims and other income and outgoings (analysed by underwriting year) together with the adjustment for the profit or loss distributed/covered on the previously closed year. Against this could be shown how the size distribution of funds between investments, cash and other assets, less creditors, had changed. Example 3 gives a possible pro forma along these lines.

Although compliance with SSAP10 by 'ordinary companies' is high, the presentations used by them are often not the most useful (see Tonkin & Skerratt, 1984, pp. 217–242 by I. Brindle). In the case of insurance companies the 'Royal' gives a presentation along the lines outlined above (Peat, Marwick, Mitchell & Co., 1984: Section 6.16–18).

EXAMPLES

■ Example 1 is the specimen that was recommended by the Fisher Task Group 4 Report.

■ Example 2 is the format presented by the one agent including such a statement with the 1984 and 1983 accounts.

■ Example 3 gives a possible pro forma for a calendar year statement of underwriting and the movement of funds.

Example 1

EXAMPLE UNDERWRITING AGENCY LTD
NON MARINE SYNDICATE NO. 1000

Statement of Source and Application of Funds
for the Year Ended 31 December 19X3

	£	£
Source of Funds		
Increase in technical balance – 19X1 Account		(522,338)
19X2 Account		309,560
19X3 Account		724,773
		511,995
Sale of investments		133,208
Investment income		20,068
Application of Funds		665,271
Purchase of investments	192,313	
Syndicate expenses paid	150,161	
Personal expenses paid	103,739	
Closed year profits paid to Names	26,608	
Taxation paid	14,303	
		487,124
		178,147
Increase in Working Capital		
Increase in brokers' balances	118,433	
Increase in sundry debtors	789	
Increase in amounts due to		
the managing agent	(119,643)	
	(421)	
Increase in net liquid funds	178,568	
		178,147

Note The comparative figures for 19X2 have been excluded from this illustrative statement.

...

EXAMPLE UNDERWRITING AGENCY LTD
NON MARINE SYNDICATE NO. 1000
Balance Sheet at 31 December 19X3

	19X3		19X2	
	£	£	£	£
Assets				
Investments – fixed interest				
government securities		990,725		868,086
Brokers' balances		297,291		178,858
Sundry debtors		10,055		9,266
Bank balances		205,332		26,764
		1,503,403		1,082,974
Liabilities				
Taxation –				
payable within twelve				
months	18,503		10,997	
payable thereafter	16,104		12,241	
	34,607		23,238	
Amounts owing to the				
managing agent	175,001	209,608	55,358	78,596
Net assets		£1,293,795		£1,004,378
Represented by:-				
Open underwriting account balances				
19X2 underwriting account	753,886		631,074	
Less: Names' personal				
expenses	51,819		38,026	
		702,067		593,048
19X3 underwriting account	605,088		424,334	
Less: Names' personal				
expenses	69,285		39,612	
		535,803		384,722
		1,237,870		997,770
Closed underwriting account balances				
19X1 underwriting account	116,198		59,931	
Less: Names' personal				
expenses	60,273		33,323	
Credit balance dealt with in				
Names' personal accounts		55,925		26,608
		£1,293,795		£1,004,378

Example 2

MARINE SYNDICATE 434,437/438

Balance sheet at 31 December 1984

	1984 £	1984 £	1983 £	1983 £
Debtors (Note 13)		2,362,859		1,353,593
Investments (Note 12)		19,509,681		12,374,997
Balances at bank		513,838		1,861,361
Total assets		22,386,378		15,589,951
Creditors (Note 14)		1,006,259		744,965
Profit for closed year account				
1982 year of account	1,307,892		1,000,958	
Personal expenses (Note 16)	393,370		322,417	
Profit after personal expenses		914,522		678,541
Total assets *less* **liabilities**		£20,465,597		£14,166,445
Open year of account balances				
1983 year of account	15,263,879		10,364,801	
Personal expenses (Note 16)	194,958		159,183	
1983 balance after personal expenses		15,068,921		10,205,618
1984 year of account	5,677,049		4,154,354	
Personal expenses (Note 16)	280,373		193,527	
1984 balance after personal expenses		5,396,676		3,960,827
		£20,465,597		£14,166,445

The Syndicate Financial Statements, comprising the Personal Account on page 1 and
the Annual Report on pages 6 to 22, together with the Managing Agent's Report
on pages 2 and 3 were approved on behalf of the Managing Agent, Lambert Brothers
(Underwriting Agencies) Limited, on 24th May, 1985 and are signed on behalf of
the Company by:-

P.T.Daniels   A.F.Ehrhart
Managing Director   Underwriter

...

MARINE SYNDICATE 434,437/438

Statement of source and application of funds for the year ended 31 December 1984

	1984		1983	
	£	£	£	£
Source of Funds				
Increase in insurance funds		7,213,674		1,952,534
Increase in taxation provisions		594,832		384,294
Decrease in investments:-				
Non US residents		—		606,108
Total source of funds		7,808,506		2,942,936
Application of Funds				
Taxation paid	(426,611)		(539,416)	
1981 personal account balance paid	(678,541)		(1,151,132)	
Increase in investments:-				
Non US residents	(6,659,305)		—	
US residents	(475,379)		(45,643)	
Total application of funds		(8,239,836)		(1,736,191)
Net (application)/source of funds		£(431,330)		£1,206,745
(Decrease)/Increase in Working Capital				
(Increase)/decrease in amounts due to the managing and members' agents		(93,584)		147,591
Decrease in sundry creditors		511		923
(Decrease) in sundry debtors		(49,707)		(8,044)
Increase/(decrease) in brokers' balances		1,058,973		(504,599)
		916,193		(364,129)
Movement in net liquid funds (Decrease)/increase in bank balances		(1,347,523)		1,570,874
Net (decrease)/increase in working capital		£(431,330)		£1,206,745

Example 3

Pro-Forma Source and Application of Funds Statement
for Year Ended 31 December 1984

+ Premiums in 1984:

    1982 underwriting account (closed)
    1983 underwriting account (open)
    1984 underwriting account (open)

− Claims paid in 1984
    (analysed as premiums)

+ Investment income and appreciation/depreciation in 1984
    (analysed as premiums)

+/− Profit/loss on exchange in 1984
    (analysed as premiums)

− Syndicate expenses in1984
    (analysed as premiums)

−/+ Distribution of profit/loss for closed year 1981

= Net change in investments, cash, other assets and sundry liabilities during 1984

Notes
1. 1982 account items could be analysed into 1982 pure and amounts in respect of prior closed years.
2. Amounts as recorded in underwriting accounts could be further adjusted to separate accruals from amounts received/paid during 1984.

CHAPTER 14

DISCLOSURE OF INTERESTS

INTRODUCTION

Interests, of those involved with the management of a syndicate, in other syndicates or businesses that have dealings with the syndicate can lead to conflicts of interest and the danger that Names on the syndicate receive unfair terms with regard to this related business. Relationships of particular concern have been where the managing agent is connected with a Lloyd's broker; where reinsurance is placed with a 'connected' reinsurer; and where more than one syndicate is managed in the same market. Under the divestment rules of the Lloyd's Act 1982 (see, e.g., Cockerell, 1984) broker relationships will have to be severed as it was judged, following the Fisher Report (1980), that the conflict of interest was too great. The abuses that have in some instances arisen from the placing of reinsurance with connected insurers overseas are also well known (see, e.g., Hodgson, 1984) and Lloyd's announced in February 1985 that rules are to be introduced to ban related party reinsurance. Where more than one syndicate is managed in the same market there is the opportunity for preferential treatment of one syndicate's Names and in December 1985 Lloyd's issued a new byelaw (No.7 of 1985) restricting multiple syndicates, together with a code of practice on how to deal with potentially conflicting interests of this kind. (The recent Inland Revenue investigation into reinsurance contracts is discussed further in Chapter 15.)

The purposes of the disclosure statements are therefore: (i) to bring into the open those arrangements that might be regarded as leading to a potential conflict of interest, so that Names are aware of the position, and (ii) to discourage agents and others from entering into doubtful arrangements, knowing that they will be obliged to disclose the details.

Because of the difficulties of standardising presentation, given the individual circumstances of each agent and syndicate, much of the value of the disclosure requirements depends on the agent's and auditor's approach to: (a) ensuring that the information is presented by the agent as clearly and informatively as is practicable (including seeing that non-disclosable interests are either excluded, or segregated from those that may be significant), and (b) as far as possible, satisfying themselves as to the completeness of the information obtained by the agent as a basis for preparing the statement. (Some further aspects of the audit of these disclosures are dealt with in Chapter 17.)

REQUIREMENTS

The requirements have gone through various stages of proposals before emerging in their final form in 'The Disclosure of Interests Byelaw' (No.3 of 1984) and in SAB. They are of two kinds:

(A) Managing agents have to include in the audited annual report a statement giving a fair presentation of any transactions or arrangements affecting syndicate members in which

1.   the managing agent
2.   any related company of the managing agent
3.   any executive of the managing agent (i.e. director or partner or the active underwriter)

had, directly or indirectly, a material interest (other than their agreed remuneration by syndicate members). The disclosable interests include interests of connected persons, companies and partnerships.

Materiality is to be judged by whether a reasonable Name might regard the interest as one which might influence the agent's actions. 'Fair presentation' of a person's interests requires the inclusion of the name of the interested party and appropriate financial information about the transaction, the interest, and the extent to which activities were conducted other than on an 'arms length' basis.

Where there have been no such transactions or arrangements the annual report has to state that fact.

I call these disclosures the 'Byelaw 3' disclosures, although the requirements have now been incorporated into SAB.

(B) In addition, where a managing agent manages more than one syndicate operating principally in the same market, SAB requires details to be given, for each syndicate, of the syndicate number, syndicate allocated capacity, and results for the stated standard share, together with the number and aggregate participation of the executives of the managing agent, and of directors of any holding company, who were members of that syndicate and their aggregate share of its results. This requirement is aimed to expose situations of 'preferred' underwriting whereby an agent might channel the 'better' business he is offered to syndicates in which connected parties are interested and leave 'worse' business to the other syndicate, or might cream off business or arrange cash flow advantages by reinsurance to the connected syndicate at the expense of the other syndicate, or arrange reinsurance protection in such a way as to favour one syndicate over the other. The managing agent's report is also required by SAB to identify, and explain the basis on which business is allocated between, such syndicates. The code of practice issued in December 1985 now states that these disclosures should include all such syndicates managed within a group of agency companies, and should embrace their reinsurance arrangements as well.

For the 1983 reports there were no specific requirements relating to (B) but the 'Byelaw 3' disclosures, as in (A), were required. However, no audit was required for that year and the disclosures could be provided separately from the annual report itself.

ANALYSIS

(A) 'Byelaw 3' Disclosures
The presentation of the 'Byelaw 3' disclosures with the random sample of 100 reports for 1984 and 1983 is analysed in Table 1. It is now rare to include these disclosures in the managing agent's report, and normal to give them in the notes to the accounts, together with the required disclosures about any other managed syndicates.

As the table shows, there was full compliance with the requirement to include a statement in the 1984 reports, but much weaker compliance with regard to the 1983 reports. It was a feature of a few of the 1984 reports that in addition to the disclosure section covered by the auditor's report, disclosures of further transactions or interests were also given, usually in the managing agent's report. This seems potentially confusing to Names, although it may be that, after consultation with the auditors, it was decided that disclosures were not required under the syndicate accounting rules, but the agent wished to inform Names, or had been accustomed to doing so in previous reports. It is inevitably a matter of judgement which items are considered disclosable.

It should, however, be noted that it is only where there have been transactions or arrangements in which the relevant parties have material interests that any positive disclosure is required and there is no general requirement to disclose all interests. However, earlier proposals (e.g. those of the 'Plaistowe Working Party' 1983) had included the keeping of a central register of all interests; and the report of Task Group 4 of the Fisher Working Party (1982) had proposed that the managing agent's report include certain details of the other directorships of directors or partners of the managing agent. A number of statements filed in respect of the 1983 reports (but fewer for the 1984 reports) included this kind of information even where there did not appear to be any transactions involving the syndicate and these other companies.

Table 1. Presentation of 'Byelaw 3' disclosures in annual reports

% of sample 1984	1983	
48	1	included their relevant disclosures in the notes to their accounts (notes 1 and 2)
20	48	gave a separate statement of disclosure of interests (note 3)
6	16	included their relevant disclosures in their managing agent's report
18	16	gave a statement that there were no interests to disclose (either separately or in the managing agent's report or in the notes to the accounts) (note 1)
100	81	
—	19	contained no statement relating to disclosure of interests
100	100	

Notes
1. In the 1984 reports, all the statements of 'nothing to disclose' were in the notes to the accounts except in one case where there was a separate statement.
2. The 1984 disclosures were required to be audited, so where the disclosures were not in the notes to the audited accounts there was generally either a cross-reference from the notes to the statement or to the relevant parts of the managing agent's report, or the stated scope of the auditor's report embraced the disclosure pages. However, neither of these was present in three cases (involving two agents) where the disclosures were in the managing agents' reports, so that the disclosures were formally unaudited. The 1983 disclosures were all unaudited except in the case of three syndicates (involving two agents).
3. In all these cases for 1984 a section of the annual report was labelled in terms such as 'Disclosure of Interests'. In many cases for 1983, the statement was a separate document and sometimes a managing agent produced a statement to cover all the syndicates managed and a copy was filed with each syndicate's annual report.

Interests Disclosed

Because of the individuality of circumstances of different agents, no standard format or specimens of the required disclosures were given in SAB or PAM and, particularly in the 1983 reports, there appeared to be many cases of 'over disclosure'. This was not always apparent because only rarely were financial details given in that year of the transactions or arrangements in which there was an interest. Thus giving details of directors' shareholdings in companies that perform insurance, investment or office services is not in itself the disclosure that is required. If the level of services performed by these companies for the syndicate, or if the size of the directors' holdings, is such that it is unlikely that the agent's directors might be influenced thereby in their employment of the company, there is no need to make a disclosure. If there is a need to make a disclosure, then quantification of the service provided and of the relevant interests therein should be given too to enable readers to understand their significance.

As Tables 3 to 6 show there was improvement in presentation in the 1984 reports, in particular with regard to financial quantification of the transactions, and to a lesser extent of the interests, involved. Many of the 1984 statements were also much shorter than their 1983 counterparts; in some cases coming down from about 10 pages to a page or less, or even to 'nothing to disclose'. Whether this reflects the greater opportunity agents had to digest the requirements (which were only published in April 1984) or the influence of the auditors in advising what disclosures are required, one cannot tell: but there are still cases where it is not entirely clear to me why it was considered necessary to make the disclosures in the absence of further financial information about the transactions, interests and terms involved.

In interpreting the information in the tables about levels of disclosure it should be realised that in several cases disclosures made in the 1983 reports were not repeated in the 1984 reports, while in other cases disclosures were made for the first time in the 1984 reports even though the transactions, arrangements or interests had been in existence in the earlier year.

Where a managing agent manages more than one syndicate, much of the disclosure information is repeated for each syndicate. The following tables therefore refer to the relevant number of agents from those having reports in the sample.

It must also be recognised that of the total number of agents (see Appendix I) several are related to each other by group and other shareholdings, so that the disclosures overlap. Except in the more obvious cases (e.g. where a standardised format of report is provided for all the agent companies in a 'group'), no attempt has been made here to unravel these relationships – a subsidiary or associate acting as a managing agent may therefore be counted as a separate agent. For the purpose of this analysis, I have recognised 74 seperate agencies as represented in the sample (covering 80 (42%) of the total of 192 agents in Appendix I). It should also be remembered that the sample was selected as a sample of syndicates, not of agents, so there may be some tendency for more extensive and complex agencies, involved with the management of more syndicates, to be represented in the sample. The information analysed is that disclosed by the agent in the information filed for the sampled syndicates only.

For the 74 separate agencies recognised in the sample, the disclosures filed were as shown in Table 2. In the case of 37 (1983:25) agents (62% of the 60 agents giving affirmative disclosures (1983: 54% of 46)), the disclosures given were accompanied by a statement that there were no other interests to disclose, or included disclaimers of specific interests, transactions or arrangements (e.g. that no executives had any interests in the connected insurance entities, or only had non-material holdings in listed companies).

Table 2. Agents' disclosures

	1984	*Agents in sample* (%)	1983	(%)
Affirmative disclosures	60	(81)	46	(62)
'Nothing to Disclose'	14	(19)	12	(16)
Nothing filed	—	—	16	(22)
	74	(100)	74	(100)

Table 3 analyses the types of interest, and Table 4 the types of transactions or other arrangements identified in the disclosures. The totals are greater than the number of 60 agents (1983: 46) in the sample filing affirmative disclosures because several interests, or transactions/arrangements were often reported. The percentages given are of these agents who filed *affirmative* disclosures only; these were 81% (1983: 62%) of the 74 'separate' agents whose annual reports were included in the sample of 100 reports. The classifications are inevitably subjective in many instances as it was sometimes hard to ascertain their precise nature from the information given.

Table 3. Types of interests identified

	1984	*Agents in sample* (%)	1983	(%)
Relationships between managing agent and other companies (e.g. holding companies, fellow subsidiaries, associated companies etc.)	33	(55)	32	(70)
Shareholdings, directorships, partnerships or other management interests in other companies or enterprises, held by identified executives of the managing agent (notes 1 and 2)	44	(73)	43	(93)
Involvement of identified executives in management of other syndicates (note 1)	14	(23)	17	(37)
Interests held by connected persons	9	(15)	10	(22)

Notes
1.   The data excludes data information about the shareholdings of executives in the managing agency company itself, or mere participations in other syndicates which might also be given as the measure of their interest in certain related party transactions.
2.   In one case no information was available in respect of certain former directors.

Table 4. Types of transactions or other arrangements identified

	1984	Agents in sample (%)	1983	(%)
Insurance cover (including reinsurance) of related companies, executives, or connected persons provided by the syndicate	9	(15)	8	(17)
Management of, or underwriting for other syndicates (including syndicates in the same market from or through whom business is accepted) (note 1)	46	(77)	24	(52)
Reinsurance for the syndicate placed with connected syndicates or insurers	15	(25)	13	(28)
Reinsurance for the syndicate placed through connected broker or intermediary	32	(53)	23	(50)
Business for the syndicate accepted from connected broker or intermediary	31	(52)	26	(57)
Provision to syndicate of:				
investment services	14	(23)	12	(26)
other financial/banking services	3	(5)	3	(7)
underwriting/agency services	5	(8)	2	(4)
other services (e.g., office accommodation or administration; accounting; data processing)	26	(43)	22	(48)
services to Names (e.g. members' agency)	14	(23)	17	(37)

Notes
1. The figures exclude three agents who gave the details now required about other managed syndicates (see (B) below), but otherwise had no interests to disclose.
2. The figures include one agent (1983: two) who mentioned that connected parties have transactions with other syndicates on which Names may participate.

Table 5 analyses the number of instances of financial quantification provided about the transactions and arrangements disclosed and the interests
therein. As it was common for agents to disclaim the existence of any
financial benefit in respect of many of the transactions or arrangements
disclosed, Table 6 analyses the disclaimers made. The percentages have been
calculated in the same way as for Tables 3 and 4.

Table 5. Provision of financial quantification relating to at least one item disclosed

	1984	Agents in sample (%)	1983	(%)
Transactions or arrangements (note 2)	36	(60)	15	(33)
Interests therein (note 3)	14	(23)	7	(15)
Extent to which not 'arms length'	1	(2)	2	(4)
Statement that not possible to quantify some or all transactions or interests	6	(10)	2	(4)
Statement that not possible to quantify extent to which not 'arms length'	1	(2)	—	(—)

Notes
1. If no quantification or statement was given, the agent is excluded from this table. If agents quantified disclosures under more than one heading, or quantified some and said others were impossible, they are included more than once in this table.
2. As an alternative, or in addition to financial quantification, 13 agents (22%) (1983: 11 – 24%) gave statements indicating the relevant percentage (e.g. of premiums received or paid, or of commissions) involved in the transactions or interest. In one case for 1983 the full details of the transactions had been sent to Names but were not included in the filed report.
3. The data excludes the information required to be given about syndicates managed in the same market, which is dealt with in (B) below.

Table 6. Disclaimers of financial benefit

	1984	Agents in sample (%)	1983	(%)
Statement that all transactions and arrangements disclosed were at 'arms length' or 'in ordinary course of business'	17	(28)	13	(28)
Statement in regard to all insurance transactions and arrangements disclosed that they were 'at arms length' or 'in ordinary course of business'	13	(22)	11	(24)
Statement in regard to one or more transactions or arrangements disclosed that they were at 'arms length' or 'in ordinary course of business'	12	(20)	6	(13)
	42	(70)	30	(65)
Statement that auditors check that all charges are fair and reasonable	—	(—)	1	(2)
Statement that services are provided at cost	6	(10)	8	(17)
Statement that one or more disclosures had been made even though the transactions or interests were not considered material (note 2)	18	(30)	12	(26)
Statement that one or more relationships had now been terminated or would shortly be (of which 15 (1983: 9) related to broking connections)	24	(40)	14	(30)
Statement in respect of one or more transactions or interests disclosed that no financial benefit had been received (e.g. by executives of the managing agent)	17	(28)	14	(30)

Notes
1. If no disclaimers were made the agent is excluded from this table. If more than one of these disclaimers was made the agent is included more than once in this table.
2. The data excludes cases where merely the size of the figures or percentages disclosed implied that the items were not material.

(B) Other Syndicates Managed in the Same Market

The following data apply to the 100 syndicates whose reports were included in the random sample. In 51 cases the managing agent managed one or more other syndicates in the same market, and (except in one case where one of the five other syndicates was omitted) in all cases the appropriate disclosures were made in their audited 1984 reports. However, the details required in the managing agent's report were not always given (see Chapter 15).

The information was normally given in a tabular form; in some cases including the data for the reporting syndicate itself, and in some cases giving figures for both US and UK Names' subgroups. One difference of interpretation arose where the reporting syndicate had started after 1982 and therefore had no closed year result itself – of three such syndicates in the sample, one had no related syndicates; one included the details of the 1982 result for the other syndicate, and one did not.

The Code of Practice issued in December 1985 (after these reports were published) now states that similar details should be given for other syndicates in the same market managed by other agents in the same group of companies – this was done in the 1984 reports of two syndicates by their agents (who were both in the same group). Other voluntary disclosures of the same details about syndicates not covered by the byelaw were: the reports of four syndicates (involving two agents) contained the details for all the other syndicates managed by the managing agent; two (involving two agents) for the other syndicates for whom the underwriter acts; one for another syndicate from which a quota-share is taken; and one (non-marine syndicate) for an incidental non-marine syndicate also managed by the agent (for which an annual report had also been filed separately from that for the 'main' marine syndicate).

EXAMPLES

Some of the interlocking arrangements are extremely complex and it is difficult to give 'typical' examples. The length of some statements (some of the 1983 statements were over fifteen pages long and some of the 1984 statements ran to seven pages) also precludes extensive reproduction, and, as noted above, financial quantification of the amount of the transactions, arrangements and interests involved was often not given. PAM did not give any specimen statement.

- Example 1 is a clearly written example of the kind of statement commonly given.

- Examples 2 to 4 give an above average amount of financial quantification (see also, for example, Merrett, 799; S.A.Meacock, 727; Safeguard, 758; Stewart & Hughman, 337).

- Example 4 includes transactions that appear to be of a kind that would in future fall under the planned rules about prohibiting 'related party' reinsurance.

- Example 5 refers to 'non-arms length' transaction, by which syndicate members have benefitted (see also, for example, Holmwoods & Back & Manson, 144).

- In Example 6, the first extract, while not part of the audited disclosures, uses an effective method of illustrating relationships. The second extract, from the audited notes, gives the details required about another managed syndicate in the same market.

For reports which give, in addition to the information required in SAB about syndicates managed in the same market, similar tabular information about other managed syndicates, or about syndicates managed by other group companies, or for which the underwriter also acts, see, for example, Brooks and Dooley, 861; Dugdale, 508; R.J.Kiln, 557; Richard Beckett, 918; Towergate, 588.

Example 1
VERRALL TURNER & CO. (UNDERWRITING AGENCY) LTD.
MARINE SYNDICATE 888/889
Disclosure of Interests

In accordance with the disclosure of interests byelaw (number 3 of 1984) the managing agent is required to disclose all transactions and arrangements entered into by the managing agent on behalf of the syndicate during the period covered by the accounts and in which
 (i) the managing agent;
 (ii) any related company of the managing agent; or
 (iii) any executive of the managing agent;
had directly or indirectly a material interest. Managing agents' remuneration is exempted. An interest is defined as material if a reasonable underwriting member might regard it as something which might influence the managing agent (or in the case of (iii) above its executive) in the performance of its duties.

   The syndicate's managing agent has, through certain of its directors and shareholders and a working arrangement with Pulbrook Underwriting Management Ltd, a close affiliation with Stewart Wrightson Holdings plc a company listed on the London Stock Exchange with many subsidiary companies. Five of the subsidiaries are Lloyd's brokers and the remainder are largely broking and insurance companies. These subsidiary companies are regarded as related companies for the purpose of disclosure.

   Under (ii) it is disclosed that regular insurance transactions are made with the group's Lloyd's broking companies, who may in the normal course of their broking activities place insurances with the syndicate on the same basis as they do with other Lloyd's syndicates and/or place reinsurance on behalf of the syndicate on the same basis as they do for other Lloyd's syndicates. At 31st December 1984 the cumulative totals of premiums, net of deductions, in respect of such business for the three years of account were

Account	1982	1983	1984
Premiums	£13,320	£19,520	£32,982
Reinsurance premiums	£11,505	£14,964	£13,331

Insurance transactions with the group's insurance companies were not material.

   All insurance transactions with group companies have been at arms length. No special terms or brokerage have been accorded to a company by reason of its group status, nor has any insurance transaction or arrangement been entered into with a related company upon the instruction of the managing agent.

   With regard to (iii) Messrs. M.Turner and W.D.Carrington were during the period covered by the accounts directors of Pulbrook Underwriting Management Ltd (PUM) as well as of Verrall Turner & Co. (Underwriting Agency) Ltd (VT). PUM is the managing agency of syndicate 334/427. Mr Turner is the Underwriter of syndicate 334/427 as well as of syndicate 888/889. Mr C.A.Merrett, a minority shareholder in VT, is a senior member of syndicate 334/427's staff. Messrs. Turner, Carrington and Merrett are members of syndicate 334/427. The Underwriter and staff of syndicate 334/427 write the business of syndicate 888/889 from syndicate 334/427's box, using its office and allied facilities. Common expenses are shared between the syndicates pro-rata to written premium income. Insurance transactions between the syndicates amount to less than £7,000.

   Under the remaining section (i) nothing falls to be disclosed.

W.D.Carrington (Director)
M.Turner (Underwriter)

14th June 1985

Example 2

THE SERVICE MOTOR POLICIES
SYNDICATE NUMBER 979

Disclosure of Interests — 31st December 1984

The following report has been prepared in compliance with The Disclosure of Interests Bye-law (No.3 of 1984), and covers the period from 1st January 1982 to 31st December 1984.

Interests of Norman Frizzell Underwriting Limited

Norman Frizzell Underwriting Limited has no interest in any transactions or arrangements entered into for the account of or otherwise concerning underwriting members underwriting through Syndicate Number 979, apart from the receipt of remuneration in respect of its duties as managing agent of that syndicate.

Interests of Related Companies of Norman Frizzell Underwriting Limited

Norman Frizzell Underwriting Limited is a subsidiary of The Frizzell Group Limited, a company which together with other subsidiaries, has various interests in transactions or arrangements entered into for the account of or otherwise concerning underwriting members underwriting through Syndicate Number 979. The interests are listed below.

1. **Service Interests**

   The Frizzell Group Limited and its related companies provide a number of services to Syndicate Number 979. The services provided and the charges made for each of the underwriting accounts are as follows:

	1982 Account £	1983 Account £	1984 Account £
Scheme Administration Fee	3,279,924	3,135,197	3,176,106
Provision of accommodation	58,247	101,521	101,924
Data processing	28,180	37,191	30,996

   In addition, some printing services are provided, but the amounts concerned are not material.

2. **Insurance Interests**

   (i)   A large proportion of the business written by Syndicate Number 979 emanates from Norman Frizzell Motor and General, a division of Norman Frizzell Insurance Brokers Limited, a wholly owned subsidiary of the Frizzell Group Limited. The arrangement, which has been in existence for over 50 years, is based on normal commercial terms in respect of premium rates and brokers commissions, and profit commissions. The total arrangement is governed by a binding authority granted to Norman Frizzell Insurance Brokers Limited by the syndicate.

   The total amount of brokerage and commission earned in respect of this business is as follows:

   1982 Account   £5,310,581
   1983 Account   £4,683,738
   1984 Account   £4,743,765

   (ii) Other business is received by the syndicate in addition to the above, from wholly owned insurance broking subsidiaries. Brokerage earned by the companies in respect of this business, is as follows:

   1982 Account   £2,413
   1983 Account   £13,080
   1984 Account   £18,555

...

THE SERVICE MOTOR POLICIES
SYNDICATE NUMBER 979

Disclosure of Interests — 31st December 1984

(iii) The syndicate also employs Frizzell International Limited, a 51% subsidiary of The Frizzell Group Limited, to arrange the excess of loss reinsurance protection and, until the 1984 account, quota share reinsurance protection.

Brokerage earned by the company in respect of this business for the underwriting accounts concerned is as follows:

1982 Account   £78,999
1983 Account   £66,525
1984 Account   £38,293

In none of the instances mentioned above, nor in respect of any other arrangements made by the syndicate or the managing agent, do we regard the circumstances as material as envisaged in Bye-law No. 3, in that the terms applicable are totally consistent with those which it is reasonable to expect could have been obtained in the case of a like for like transaction or arrangement, entered into on an arms length basis; no secret profits or benefits have been made or derived from any transaction or arrangement entered into by the agency or its executives on behalf of syndicate members.

Interests of Executives of Norman Frizzell Underwriting Limited

1. In recognition of the fact that the arrangements outlined above ultimately form part of the revenue of The Frizzell Group Limited, the interests of the executives of Norman Frizzell Underwriting Limited in the issued shares of The Frizzell Group Limited during the period covered by this report and whilst holding office, were as follows:

	Ordinary shares of 25p each			
	1st January 1982	31st December 1982	31st December 1983	31st December 1984
C.F. Frizzell				
Beneficial	1,541,030	1,441,030	1,686,830	885,400
Other	1,569,807	1,527,807	1,258,412	1,578,145
N.R. Frizzell (Resigned 11.7.83)				
Beneficial	1,304,380	1,304,380	1,304,380*	—
Other	1,697,807	1,797,807	1,308,152*	—
W.H.J. Ritchens (Appointed 12.1.84)				
Beneficial	—	—	—	6,030

(* As at date of resignation)

2. Messrs C.F. Frizzell, W.H.J. Ritchens and K.J. Sharpe are directors of S.M.P. Insurance Services Limited. In addition, Messrs W.H.J. Ritchens and K.J. Sharpe each hold one ordinary £1 share in the company, in non-beneficial capacities.

Mr. K.J. Sharpe is also a director and holder of fifty ordinary shares of 10p each, in a non-beneficial capacity, of Horncastle Insurance Services Limited.

These companies act as insurance brokers and place all business with Syndicate Number 979. The companies are non-profit making in that any profits are transferred to Syndicate Number 979 by way of reduced brokerage. None of the directors have received fees or any other form of benefit in respect of their directorships.

Example 3

M.E.CHARLESWORTH (UNDERWRITING AGENTS) LIMITED

M.E.CHARLESWORTH & OTHERS MARINE SYNDICATE 24

Notes to the Annual Report

8. Disclosure of Interests

The directors of M.E.Charlesworth (Underwriting Agents) Limited (the Agency) and their interest as Names on syndicates 734, 678 and 24 are shown in the Managing Agent's report.

Mr M.E.Charlesworth holds 70.74% of the issued ordinary £1 shares of the Agency. As discussed in the underwriter's report for syndicate 734, Mr M.E.Charlesworth and persons connected with him hold 90% of the equity in London Aviation Underwriters Inc. (L.A.U.), Seattle, Washington, U.S.A. The main purpose and function of L.A.U. is to attract aviation business to syndicate 734 and the London aviation market in general. The amount of brokerage and other income received by L.A.U. during 1982 was U.S.$90,051, 1983 U.S.$127,357, 1984 U.S.$171,716, of which approximately 50% was in respect of business placed with syndicate 734. Mr Charlesworth has not received any remuneration from L.A.U. in those years, on the contrary there is an outstanding unsecured loan of U.S.$64,500 due from L.A.U., provided personally by Mr. Charlesworth.

Up to and including 1984 the Agency owned 65% of the issued share capital of Holmoak Services Limited (formerly Teville Insurance Services Limited), with the remaining 35% owned by directors and executives of the Agency and Holmoak. Since 31st December 1984 the Agency has acquired the 35% interest of the directors and executives at par and now owns 100% of Holmoak's equity. The main purpose of Holmoak was to attract motor business to syndicate 678 and assist in meeting some of syndicate 678's expenses. The amount of brokerage earned on the business passed to syndicate 678 by Holmoak was approximately £160,000 in 1981, £131,000 in 1982 and £126,000 in 1983.

Messrs M.E.Charlesworth and A.C.Charlesworth are trustees of E.F.Charlesworth's daughter's settlement. The trust has lent the Agency £40,000 to finance the purchase of the freehold property in Eastbourne. The loan is secured by a mortgage over the freehold premises and interest on the loan is charged at a commercial rate.

It is considered that no material interest was gained by the individuals concerned in connection with the above arrangements.

Example 4

K.F. ALDER
(UNDERWRITING AGENCY) LIMITED
NON-MARINE SYNDICATE No. 122
DISCLOSURE OF INTERESTS

The managing agent, related companies of the managing agent and/or executives of the managing agent had interests in the contracts disclosed in this report.

A   INWARDS REINSURANCE
1982 ACCOUNTS

(i) Contract protecting the Personal Accident Account of the Midland Reinsurance Company Limited

Limits: £5,000 excess of £5,000 any one accident
Deposit Premium: £1,000 plus US$2,000 adjustable at 4% of premium income.
Adjustment Premium added £4,919 plus US$9,370 plus Can.$1,802.
Claims Paid & Outstanding: NIL
Syndicate Share: 50%

(ii) Contract protecting the Whole Account of the Midland Reinsurance Company Limited.

Limits: £50,000 excess of £50,000 any one loss.
Premium: £750 plus US$1,500
Claims Paid & Outstanding: NIL
Syndicate Share: 25%

1983 ACCOUNT

(i) Contract protecting the Personal Accident Account of the Midland Reinsurance Company Limited.

Limits: £5,000 excess of £5,000 any one accident.
Premiums: £1,000 plus US$2,000 adjustable at 4% of premium income.
Claims Paid & Outstanding: NIL
Syndicate Share: 50%

1984 ACCOUNT — NIL

These contracts were placed by Bellew, Parry and Raven Limited (Lloyd's Brokers).

B.   OUTWARDS REINSURANCE
1982 ACCOUNT
With Bermuda Reinsurance Company Limited
(placed through Bellew, Parry & Raven Limited)

(i) Whole Account Excess Aggregate Stop Loss

Limit: £600,000 plus US$805,000 excess of 93% settlement.
Premium Paid: US$25,250
Claim made as at 31st December, 1984: £600,000 plus US$805,000

This policy was a renewal from previous years and the sum insured reflects the loss experience on those years. An amount equivalent to 60% of accrued interest earned the Reinsurer has been taken into account by the Reinsurer in calculating the cover that it gives under the policy.

(ii) Contract to pay in the event of non-availability of other reinsurance contracts, they being unable to respond due to default, insolvency or any other reason. The contract losses occurring during the twelve months to 31st December, 1982, irrespective of the year of account.

Limit: US$635,000 excess of US$50,000 each and every loss, with one free reinstatement.

Premium Paid: £2,020 plus US$16,160.

No claims were made on this policy, which was a renewal from previous years and the sum insured reflected the loss experience on those years. An amount equivalent to 75% of the accrued interest earned by the reinsurer had been taken into account by the insurer in calculating the cover that it gave under the policy.

...

K.F. ALDER
(UNDERWRITING AGENCY) LIMITED

NON-MARINE SYNDICATE No.122

DISCLOSURE OF INTERESTS

CONTINUED

B. OUTWARDS REINSURANCE (continued)

1982 ACCOUNT

With Bermuda Reinsurance Company Limited

(placed through Bellew, Parry & Raven Limited)

(iii) Quota Share contract in respect of open cover for Canadian Auto business – 20% of Syndicate's retention.

Terms: Original net rate with 100% profit commission.
Premium Income at 31st December, 1984: Can.$510,857
Claims paid at 31st December, 1984: Can.$363,769
Claims outstanding at 31st December, 1984: Can.$39,767 (Estimated)

(iv) Quota Share contract in respect of Errors & Omissions cover for Chartered Accountants.

Limits: £250,000 any one claim
Reinsurer reinsured 25% part of 55% of the Syndicate's line.
Terms: Original net rate with 20% profit commission.
Premium Income at 31st December, 1984: £277,417
Claims paid at 31st December, 1984: £129,876
Claims outstanding at 31st December, 1984: £461,641 (Estimated)

1983 ACCOUNT

With Bermuda Reinsurance Company Limited

(placed through Bellew, Parry & Raven Limited)

(i) Quota Share contract in respect of open cover for Canadian Auto business – 20% of Syndicate's retention.

Terms: Original net rate with 75% profit commission.
Premium Income at 31st December, 1984: Can.$636,016
Claims paid at 31st December 1984: Can.£402,500
Claims outstanding at 31st December, 1984: Can.$132,717 (estimated)

(ii) Reinsurance contract to pay in the event of non-availability of other contracts, they being unable to respond due to default, insolvency or any other reason. The contract covered losses occurring during the fifteen months to 31st March, 1984, irrespective of the year of account.

Limit: US$680,000 excess of US$50,000 each and every loss, with one free reinstatement.
Premium paid: £2,020 plus US$16,160
Claims paid at 31st December, 1984: US$1,360,000 of which US$680,000 was credited to the 1978 Account and US$680,000 to the 1979 Account.

The risks for which this policy was taken out are still in existence and provision is now included in the reinsurance to close.

(iii) Quota Share contract in respect of Banker's Comprehensive Insurance For Sun Banks Inc.

Limit: US$10,000,000 any one loss. Quota Share 1.72% part of 8.05% of the Syndicate's line.
Terms: Original net rate.
Premium Income at 31st December, 1984: US$2,350
Claims Paid at 31st December, 1984: US$4,455
Claims Outstanding at 31st December, 1984: US$8,600

1984 ACCOUNT

With Bermuda Reinsurance Company Limited

(placed through Bellew, Parry & Raven Limited)

(i) Quota Share contract in respect of Bankers Comprehensive Insurance For Sun Banks Inc.

Limit: US$10,000,000 any one loss. Quota Share 1.72% part of 8.05% of the Syndicate's line.
Terms: Original net rate.
Premium Income at 31st December, 1984: US$1,572
Claims Paid at 31st December, 1984: US$NIL
Claims Outstanding at 31st December, 1984: US$NIL

Note: The Underwriter believes that the terms of the contracts in Section A and B above were the equal of, or better than, those which could have been expected at the same time as an arm's length transaction in the absence of the connected interest.

...

K.F. ALDER
(UNDERWRITING AGENCY) LIMITED
NON-MARINE SYNDICATE No.122
DISCLOSURE OF INTERESTS
CONTINUED

C. TRANSACTIONS WITH BROKERS

The Syndicate writes business placed by Bellew, Parry & Raven Limited, (a wholly owned subsidiary of Bellew, Parry & Raven (Holdings) Limited) and places certain reinsurance contracts through that company. The managing agent does not consider that the contracts written by the Syndicate, except those in Section A above, fall within the definition of "material" in Disclosure of Interests Byelaw No. 3 of 1984.

The Syndicate has placed certain reinsurance contracts through Bellew, Parry & Raven Limited, which has accounted for brokerage on these contracts in its accounts to 30th September each year as follows:-

1982 approximately £ 69,300
1983 approximately £ 87,100
1984 approximately £124,500

It is not practicable to allocate these figures between Underwriting years.

Bellew, Parry & Raven Limited, had an agreement with Bellew, Parry & Raven (Agencies) Limited, whereby the latter company received commission equal to 25% of the brokerage earned by Bellew, Parry & Raven Limited, on these contracts. This agreement terminated in October 1982.

Surplus Reinsurance Management Limited had a contract with Bermuda Reinsurance Company Limited by which it received commissions in respect of contracts B(i) and (ii) above relating to the 1982 underwriting account and B(ii) relating to the 1983 underwriting account. It is not possible to determine the exact amount of the consideration, but the Directors estimate the figure to be not greater than £85,000.

D. EXPENSE TRANSACTIONS

The Syndicate paid leasing rentals to Bellew, Parry & Raven (Leasing) Limited, a wholly owned subsidiary of Bellew, Parry & Raven (Agencies) Limited, in respect of office equipment, motor cars etc. The amounts charged to Syndicate expenses were as follows:-

1982 Account £34,441
1983 Account £27,132
1984 Account £25,568

The Directors believe the terms of these leasing contracts were those which would have been expected as an "arm's length" transaction.

The Syndicate made rental payments to Bellew, Parry & Raven (Holdings) Limited, for use of office space. The amounts charged to Syndicate expenses were as follows:

1982 Account £ 8,381
1983 Account £ 8,829
1984 Account £18,184

Rental payments were based on a valuation by Savills.

Management fees and expenses at "arm's length" terms were paid to Bellew, Parry & Raven (Holdings) Limited in respect of the Syndicate's share of certain communal facilities:-

1982 Account £29,143
1983 Account £30,729
1984 Account £27,006

R.P. Milligan (Underwriting Agencies) Limited writes Livestock business on behalf of Syndicate 122.
R.P. Milligan (Underwriting Agencies) Limited are credited with 5% overrider plus 50% profit commission after allowing 10% for Syndicate 122's expenses.

1982 Account at 31st December, 1984

Net premium signed: £392,114	Plus US$1,380,645	Plus Can.$18,723
Claims Paid: £355,766	Plus US$ 673,521	Plus Can.$44,888
Claims Outstanding: £2,620	Plus US$ 36,000	Plus Can.$ NIL

1983 Account at 31st December, 1984

Net premium signed: £349,547	Plus US$1,020,144	Plus Can.$10,643
Claims Paid: £253,294	Plus US$ 650,382	Plus Can.$10,403
Claims Outstanding: £1,875	Plus US$ 53,799	Plus Can.$ NIL

...

K.F. ALDER
(UNDERWRITING AGENCY) LIMITED
NON-MARINE SYNDICATE No.122
DISCLOSURE OF INTERESTS
CONTINUED

D. EXPENSE TRANSACTIONS (continued)
1984 Account at 31st December, 1984

Net premium signed: £240,843	Plus US$736,111	Plus Can.$7,575
Claims Paid: £133,840	Plus US$245,599	Plus Can.$ NIL
Claims Outstanding: £19,140	Plus US$ 55,400	Plus Can.$ NIL

...

K.F. ALDER
(UNDERWRITING AGENCY) LIMITED
NON-MARINE SYNDICATE No. 122
DISCLOSURE OF INTERESTS
CONTINUED

E. EXTENT OF INTERESTS

The proportion of shareholdings of the excecutives (or their connected persons as defined in the Disclosure of Interests Byelaw No. 3 of 1984) in the companies mentioned above were as follows:-

PERCENTAGE OF EQUITY

	A.H.B. Grattan-Bellew	*E.E. Nelson	J.R. Parry	F.C. Raven	D.G.L. Mott
1st January, 1982	%	%	%	%	%
Bellew, Parry & Raven (Agencies) Limited	14.08	60.95	14.09	5.15	—
Bellew, Parry & Raven (Holdings) Limited	20.42	—	20.41	24.99	—
Bermuda Reinsurance Company Limited	4.33	14.00	4.34	8.67	—
Midland Reinsurance Company Limited	16.66	—	16.66	33.34	—
R.P. Milligan (Underwriting Agencies) Limited	10.00	—	—	10.00	10.00
Surplus Reinsurance Management Limited	11.00	35.00	11.00	21.00	—
1st January, 1983	%	%	%	%	%
Bellew, Parry & Raven (Agencies) Limited	12.69	60.95	14.09	5.15	—
Bellew, Parry & Raven (Holdings) Limited	15.83	—	20.41	24.99	—
Bermuda Reinsurance Company Limited	—	14.00	4.34	8.67	—
Midland Reinsurance Company Limited	—	—	16.66	33.34	—
R.P. Milligan (Underwriting Agencies) Limited	10.00	—	—	10.00	10.00
Surplus Reinsurance Management Limited	—	35.00	11.00	21.00	—
1st January, 1984	%	%	%	%	%
Bellew, Parry & Raven (Agencies) Limited	12.69	60.95	13.40	4.22	—
Bellew, Parry & Raven (Holdings) Limited	15.83	—	18.12	21.94	—
Bermuda Reinsurance Company Limited	—	14.00	2.16	5.78	—
R.P. Milligan (Underwriting Agencies) Limited	10.00	—	—	6.67	10.00
Surplus Reinsurance Management Limited	—	35.00	5.50	14.00	—

* In respect of Mr. E.E. Nelson, the shareholding shown is in respect of an indirect contingent interest, other than B.P.R. (Agencies) Limited, which is a direct interest.

Example 5

I.C.AGNEW UNDERWRITING LTD
SYNDICATE 672·673

Disclosure of Interests

I   Interests of the Managing Agent.
NONE

II   Interests of related companies of the Managing Agent.
NONE

III   Interests of the executives.
R.H.M. Outhwaite
R.M.H. Gilkes

R.H.M. Outhwaite and R.M.H. Gilkes are directors of R.H.M. Outhwaite Holdings Limited (Holdings) and R.H.M. Outhwaite (Underwriting Agencies) Limited (Agencies).

In the first few months of trading by Syndicate 672.673, Holdings provided interest free loans to the syndicate which have now been repaid.

Syndicates 317 and 661, which are managed by Agencies, have insurance transactions with the Company managed syndicate which are placed through Lloyd's brokers on normal commercial terms.

Example 6

M.W.E. UNDERWRITING AGENCIES LTD.
(MARINE SYNDICATES NUMBERS 275/6)

Extract from Agency Information

1.12   The structure of the Lloyd's activities of the John Townsend Group

The Lloyd's activities of the John Townsend Group and the respective shareholdings are set out below:

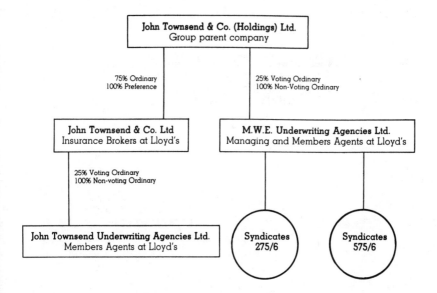

In accordance with the regulations of Lloyd's requiring overall voting control of underwriting agencies to be in the hands of members of Lloyd's, Messrs J.R.C. Townsend, J.A.V. Townsend and N.R.P. Townsend each own 25% of the voting shares in John Townsend Underwriting Agencies Limited. They are all directors of John Townsend & Co. (Holdings) Limited, John Townsend & Co. Limited and John Townsend Underwriting Agencies Limited. Mr. J.A.R. Moller is a director of John Townsend Underwriting Agencies Limited but neither he nor Messrs. J.H. Chappell nor M.A. Lewis holds any other directorships or interests in the shares of any John Townsend Group companies.

The directors of the Agency have shareholdings in the ultimate parent company, John Townsend & Co. (Holdings) Limited, as follows:-

Director	No. of Ordinary Shares of £1 each	Percentage of total in issue
J.R.C. Townsend	114,750	48.3
J.A.V. Townsend	20,000	8.4
N.R.P. Townsend	18,000	7.6

...

M.W.E. UNDERWRITING AGENCIES LTD.
(MARINE SYNDICATES NUMBERS 275/6)

Extract from Notes to the Accounts

16.   Other syndicates managed by M.W.E. Underwriting Agencies Limited

M.W.E. Underwriting Agencies Limited is also responsible for managing the marine syndicates 575/6, J.H. Chappell and Others, which commenced underwriting for the 1983 year of account. Details of the participations by directors and executives of the agency in those syndicates for the last two years are as follows:-

	1983 Account	1984 Account
Syndicate allocated capacity	£1,330,000	£2,780,341
Standard share	£20,000	£20,000
Participants in syndicate:-		
Executives of the agency	6	6
Directors of John Townsend & Co. (Holdings) Limited other than those included in above	3	3
Aggregate percentage participation of executives of the agency and directors of John Townsend & Co. (Holdings) Limited	15.04%	8.27%

CHAPTER 15

MANAGING AGENTS' REPORTS

INTRODUCTION

Full understanding of the performance of a business, and of the nature and risks of its activities, requires more information than the financial accounts alone can reveal. In the case of Lloyd's syndicates much of this kind of information is provided by the managing agents' and underwriters' reports. In this Chapter I deal with the first of these together with certain other information that was disclosed, and in Chapter 16 I deal with the underwriters' reports.

REQUIREMENTS

SAB requires the filing of a 'managing agent's' report (which may be combined with the underwriter's report), attached to the annual report. The auditors are required to check that the report is consistent with the syndicate accounts.

The report is to include information similar to that in a company's directors' report, including names of directors, or partners, and underwriters and their participations in the syndicate; the auditors and details of any change of auditors; together with the location of the accounting records (if not at the registered office). Managing agents are also required to comment on the investment policy and results; give details of major subcontracted functions, and discuss any plans for material expansion or contraction of the syndicate. Details of members' agents who have contributed a significant amount of the syndicate's stamp capacity are required; and also explanations of the basis on which business has been allocated between the syndicate and any other syndicate operating principally in the same market and managed by the managing agent. A 'catch-all' provision calls for any other matters it is considered appropriate to include.

For the 1983 accounts, while there was a requirement to send a managing agent's (and underwriter's) report to Names, and a specimen was included in PAM, there was no requirement to file it. The guidelines in PAM were largely the same as those in SAB, the main differences being that the matters

(i) major subcontracted functions, and
(ii) allocation of business between managed syndicates

were not mentioned, while it was suggested that there should be given details of major commitments which would affect future years (e.g. leases).

The 'catch-all' provision in PAM referred to other information considered necessary for proper understanding and proper accountability (as opposed to considered 'appropriate').

PAM also envisaged that the report might normally be combined with the underwriter's report, although the two could be separate, while SAB now envisages separate reports as 'normal', although they may be combined.

ANALYSIS

The filing of managing agents' reports with the 457 1984 annual reports (1983: 468) is analysed in Table 1.

Table 1. Filing of managing agents' reports

1984	(%)	1983	(%)	
415	(91)	192	(41)	included a separate managing agent's report
42	(9)	104	(22)	included a combined managing agent's and underwriter's report
457	(100)	296	(63)	
—	—	172	(37)	did not include their managing agent's report
457	(100)	468	(100)	

Note
For 1983 those syndicates that included some, or all, of the information in pages headed 'Management Agency Information' or 'Dislosures' or similar have been included as filing a report.

In respect of the random sample of 100 annual reports, 88 (1983: 40) included a separate report, and 12 (1983: 22) a combined report.

The disclosure of information in the 1983 annual reports was essentially voluntary. In both years much of the presentation dealt with the 'formal' information about directors, underwriters, percentages of stamp capacity, etc. Several 1983 reports discussed future commitments such as the effect of leases of premises or equipment. In both years, the most commonly mentioned subcontracted functions were investment management, accounting, data processing and other administrative services.

In relation to agency executives, several reports also gave their shareholdings in the agency; indicated who were the trustees of the Premiums Trust
Fund; and stated whether or not individuals had personal (stop loss) reinsurance policies on their underwriting participations.

With regard to investment results and policy the kind of information
given in the reports in the sample was as set out in Table 2.

Table 2. Comments on investment policy and results of investment management

	% of sample 1984	1983
Nothing said	1	2
'Nil' return (i.e. no, or minimal, investment funds)	1	2
Some	44	45
Full	41	40
Very full	13	11
	100	100

Notes
1.   The percentages for 1983 relate to the 62 managing agents' reports voluntarily filed for
     that year in respect of the 100 syndicates in the sample.
2.   In a few cases this information was given in the underwriter's report where this was not
     combined with the managing agent's report. In some cases the comments were provided
     by the investment manager to whom the agency had subcontracted the management of
     the syndicate investments.
3.   'Some' indicates a brief mention of portfolio make-up with a comment such as 'Returns
     are satisfactory'.
     'Full' indicates some comment about reasons for the level of returns achieved and factors
     influencing investment choice (as in PAM's specimen).
     'Very full' indicates a lengthy discussion (sometimes in a separate Investment Manager's
     report) on the reasons for past and current investment policy and results, and the likely
     factors influencing future investment strategy. (See Examples 1 and 2.)

In several cases there was comment only on the choice of investments,
and not on the results, so there is considerable scope for additional interpretation to be provided.

With regard to the information required by SAB about the allocation of
business between syndicates managed in the same market, 51 of the syndicates in the sample had one or more such parallel syndicates. But although
the required details about results, participations etc. were given in the 1984
audited disclosures of interests (see Chapter 14), some or all of the relevant
syndicates were not identified in 11 of the 1984 managing agents' reports.
For the remainder information was given about the basis of allocation of
business as required by SAB: in some cases there was a fixed percentage

allocation of business between the syndicates; in other cases they were stated to operate independently, or to take different types of business, or to have different underwriters, or some explanation was given of how the underwriter would choose the business to be written by each. In three instances the other syndicate was stated to have ceased business or to have been absorbed into another syndicate. In addition, 31 reports volunteered information about other syndicates than those for which disclosure was required: e.g. about the other syndicates or incidental syndicates managed by the same agent or agency group, or for which the underwriter also acted, or with which the syndicate wrote business on a percentage share. In some cases there was also discussion of the reinsurance arrangements between the syndicates, as will in future be required by the December 1985 Code of Practice on multiple syndicates.

Two reports stated that there were no other syndicates managed in the same market.

Other Information in Managing Agents' and Underwriters' Reports
In addition to the items recommended by PAM, or that are now required by SAB, the reports filed often contained other information on matters of interest to Names. This was mainly non-quantified information. The following were certain of the items commonly discussed in the reports in the sample (the percentages calculated for 1983 being of the 62 managing agents' reports filed for that year, although the information might be given elsewhere in the annual report).

(a) Inland Revenue Inquiries
Thirty-six (1983: 26=42%) mentioned the Inland Revenue investigations and the problems of 'rollover' policies of offshore reinsurance, often commenting on how this could delay the final computation of Names' tax liability. (A settlement between Lloyd's and the Inland Revenue was subsequently reached in October 1985 in respect of years up to the end of 1982.)

(b) Expenses and Their Allocation
Twelve reports (1983: 24=39%) gave some further amplification of the kinds or level of expenses incurred by the managing agent for the syndicate, or discussed special circumstances relating to the allocation of expenses (e.g. for a new syndicate, that a higher proportion had been borne by the agency; or that a particular syndicate had been lightly or heavily treated under the terms of a previous underwriting agency agreement which had now been changed) or gave further information about personal expenses charged.

(c) Litigation
Fourteen reports (1983: 20=32%) referred to, or gave further details about, litigation pending against or by the syndicate. Of these seven (1983: 8=13%)

and two (1983: 2=3%) that there was no significant litigation.

(d) 'Bondwashing'
Twenty-nine of the 1984 reports referred to the proposals in the 1985 Finance Bill to change the taxation of the accrued interest element of capital gains, often commenting on how this might affect investment strategy and returns in future.

(e) Divestment
Eighteen of the 1984 reports referred to the steps that had been or would have to be taken to enable the managing agent to comply with the divestment requirements of the Lloyd's Act 1982, in particular to separate broking and management agency interests. In several cases the syndicates' management was to be transferred to a different agency.

(f) Audit Arrangements
Fourteen reports referred to the changes that had been or would have to be made to comply with the requirements (under Byelaw 10 of 1984) to have separate auditors for the managing agency and the managed syndicate with effect from the 1985 annual reports, and for the syndicate auditors to have no involvement with the syndicate's accountancy functions.

In view of the topicality and significance of these imminent changes it is perhaps surprising that they were not more frequently discussed. There were also references in some reports to the expected impact of moving to the new Lloyd's building, or to computerisation of statistical and accounting systems. In some cases a 'Chairman's Report' was also provided.

EXAMPLES

■   Examples 1 and 2 are extracts giving 'very full' investment reports (see also, for example, Merrett, 799; Stewart & Hughman, 4).

■   Example 3 includes discussion of the allocation of business and expenses shared with a parallel syndicate; divestment; 'rollovers'; and the auditing byelaw.

For an example of a combined managing agent's and underwriter's report see, for example, J.D.Boyagis, 227.

Example I

R.W.STURGE & CO

Report of the Managing Agent 31st December 1984

This Managing Agent's Report covers all of the twelve syndicates managed by A.L.Sturge (Management) Limited, which trades as R.W.Sturge & Co.
[Introduction to report not reproduced]

Investment Policy, Management and Results

(a) POLICY

The funds from all our managed syndicates are grouped together and invested as a single amount. This reduces the cost of investment and allows us to obtain better investment opportunities. In accordance with the Lloyd's system of accounting, investments are revalued at the end of each calendar year. Any profit or loss, together with that arising on transactions during the year, is apportioned over the three open underwriting accounts in accordance with a consistently applied formula. Approximately two thirds of the result in calendar 1984 has generally been allocated to the 1982 underwriting account. The allocation of investment income and capital gains or losses arising from the investment fund as between each of the participating managed syndicates is determined on a weighted cashflow basis.

The fund is maintained in three separate currencies: sterling, US dollars and Canadian dollars. Cash funds required to service each syndicate are placed in interest-bearing accounts on advice from our bankers. We have for many years transferred cash which is surplus to the day-to-day requirements of our syndicates into a combined investment account with our investment advisers, Lloyds Bank Plc, with whom we have a close working relationship. Broad investment policy is set by ourselves and our investment advisers effect individual investment transactions within these policy guidelines, meeting with us monthly to review the previous month's transactions and future developments.

A low risk policy is followed by restricting the maturity of any fixed interest investment to 5 years (with the average maturity of the portfolio never in excess of 2–3 years) and avoiding equities. Investments are chosen in light of the average taxation position of Names with the aim of maximising capital gains.

Details of the investment funds at 31st December 1984 and of the syndicates' participation therein, are given on pages 86 and 87.

(b) INVESTMENT BACKGROUND IN 1984

UK Interest rates rose over the year in response to sterling weakness induced by oil price fears and excessive domestic monetary expansion. In July there was a succession of base rate increases to stabilise sterling in the face of an apparently deteriorating industrial relations environment, which was later reversed. Nevertheless the pound remained under pressure at the end of the year, resulting in a weak gilt market.

USA Interest rates rose very sharply until August in response to a booming economy evidenced by burgeoning loan demand and industrial production. Bond yields rose significantly as no measures seemed likely to be taken to curb the budget deficit. The investment climate improved as the economy showed evidence of slowing in the 3rd quarter and the authorities indicated an easing of monetary policy, especially as the dollar's strength was inhibiting inflation. President Reagan's re-election further boosted confidence, enabling bonds to end the year at levels higher than they started.

...

R.W.STURGE & CO

Report of the Managing Agent 31st December 1984 – continued

CANADA   Canadian bonds largely mirrored US trends although interest rates rose relative to US rates in order to protect the weakening currency. The election of a Conservative administration, however, boosted confidence and bonds ended higher than they began the year.

(c) 1984 PERFORMANCE
In this volatile market environment, the results for the year are satisfactory (and in excess of those for the previous year) as well as above the returns achieved by an appropriate (tax efficient) benchmark 1-year investment notionally made at the beginning of the year. The pre-tax capital gain expressed as a percentage of average capital investment over the year was 9.57% (£), 8.44% (US$) and 8.68% (Can$). This produced a weighted overall return for the fund of 8.62%.

(d) 1985 PROSPECTS
UK interest rates in 1985 have so far been dominated by the volatility of exchange rates. Against an end-year value of US$1.16 per £, the dollar rose to $1.04 at the end of February before falling to a rate of $1.26 at the time of writing. These moves led to sterling interest rates rising rapidly at the start of the year before declining slowly. They are still not back to the levels pertaining at the start of the year, but the value of your sterling investments has been protected by our policy of being invested in short dated bonds which are now earning a satisfactory rate of return. Interest rates are expected to fall further over the year, although much of this is already discounted in bond yields. US interest rates rose slightly from their year-end levels, but with evidence of slower economic growth they have now declined to below these levels, thus vindicating our policy of slightly lengthening the maturity of the portfolio. Although the budget deficit militates against any significant fall in rates the outlook for bond prices is modestly optimistic in a low inflation environment provided the dollar does not fall precipitously.

The proposed change in the basis of taxation of accrued income from capital to income contained in the 1985 Finance Bill is bound to have some after-tax effect on the 1985 calendar year which will affect the returns for the 1983, 1984 and 1985 underwriting years. We are reviewing the longer term implications of this change carefully with a view to minimising, where possible, the consequent after-tax decline in your investment returns. It is as yet too early to comment on this in any detail.

[Rest of report not reproduced]

Example 2

J.M.POLAND & OTHERS

MARINE SYNDICATE NO: 108/768

Investment Report: 31st December 1984

For a £5000 share, the 1982 account has returned an investment appreciation, net of capital gains tax, of £338, compared to £366 for 1981. Net interest income of £143 compares to £128.

General
1984 was a difficult year for investments and it is hard to generalise on its record. In the U.S., we witnessed a confused year as, initially, interest rates rose due to worries about the economy over-heating, the size of the Government deficit and banking problems resulting from Third World debts. The year stabilised, however, and improved towards the end, but the pressures on interest rates have not entirely disappeared.

At home, one can perhaps describe the markets as akin to riding on a roller coaster – sharp, sudden and fast climbs and falls, each experienced with breath-taking ferocity. The Government hoped that it would be a year of declining interest rates but witnessed the reverse. The Budget strategy in March 1984 based on a stable currency and reducing interest rates was to be completely confounded. The market was at the mercy of the U.S. scenario, a sharply declining currency, oil price fears, the miners' strike and the change of tax status for building society investments.

It was only by investing in very short-dated bonds that we were able, against general market trends, to return a profit on our portfolios.

Equities
You will have read of the intended sales of Lloyd's Life. Your Syndicate holds 49,500 shares and, if successful, the company's sale will represent a once and for all windfall of major proportions. The profits will be distributed over the 1983/84/85 years of account.

Your Syndicate holds no other U.K. equities but is party to a U.S. portfolio managed by Bankers Trust. In the early part of the year its performance was disappointing but after a review with our Fund Managers has now shown an improvement.

The Future
I must advise you that although, due to Lloyd's Life, investment appreciation earned this year should be comparable to last's, the general outlook for the future is much bleaker and I can only predict reduced investment returns for the long term.

Firstly, in February, the Chancellor introduced a measure to prevent bond washing – hitherto, the source of much of our profits. It will involve our investments in all currencies, with the U.S. being most affected. From next February onwards, for appreciation, we will have to rely almost entirely on profits earned from low coupon and index-linked stocks and on correctly judging overall market movements. The Chancellor's action will progressively show in our accounts; the 1983 account will be barely affected, with it beginning to bite into the 1984 profits until 1986 when the effect will be complete.

Secondly, because of the poor Underwriting cycle and the need to take out protective reinsurance policies, there has been a sharp reduction in the funds available for investment.

M.D.POLAND – Director
31st May 1985

Example 3

R. E. W. LUMLEY AND OTHERS
MARINE SYNDICATE No. 247/133

MANAGING AGENT'S REPORT

Directors of the Managing Agent

The Directors of Edward Lumley & Sons (Underwriting Agencies) Limited, the Managing Agent, and their member's syndicate premium limits allocated to the Syndicate are as follows:

	1982 Account	1983 Account	1984 Account	1985 Account
R. E. W. Lumley	£80,000	£80,000	£70,000	£60,000
H. R. L. Lumley	£60,000	£60,000	£60,000	£60,000
J. S. Harvey	£30,000	£30,000	£60,000	£60,000
T. K. Belton	£20,000	£25,000	£25,000	£20,000

The Directors have all held office since before 1st January, 1982

Underwriting

The underwriting for the Syndicate is delegated to Street (Underwriting Agencies) Limited, which is the Managing Agent of Syndicate 123/132.

The active underwriter for both Syndicates 123/132 and 247/133 is Mr D. A. Pollock, a director of that company. Mr Pollock is a member of the Syndicate, and his member's syndicate premium limit allocated to the Syndicate for the 1982, 1983, 1984 and 1985 Accounts is £15,000.

The deputy underwriter for both syndicates is Mr W. M. Mitchell, also a director of that company, who is not a member of the Syndicate.

Both Mr Pollock and Mr Mitchell are members of Syndicate 123/132.

All business written by the active underwriter is allocated between the two syndicates in the ratio of 80% to Syndicate 123/132 and 20% to Syndicate 247/133. The expenses of the Underwriting Box in the Room at Lloyd's and the Box Staff are shared in the same proportions. However, both Syndicates have substantial other expenses which are borne by each separately, although no expenses of Edward Lumley & Sons (Underwriting Agencies) Limited are charged to the Syndicate.

Prior to 15th November, 1984 the whole of the issued share capital of Street (Underwriting Agencies) Limited was held by Mr Pollock and Mr Mitchell. On that date a controlling interest was sold to R. J. Kiln & Co. Limited, a prominent firm of Lloyd's underwriting agents, and directors of that company.

Members' Agents' Participation

The proportion of the total syndicate allocated capacity attributable to Names participating in the Syndicate through the agency of Edward Lumley & Sons (Underwriting Agencies) Limited is 88% for both the 1982 and 1983 Accounts, 79% for the 1984 Account and 73% for the 1985 Account. No other member's agency accounted for a significant proportion.

...

R. E. W. LUMLEY AND OTHERS
MARINE SYNDICATE No. 247/133

MANAGING AGENT'S REPORT

continued

Underwriting Result

The 1982 Underwriting Account has closed with a much improved result as compared with 1981. The principal reasons for this are given in the Underwriters' Report which has been prepared by Mr Pollock and Mr Mitchell and is attached hereto. When satisfactory investment gains and income are added the overall result for a Name with a £40,000 share is £3,441 (1981: £781) after all expenses but before U.S. tax and any retentions for Personal Reserve are taken into account.

As newspaper reports have emphasised only too stridently the 1982 Underwriting Account was not a good one for Lloyd's as a whole. Given this backdrop the Syndicate's own result can be regarded with satisfaction.

In pure underwriting terms the 1983 Account is showing a slight improvement over 1982 after 24 months.

1984 has made a reasonable start but 12 months is always too short a time span to be of practical value.

Investments

The Syndicate's investments are managed by Edward Lumley & Sons (Underwriting Agencies) Limited, whose consistent policy has been to hold only short-dated securities issued by the British, U.S.A., and Canadian Governments and U.S.A. federal agencies.

The capital appreciation credited to the 1982 Account is approximately 23% higher than for the previous year, reflecting increased interest rates during 1984.

Divestment

It is a requirement of the Lloyd's Act 1982 that Lloyd's Underwriting Agents which are associated with a Lloyd's Broker shall not continue to act as Managing Agents for any Lloyd's syndicates after 22nd July, 1987. Edward Lumley & Sons (Underwriting Agencies) Limited is associated with three Lloyd's Brokers, and proposes to cease to act as Managing Agents for the Syndicate before that date. A proposal has been made that the business of the Syndicate should be taken over by Syndicate 123/132 with effect from 1st January 1986, and that all members of the Syndicate will be offered similar participation in that Syndicate, through their present Agents, for the 1986 Account.

This proposal is under active discussion, and, if it becomes effective, will result in Edward Lumley & Sons (Underwriting Agencies) Limited acting solely as Member's Agent in respect of all Syndicates on which it places Names.

...

R. E. W. LUMLEY AND OTHERS
MARINE SYNDICATE No. 247/133

MANAGING AGENT'S REPORT

continued

Inland Revenue Enquiry

As you are aware, certain reinsurances placed by this Syndicate are being questioned by the Inland Revenue and assessments to additional tax have been sent out. We have written to Names and Member's Agents about this situation and expect to do so again when we have anything further to report.

Accounting Records

The accounting records of the Syndicate are maintained by Sherwood Computer Services PLC at 11, St. Edward's Way, Romford, Essex.

Syndicate Auditors

For many years Peat, Marwick, Mitchell & Co., have acted as auditors of both the Syndicate and Edward Lumley & Sons (Underwriting Agencies) Limited. This double function is no longer permitted, following the introduction of Lloyd's Byelaw No. 10 of 1984. Since Peat, Marwick, Mitchell & Co., act as auditors of most of the companies in the Edward Lumley Group, it is appropriate that they should continue to act as auditors of Edward Lumley & Sons (Underwriting Agencies) Limited, and they have agreed to do so.

Messrs. Littlejohn de Paula, who act as auditors of Syndicate 123/132, have been appointed auditors of the Syndicate in respect of the accounts for the year ending 31st December, 1985.

R. E. W. LUMLEY
Chairman

11th June, 1985

CHAPTER 16

UNDERWRITERS' REPORTS

REQUIREMENTS

Starting with the 1984 annual reports, the filing of an underwriter's report (which may be combined with the managing agent's report) is required and the auditor is required to check its consistency with the annual accounts. SAB (Schedule 8) requires it to cover the following information:

(a) a description of the business underwritten and, in general terms, of the reinsurance arrangements in force, together with a commentary on significant changes since the last annual report;

(b) a review of the year of account closed at the reference date;

(c) a review of each open year of account;

(d) a commentary on the level of premium income arising out of the business underwritten on behalf of the members of the syndicate in respect of each year of account to which the annual report relates;

(e) an outline of likely future developments, including comments in general terms on any proposed or anticipated material changes in:

  (i) the business to be underwritten for the members of the syndicate; and

  (ii) the reinsurance protection effected for the members of the syndicate; and

(f) any other matters which the active underwriter considers it appropriate to include in his report.

The explanatory notes to SAB point out, in regard to (a), that it will be normal for the description of business underwritten to cover both (i) the categories of business written and (ii) the manner of acceptance.

The underwriter may also wish to comment on (iii) the source of business, e.g. by geographical area or by the currency in which it is transacted.

How detailed a description of reinsurance policy is given is regarded as a matter for the underwriter's judgement in striking a balance between providing useful information to Names and protecting commercial confidentiality.

With regard to (b), it is suggested that the underwriter may comment on:

(i) the contribution of the various categories of business to the closed-year result
(ii) significant claims
(iii) the performance of the reinsurance to close prior years
(iv) any significant change from previous indications.

With regard to (c), the review may include comments on the expected outcome, especially when this is significantly different from previous indications; but making clear the inherent uncertainties.

With regard to (d), it would be normal to compare the actual level of premium income with the allocated capacity for each year, and the underwriter may wish to explain excesses.

These final requirements are less demanding than earlier proposals had been. PAM had envisaged a fairly detailed report which would be likely to include tables analysing the net premium income by the three subdivisions mentioned with regard to (a) above, and which would include an analysis of the result of the closed year by the categories of business mentioned with regard to a (i) above. It was envisaged that most of the other information which the notes now suggest the underwriter 'may' include would be included, and the specimen in PAM gave such a full analysis (albeit flagged 'non-mandatory').

There was, however, considerable disagreement in the market about the appropriate level of disclosure, and the strict requirement for the 1983 reports was that, while no underwriter's (or managing agent's) report needed to be filed, they had to be sent to Names, and the Chairman requested that, as far as possible, underwriters make use of PAM's suggestions 'which only reflect best practice'.

ANALYSIS

The filing of underwriters' reports with the 457 1984 annual reports (1983: 468) is analysed in Table 1.

In respect of the random sample of 100 1984 annual reports, 88 (1983: 26) included a separate report and 12 (1983: 22) a combined report.

For 1983, as with the managing agents' reports, it must be remembered that the information was required to be sent to Names, even though it did not have to be publicly filed. Also some of the information was sometimes given elsewhere in the annual report. In both years Names may have received further information about the syndicate's business in addition to that included in the filed report (for example underwriters sometimes refer to interim or preliminary reports on the year's progress sent to Names).

The underwriters' reports that were filed usually gave some discussion of the nature of the syndicate's business and how it was protected by reinsurance, together with a review of the closed year's result and how the open

Table I. Filing of underwriters' reports

1984	(%)	1983	(%)	
415	(91)	110	(24)	included a separate underwriter's report
42	(9)	104	(22)	included a combined managing agent's and underwriter's report
457	(100)	214	(46)	
—	—	254	(54)	did not include their underwriter's report
457	(100)	468	(100)	

years were developing (often by comparison with earlier years at the same stage). The quantity and quality of the information provided varied greatly in both years. The reports varied in length from a few paragraphs taking half a page to seven or eight pages. Several were highly individualistic (and arguably giving readers some impression of the underwriter's character and attitude to risk is one of the most valuable features of such a discussion). Because of their variety, and mainly verbal analysis, it is difficult to give 'typical' examples.

In the following analyses, the percentages given for 1983 are of the 48 underwriter's reports voluntarily filed for that year in respect of the 100 syndicates in the sample. In interpreting the comparative statistics it should be remembered that only syndicates filing 1984 annual reports were included in the sample selection (i.e. most of those that ceased business at the end of 1981 were excluded) and those starting business in 1982 would have no closed year data in their 1983 reports. Some of the information that might be included in an underwriter's report (and/or managing agent's report) might also, or alternatively, appear elsewhere in the annual report or attached documents (e.g. some syndicates gave settlement ratios on the face of the underwriting accounts or additional analyses of premium income and settlement percentages in tables appended to the accounts). These instances have not been counted here unless referred to by the underwriter.

Segmental Analysis
Table 2 analyses the extent to which a *quantified* analysis was provided of the kinds of business written, normally by percentage breakdown of the closed year net premium income. This excludes comments such as 'Our business is predominantly UK', but 'Our business is wholly UK' does count as a 'nil return' in regard to geographical origin ('nil return' indicating there

is only one segment). '35% of our business is in Canada' counts as 'partial quantification' if the remaining 65% is not fully analysed.

Table 2. Instances of quantified segmental analysis

	% of 1984 sample (1983)		
	'Nil' return	Partial	Full
(a) Category of business	5 (6)	19 (12)	38 (31)
(b) Long/short-tail	3 (4)	4 (4)	18 (10)
(c) Type of acceptance	3 (4)	8 (6)	5 (8)
(d) Geographical origin	7 (6)	4 (6)	2 (—)
(e) Currency	2 (2)	11 (10)	30 (25)

Notes
1. Some reports provided more than one of the above analyses and are therefore included more than once in the table.
2. Twenty-four reports (1983: 7=15%) provided some analysis of changes in the size of segments as between years. Ten (1983: 2=4%) said there had been no changes.
3. Twenty-two reports (1983: 7=15%) gave some figures or percentages in regard to reinsurance protection. Five reports (1983: 2=4%) quantified some aspects of changes in the reinsurance protection, and 10 (1983: 1=2%) said there had been no changes.

Closed Year Result

(a) Quantified

Of the sample, three had started business after 1982 and five started in 1982. Five reports (1983: 1=2%) gave some quantified analysis of the closed year result by category of business (see Examples 5 and 6, neither of which was in the sample); one report (1983: none) gave some quantification of how the result differed from that forecast; and 16 (1983: 5=10%) gave some quantification of the 'pure year' result (e.g. gave the loss ratio for the pure year). Seven gave some figures relating to the computation of the reinsurance to close the 1982 account (1983: 2=4% for the 1981 account) (e.g. gave the amount relating to certain past years or lines of business; or the amount allowed for IBNR or paid for certain external reinsurance; or the provision for latent diseases; or the percentage for the pure closed year); 41 (1983: 11=23%) quantified the difference between the actual net premium income for the closed year and the allocated capacity (for 1983 allocated capacity had not been required to be stated in the underwriting accounts). In several cases a much fuller analysis was provided in the 1984 than in the 1983 reports in order to explain unexpectedly severe losses that had emerged for 1982.

(b) Verbal Comments

Although generally not quantified, 28 (1983: 13=27%) reports included comments on the effect of investment returns on the overall result; 43 (1983: 12=25%) commented on the effects of currency movements on the utilization of allocated capacity (this was quantified in four cases (1983: 1=2%)) and 17 (1983: 2=4%) on their effects on other aspects of the final result.

Although not quantified (except in two cases in each year – see Example 1 for one of these for 1984), 46 reports (1983: 18=37%) gave some comment on the adequacy of the reinsurance to close that had been received by the 1982 (1981) account from earlier years, as shown in Table 3.

Table 3. Adequacy of reinsurance to close from earlier years

	% of sample	
	1984	1983
Indicated to be adequate/satisfactory	14	12
Indicated that had to be strengthened (note 1)	25	19
Indicated that had proved to be more than needed	7	6
	46	37

Notes
1. Eleven reports (1983: 1=2%) stated that while the provision in relation to certain past years, or certain lines of business had proved to be inadequate, the provision in relation to other years or other lines had been adequate or more than adequate.
2. Twenty-five reports (1983: 7=15%) discussed the impact of latent diseases such as asbestosis or environmental pollution claims (in one case (1983: none) quantifying the provision), while four (1983: 2=4%) reports stated that their syndicates had not been affected by the emergence of these losses, e.g. because the syndicates were fairly new. Some discussed the general problem of the attitudes of US courts to liability.

Development of Open Years

Of the sample, seven had ceased business after 1982, seven after 1983, and four after 1984; three had started business in 1983, and none in 1984.

(a) Quantified Analysis

Seven reports in the sample gave forecasts of the percentage losses anticipated for open year 1983 and one for 1984 (1983: none for 1982 or 1983). (In all the 1983 underwriters' reports filed there had only been four (2%) quantified forecasts for open year 1982 and none for 1983.)

Table 4 indicates the frequency with which certain other aspects of the open years were *quantified*. There were also several non-quantified predictions about utilisation of stamp capacity, e.g. 'will be within' or 'will be in excess of' capacity.

Table 4. Quantification of aspects of progress of open years

	% of sample	
	1984	*1983*
Stamp capacity of one or both open years	19	23
Forecast of utilisation of 1983 (1982) capacity	25	17
Forecast of utilisation of 1984 (1983) capacity	13	15
Development of open years to date (e.g. by settlement ratios)	31	12

Notes
1. Reports often gave information under several of the categories in this table, and therefore are counted more than once.
2. Nine reports (1983: 4=8%) gave figures relating to planned changes in premium income level or categories of business in future years, while 8 (1983: 4=8%) indicated that no significant changes in business were planned. There were no figures relating to planned changes in reinsurance protection (1983: 1=2%), while two reports (1983: 2=4%) said no changes were planned.

(b) Verbal Comments

Verbal information was given as analysed in Tables 5 and 6 (thus Table 5 deals with the information given in the 1984 reports about 1983, and in the 1983 reports about 1982).

Four reports (1983: 1=2%) discussed the significance of solvency audit surpluses or deficiences on open years.

Forty-eight gave some discussion of the way in which business for the 1985 year was progressing so far (1983: 24=50% about 1984).

Claims

There was often discussion of the impact of significant claims on one or more of the three years being reviewed. Four reports in the sample (1983: 3=6%) indicated that there had been no signficant impact from individual claims, while ten (1983: 4=8%) quantified the impact, gross or net, of one or more claims. It is, of course, not always straightforward to estimate the net impact

Table 5. Information about likely outcome of first open year

	% of sample	
	1984	1983
Stated that too early or too difficult to forecast	8	8
Gave some discussion of factors likely to affect the result (e.g. investment returns; premium ratings; changes of business; incidence of losses)	46	31
Gave verbal indication of kind of result expected (e.g. 'profit'; 'loss'; 'underwriting loss'; 'break-even')	50	54
Expected better result than 1982 (1981)	20	15
Expected worse result than 1982 (1981)	16	17
Expected similar result to 1982 (1981)	11	19

Note
Reports often gave information under several of the categories in this table, and therefore are counted more than once.

Table 6. Information about likely outcome of second open year

	% of sample	
	1984	1983
Stated that too early or too difficult to forecast	35	31
Gave some discussion of factors likely to affect the result (e.g. investment returns; premium ratings; changes of business; incidence of losses)	53	52
Gave verbal indication of kind of result expected (e.g. 'profit'; 'loss'; 'underwriting loss'; 'break-even)'	17	23
Expected better result than previous year(s)	27	12
Expected worse result than previous year(s)	4	6
Expected similar result to previous year(s)	6	4

Note
Reports often gave information under several of the categories in this table, and therefore are counted more than once.

of a claim because of the protection from non-proportional reinsurances. A number gave other figures relating to individual claims (e.g. their total cost to the insurance market). One of the disasters most frequently discussed was the hurricane Alicia which swept through Texas in August 1983, to be followed by severe weather in the winter (although I have a particular reason for noting Alicia as I was in Houston myself when it struck). The hurricane was referred to in terms such as 'The total cost of this incident to the insurance industry is estimated to be US$1.4 billion, the largest single catastrophe loss ever'.

Presentation of Statistics

A number of reports made use of pie charts, bar charts etc. to aid presentation of underwriting statistics (see Example 7). Of the sample, six syndicates' annual reports (1983: 4) also included tables of premium income and claims development for closed and open years that were not referred to by the underwriter and have not been included in the analyses in this chapter.

CONCLUSIONS

The aim of the underwriter's report should be to assist understanding of the risks and returns of the syndicate's business. This requires a suitable blend of verbal explanation and quantified analysis. While the 1984 under-writers' reports show evidence of a greater degree of quantified analysis than was provided in those filed for 1983, the overall level was still low. Segmental analysis concentrated mainly on classes of business and currencies. Underwriters generally need to give further consideration to how best to present useful statistics to provide performance indicators and guides to likely prospects, and how to strike a suitable balance between merely giving broad generalisations and swamping readers with an uninterpreted mass of detailed figures.

While there was an increase in the number of quantified forecasts in the 1984 reports, these were all in cases where losses were anticipated – there seems to be general reluctance to provide quantified profit forecasts even for the open years, let alone future years. While uncertainty about exchange rate fluctuations and investment returns may contribute significantly to this reluctance, there is scope for giving forecasts on the basis of stated assumptions about these factors, or for giving a likely range of outcomes, which should be considered. Generally the question of how much further disclosure of segmental data, and of expectations and assumptions about future results, should be provided to Names (taking into account the nature of each market), and how much of this should be on public file, deserves further examination.

EXAMPLES

■ Example 1 gives above average quantified analysis together with illuminating discussion of past results and future prospects. It includes appropriate quantification by segment (including changes), details of reinsurance protection and the development of claims, as well as measurement of the impact of the development of prior years' underwriting and discussion of allocation of business between syndicates.

■   Example 2 gives, in addition to other details, discussion of 'acceptance' and a forecast of the estimated size of the loss anticipated for the 1983 year of account (see also, for example, Cassidy Davis, 582; Philip N. Christie, 469; R.D.Robertson, 977).

■   Example 3 discusses the particular problems of currency fluctuations and gives the underwriter's 'philosophy' (see also, for example, Cassidy Davis, 582).

■   Examples 4, 5 and 6 are extracts illustrating various forms of quantified segmental analysis. Example 4 uses a matrix presentation (managing agent: Sedgwick Forbes (Lloyd's Underwriting Agents) Ltd.). Example 5 gives extensive segmental analysis of the development of loss ratios and premium income for a number of years (managing agent: M.F.K. Underwriting Agencies Ltd.) (see also, for example, Street, 123).

■   Example 6 is an extract giving various tabulations to present the statistics, which include an analysis of the closed year result by category of business.

■   Example 7 is an extract illustrating additional presentation of statistical information in graphical form (managing agent: Higgins & Doble Ltd, syndicate 284) (see also, for example, C.D., 529; Cotesworth, 536; R.J.Kiln, 557).

For a combined managing agent's and underwriter's report, see, for example, J.D.Boyagis, 227.

Example 1

F.L.P. SECRETAN & COMPANY

Aviation Syndicate 545

Underwriter's Report

I am relieved to be able to report that we have closed 1982 with an underwriting profit in addition to capital appreciation. The overall profit of each Name following a 35% increase in Syndicate Stamp capacity was greater than I had expected 12 months ago. Some 50% of our profit is the result of the strength of the U.S. Dollar which has boosted premium income, exchange differences, investment yield and capital appreciation to a greater extent than claims. It is thought likely that the U.S. Dollar will weaken against Sterling during 1985 and therefore a similar situation is unlikely to benefit our 1983 account.

Whereas 1981 had been a particularly safe year for airline operators this did not last and 1982 returned to a more normal loss pattern. The number of western-built jet airliners lost from all causes during 1982 was 27. This figure included 3 high valued wide-bodied aircraft and 6 other aircraft, fortunately low valued, destroyed in the fighting at Beirut Airport. This 1982 total compared with 12 aircraft lost in 1981, only one of which was wide-bodied and the subject of a hangar fire. In insurance terms the cost was $240,000,000 in 1982 compared with $120,000,000 in 1981. In addition, two satellites, valued at $90,000,000 were also lost, our own involvement being negligible.

A regrettable consequence of the increased number of Hull accidents in 1982 was a rise in the number of passenger fatalities at 553 which included many U.S. citizens compared with 358 in 1981.

In nearly every respect the closed year was a poor one for the Aviation insurance market. Rates were still being reduced and claims were heavy. For our Syndicate lack of real Premium Income growth coincided with increased retentions and reinsurance costs. In addition we suffered our fair share of losses compared with previous years resulting in incurred claims exceeding premium income.

However the overall pure year result for 1982 was an underwriting profit of £126,709 having taken into account a reinsurance recovery of £260,850 from the reinsurance which had protected the 1979 to 1983 Accounts and was specifically referred to last year.

Subsequent to our letter 12 months ago the Inland Revenue have regrettably disallowed the reinsurance premium of £125,000 in respect of the 1981 account pending their further enquiries. No doubt all Names will have appealed against this decision. The reinsurance premium for 1982 in respect of this protection was £120,578 (3% of PI) resulting in the claims recovery of

£260,850 referred to above.

In our letter last year I referred to the 1983 account being even worse than 1982 and there has been no improvement in the comparative loss ratios. Since the situation is marginal the only forecast I wish to make, somewhat hesitantly, is that we should break even, hopefully leaving capital appreciation intact for distribution. This forecast takes into account investment income, expenses and an anticipated recovery on the reinsurance which subject to a limitation of £400,000 protects the 1983 net account in respect of aggregated losses.

The downward cycle in our market began in 1972 and lasted twice as long as any previous downturn. It can be said to have culminated in 1983, a year which will not be easily forgotten by Aviation Underwriters.

The recovery was brought about by the run of losses at the end of 1983 when 14 jet airliners were lost within the last 120 days coinciding with a further reduction in market capacity. At the beginning of 1984 it became apparent that underwriters worldwide were prepared to follow the London Market leaders in increasing premiums substantially and at the same time tightening policy terms and conditions. This improvement was sustained for the whole of 1984 and applies to virtually every aspect of our business, the exception being personal accident.

Ironically as the recovery continued through 1984, with underwriters obtaining much higher premiums and applying stricter conditions for their airline business, the number of accidents again reduced dramatically with only 8 jet airliners lost and 2 passenger fatalities compared with 28 aircraft and 991 passenger fatalities during 1983. Not surprisingly our 1984 account at the end of the first year is infinitely better than the two previous years and I am certainly hopeful of a profitable outcome but again I must warn that much could happen during the next twenty-four months to dampen one's optimism.

The whole insurance world has witnessed an appalling deterioration in respect of casualty business particularly in the U.S.A. The Aviation market is no exception and many reserves established over the past 15 years for claims made against Products Liability policies now appear inadequate. Although we have been fortunate and missed many of the worst cases, the deterioration has been across the class and we have been affected.

Despite the problems outlined above the old years

...

F.L.P. SECRETAN & COMPANY

resulted in a surplus of £85,738 due in part to collection of reinsurance recoveries which had not been allowed for since reinsurers had been slow or shown reluctance to pay. Also in part to our cautious reserving over the years.

Products liability can be very long tail business and recently it has represented some 20% to 25% of our premium income. Following the deterioration mentioned earlier many underwriters world-wide have withdrawn from this class and due to shortage of capacity dramatic increases in rates of 150% to 400% have been obtained. It is possible therefore that despite increases on virtually every risk seen, and on all classes of business written, Product Liability could rise to 35% of our overall premium income.

The recovery has attracted the attention of other insurers and inevitably available capacity for our airline business has increased to the point where once again it is much greater than we would wish but although the orders to London are in many cases reduced, there is still a desire to correct the ills of the past decade. The recovery continues albeit at a slower pace assisted no doubt by the accidents which have occurred in the first four months of this year as once again the loss frequency returns to a more normal pattern.

In the current climate many underwriters are reluctant to take an optimistic stance when writing to their Names for fear of misleading them. As has been said before, we are in a risk taking business in which, there can be no room for unwarranted optimism. However I do feel that despite increased retentions and reinsurance costs the present situation is healthier than it has been for a decade.

In view of the doubts which exist regarding the exchange rate together with the increased volumes of business and therefore premium income I have decided to increase stamp capacity in 1986 to approximatley £20,000,000. Such an increase should enable us to maintain our position in the market and provide us with the necessary margins to stay within our Premium Income limits.

My role as Chairman of the L.A.U.A. finished at the end of 1984. It was an interesting period during which to be involved but two years proved quite sufficient.

Robert Swinton our Deputy Underwriter, Vincent Wallace, John Boler and Andrew Griffin who make up the team have had to contend with a great deal this past two years and I am extremely grateful for their good natured and wholehearted support.

Analysis of the Account as at 31st December 1984

The syndicate writes a broadly based aviation account both direct and by way of reinsurance. The reinsurance could be on an individual or treaty basis. In turn the treaties could be either proportional or excess of loss.

Whereas we seek to restrict our involvement in Aviation Hull and Liability binding covers to a minimum the situation is different for Personal Accident for in view of the high cost factors involved for both brokers and underwriters in handling low premium business virtually all our P.A. business is derived from reinsurance treaties, binding covers and line slips.

Our gross lines vary considerably depending on class of business and value of risk involved. Hulls vary in value up to $135,000,000. Liability policies frequently total $1,000,000,000 any one assured.

We reinsure on a surplus or quota share basis which enables us to spread the risk and remove the "peaks" which inevitably occur. It also means we have in effect additional business we can retain in a subsequent year if we expand capacity and need to increase our net premium income.

We also buy Excess of Loss reinsurance in order to protect the syndicate against major losses. These reinsurances are placed in "layers" by various brokers of our choice and are subject to reinstatement limitation at additional cost. Our retentions vary according to cost and availability of such excess of loss protections. At present they are much higher than in the past. The effects of higher retentions should be offset by rising premium income. The approximate retention per Name is $250 any one accident assuming the loss to the syndicate does not exceed overall protection purchased.

Our premium income is split approximately:—

	1981	1982
Currency		
Sterling (incl. convertible currency)	25%	18%
U.S. Dollar	72%	79%
Canadian Dollar	3%	3%
Length of Account		
Short tail	56%	55%
All other	44%	45%

...

F.L.P. SECRETAN & COMPANY

		1981	1982
Type of Business			
Hulls	All Risks	25%	25%
	War	5%	3%
Liabilities	Aircraft & Airports Etc.	12%	15%
	Products	23%	23%
Personal Accident		24%	27%
Excess of Loss		11%	7%

We retain approximately 65% of our Gross Premium Income.

The end of year percentage settlement comparisons for the open years are as follows:—

Percentage Settlement at end of

	1st Year	2nd Year
1981	18.00	40.98
1982	23.52	47.72
1983	32.79	54.37
1984	13.46	

My primary function is to underwrite Syndicate 545, a specialist Aviation Syndicate. In addition lines are written for Syndicate 684, an incidental Aviation account for our Marine Syndicate 367. The income for Syndicate 684 is considerably less than for Syndicate 545 and has a much greater proportion of Aviation Hull War than Syndicate 545. For the most part we split written lines as follows:—

	545	684
Most Aviation Business	75% of written line	25% of written line
Hull – War	retain 1½% of original limits	Balance of written line
Personal Accident	100% of written line	Nil

The Marine Syndicate writes its own Aviation Hull War account – any line written by us is either additional or on risks which would not otherwise be shown to them – the Marine Syndicate does not write Personal Accident.

If we are unable to obtain the line required we frequently retain 100% in Syndicate 545. There are risks which are less suitable for a Marine Syndicate which are written 100% by Syndicate 545.

At all times we endeavour to split the lines between syndicates on an equitable basis.

T. O. Pitron *Active Underwriter*
14th May 1985

Example 2

K.F. ALDER
(UNDERWRITING AGENCY) LIMITED
NON-MARINE SYNDICATE No.122
UNDERWRITER'S REPORT

As predicted last year, I have to report an underwriting loss for the Syndicate in respect of the 1982 account. However, I am pleased to say that the capital appreciation and dividends have more than covered the deficiency, leaving a bottom line profit.

The underwriting loss which we predicted came about as a result of the intense and unjustified competition throughout virtually the whole of our business. We have commented on this situation for the past few years and it will come as no surprise. We did have a Stop Loss Policy of the "roll-over" type for the 1982 account and this is the last year that the reinsurance will be available. We have had to make additional provision for the Asbestosis losses on the closed years, but after the benefit of applicable reinsurance, there was a surplus on the run-off of the 1981 account and prior during 1984. We have also previously reported to you the successful outcome of the litigation regarding certain Canadian Treaties, which were settled on terms most satisfactory to ourselves. I would, however, remind you that there is a second litigation underway on the same Treaties with a separate group of Reinsurers. This matter is set for Trial in April 1987.

The chart below sets out the breakdown of the account for the three years, which is self-explanatory:-

TYPE	1982	1983	1984
"Short Tail"	62%	54%	54%
"Long Tail"	32%	41%	41%
Direct Overseas Motor	6%	5%	5%
£	25%	28%	33%
US$	61%	60%	57%
C$	14%	12%	10%

STERLING ACCOUNT

40% of the business is in the "short tail" area and is mainly U.K. domiciled. Personal Lines account for a large proportion of the business written, this and the balance, being mainly Commericial Fire business, is written by way of Binding Authorities, Line Slips or Facultatively. We also participate in a number of Reinsurance Treaties domiciled in the U.K., and elsewhere on both an excess of loss and pro-rata basis.

The "long tail" account is made up almost entirely of Professional Errors & Omissions based on a "claims made" form. A substantial part of this is written for Accountants and Lawyers. We do write one important scheme for Australian Workmen's Compensation business which approximates 10% of the premium income.

UNITED STATES DOLLAR ACCOUNT

"Short tail" accounts for approximately 60% of the income and involves both direct and reinsurance business. We do utilize Binding Authorities on a carefully controlled basis for certain classes and this approximates 15% of the income. We write a catastrophe account on an excess of loss basis, covering such perils as windstorm, freeze and earthquake.

The "long tail" business includes a substantial amount of Medical Malpractice which we write by way of reinsurance of the Doctor Owned Companies. This is almost entirely experience rated, with deductibles indexed to allow for inflation. In addition, there is a general book of Casualty reinsurance for miscellaneous classes.

CANADIAN DOLLAR ACCOUNT

Lloyd's is a licenced Market for both insurance and reinsurance in Canada and we write both classes. The "short tail" income is principally Home Owners business written on Binding Authorities with a smaller proportion of Commercial Property business.

The "long tail" account is almost entirely Canadian Auto written by way of Binding Authority on the Lloyd's scheme.

...

K.F. ALDER
(UNDERWRITING AGENCY) LIMITED
NON-MARINE SYNDICATE No.122
UNDERWRITER'S REPORT
CONTINUED

BINDING AUTHORITIES

There has been considerable publicity on this subject and it is right that you should be aware that we do delegate authority to some Agents to write business on our behalf. We feel that control is of the most vital importance and we do impose conditions regarding premium income limits, policy forms and in some cases, the rates to be charged. We keep in constant communication with the London Broker and our staff regularly visit our principal Agents in the U.S.A. and Canada. Whilst it must be admitted that Binding Authority arrangements have caused problems, we have to accept that it is the only means of successfully writing small premium business overseas, and we ourselves have generally had a favourable experience.

It might well be opportune to mention two other areas where we delegate underwriting authority. Our Aviation Underwriter, John Nevitt, does write for us an excess of loss Aviation book, and Mr. Richard Milligan writes Livestock business for us. We felt that we needed professional and specialist Underwriters for these two classes and I am pleased to say that our efforts have been very well rewarded.

The Syndicate is well protected by way of reinsurance and we do take a very conservative attitude. We have to weigh-up cost against security and the amount of retention which we are prepared to run. We also purchase facultative reinsurance where the situation requires, and again we endeavour to obtain the best terms available.

Turning now to the open years, I am afraid the 1983 account will not produce an underwriting profit, due to the continuing competitive Markets and also the impact of two major catastrophes in that year. Although we expect to make a good capital appreciation, I feel it is right to warn you that we may be facing a bottom line loss for this year, which I would currently estimate as being between 5% and 10% of premium income. It is obviously too soon to be more definite in this regard, but I know you will appreciate having early notice.

1984 did see a positive improvement in the general level of rates, and it was a year relatively free of catastrophes. The paid loss ratio at 12 months is a considerable improvement on that for 1983 and it should be a better year. The general level of rate increase is substantial and continues. It promises well for 1985.

NICHOLAS D. PRITCHARD
ACTIVE UNDERWRITER

JUNE 1985

Example 3

Murray Lawrence & Partners

C. T. BOWRING (UNDERWRITING AGENCIES) LIMITED
AND FAIRWAY UNDERWRITING AGENCIES LIMITED
HARVEY BOWRING AND OTHERS
NON-MARINE SYNDICATE No. 362/444
Underwriter's Report for the year ended 31st December 1984

1982 ACCOUNT (Including run-off of 1981 and prior Years of Account)

Breakdown of Account
The breakdown of the 1982 account at 31st December, 1984 is fairly similar to that in previous years:—

Audit Code		Currency	
Short Tail (Property)	77%	Sterling inc. Convertible Currency	25%
All Other (Casualty)	15%	U.S. Dollars	58%
Overseas Motor	7%	Canadian Dollars	17%
Miscellaneous	1%		

Run-off of 1981 and prior Years of Account
The run-off should now be considered in two parts: first, the 1978 Account and prior years where we are protected by unlimited Stop Loss reinsurance covers, and second, the years of account 1979 to 1981 which, while being well insured do not have the same unlimited cover.

As regard to losses, we have had to make substantial increases in our reserves against Asbestosis and other latent disease claims, as well as increase our reserves on the Shell Oil pollution case.

Because of the Stop Loss protection these new reserves will not produce any increase in the Underwriting loss to the 1982 Year. However, because of the weakness of Sterling during 1984, there has been a further currency loss on the reserves up to the excess point of the first Stop Loss cover, a point referred to in last years report.

The 1979, 1980 and 1981 years of Account have shown a satisfactory run-off pattern during the last 12 months, and it has been possible to release a profit in respect of these years, which just outweighs the currency loss on the 1978 and prior years.

While on the subject of currency movement it must be said that the fluctuation in currencies other than the US and Canadian Dollars do have a significant influence on our results. To try and mitigate their effect we do from time to time buy and sell currency either forward or for cash delivery. The transactions are designed to protect the names against the potential adverse effect of currency movements on our underwriting result and are not speculative.

Taken together with an improving underwriting result these extraordinary items, if they materialise, have the potential to produce a worthwhile overall profit, but it must be said that currency fluctuations and late advices could still seriously affect the result.

Pure Year 1982 Account
This account, like the 1981 year, has finished with a substantial Underwriting loss, and as forecast only a very small overall profit has been declared after investment income and capital appreciation. Areas where results were particularly unsatisfactory were French Motor Liability business, Australian Workmen's Compensation Liability excess of loss and Open Market Property and Liability business. As I explained last year, we took firm action in each of these classes to ensure that they would not continue to exacerbate the effects of a very difficult market.

The final Net Premium Income was £41,471,000 which represents a utilisation factor of just over 105% of the Stamp Capacity of nearly £39,000,000. It is worth commenting that had the rates of exchange remained as they were during autumn 1981 when most of this account was written, the final Net Premium Income would have been below £32,000,000, or 82% of Stamp Capacity.

1983 ACCOUNT
The premium income shows a real increase of some 20% over the 1982 account at the same time which coupled with the revaluation of the U.S. dollar means that our final premium income for this Year of Account is expected to be in the region of £47,000,000, or 115% of the Stamp Capacity of £39,335,000 million, depending on the closing rates of exchange. At the Audit Rates of Exchange at 1st January 1983 this final premium income would be of the order of £38,750,000.

The account is now beginning to show a little improvement over the 1982 year; this we believe is largely due to the changes in our book of business, referred to last year, as the market had not really tightened. However we are still expecting substantial underwriting losses although we are hopeful that the final result after investment income and capital appreciation will show a more meaningful profit than 1981 and 1982 years.

There are some extraordinary factors which may further improve this result. The general strength of Sterling has enabled us substantially to reduce our reserves in respect of outstanding convertible currency claims since February, and we have now protected this position by purchasing currency sufficient to pay a large proportion of these claims. If this strength is maintained there will also be a profit from the 1978 and prior years.

...

Murray Lawrence & Partners

C. T. BOWRING (UNDERWRITING AGENCIES) LIMITED
AND FAIRWAY UNDERWRITING AGENCIES LIMITED
HARVEY BOWRING AND OTHERS
NON-MARINE SYNDICATE No. 362/444

Underwriter's Report for the year ended 31st December 1984 (continued)

1984 ACCOUNT

The Premium Income for 1984 is similar to that for 1983 in real terms, with an increase of over 20% in Sterling balanced by a similar reduction in the Canadian dollar account. It is very difficult to project this income to finality in view of the violent fluctuations in rates of exchange, but at current rates I would expect a final income in the region of £48,000,000. This again represents a significant overwriting but again it should be noted that at the Audit Rates of Exchange applying at 1st January, 1984 this figure would be around £42,500,000-£43,000,000 compared with a stamp capacity of £43,085,000.

Last years Balance Sheet was accompanied by a detailed breakdown of our book of business together with details of the action we were taking to improve results. It appears at this early stage that this process of re-rating and re-underwriting, together with the first signs of a hardening market are producing much improved underwriting results. These improvements can be seen in all currencies and in nearly all the classes of business we are writing. It is particularly encouraging on the US Dollar Facultative Property account which has been unprofitable for several years.

MARKET PROBLEMS

Names will have become aware of the serious losses being incurred in some areas of the Insurance Market. We feel that we have a responsibility to the Members of the Non-Marine Syndicates that we manage to comment on any potential that might exist for similar losses in Syndicates under our management. Members can readily appreciate that there are many ways of making losses in the insurance and reinsurance business, particularly if one is involved in the long tail liability classes. This Syndicate therefore tries to ensure that it has what one could call 'safety nets' in place when underwriting any long tail business. we believe these 'safety nets' fall into six distinct categories:

Risk Underwriting

While the Syndicate does write US Liability business, this broad heading covers a great number of different types of risk and policy form. Many of the Market losses have arisen out of product liability and seepage and pollution insurances and reinsurances written on an occurrence basis. This Syndicate has avoided for some years risks where exposures of this kind are identifiable.

Reinsurance Protections

The Syndicate buys comprehensive reinsurance cover against both severity and frequency of losses; the amount of cover in force has been increasing steadily since 1979.

Reserving

Our philosophy on the reinsurance to close has been to look closely at any individual contract with the potential to produce losses after the third year and to set aside heavy reserves wherever this potential is significant.

We recalculate these reserves at least annually on all such contracts, and therefore we believe that we are doing everything we can to avoid putting ourselves in the position where a reserving deficiency can accumulate over a number of years, calling for it to be covered in one year.

Spread of Account

As the breakdowns published last year show, we believe in spreading our premium income between many different classes of business. Names are aware that liability business has never been more than a minor part of our overall account and that a considerble proportion of the Casualty account we write is concentrated in these areas of business which have a shorter tail.

Co-Insurance

As a matter of Syndicate policy we believe in a co-insurance market and almost never write 100% of a slip. We feel that having at least one other underwriter subscribe to a piece of business acts as a useful check on our underwriting and adds a further 'safety net'. Our normal line on Casualty business would be 0·5% or less.

Underwriting Limits

Although we believe we are more than adequately reinsured, our gross acceptance before the reinsurance protection on any risk rarely exceeds 0.5% of our Stamp Capacity.

While these 'safety nets' do not in themselves guarantee that underwriters will never incur losses, we believe in almost every case where really serious losses have been made, at least one, and usually more, of these safe-guards have been ignored.

...

Murray Lawrence & Partners

C. T. BOWRING (UNDERWRITING AGENCIES) LIMITED
AND FAIRWAY UNDERWRITING AGENCIES LIMITED
HARVEY BOWRING AND OTHERS
NON-MARINE SYNDICATE No. 362/444

Underwriter's Report for the year ended 31st December 1984 (continued)

THE FUTURE

It is not my intention to repeat the breakdown of the account given last year, as the estimated splits of Premium Income given last Spring for 1984 account and in November for 1985 account remain substantially unchanged. Our observations about changing market conditions if anything underestimated the speed at which markets would react to the appalling underwriting results of the early 1980s, and there are now opportunities to re-rate business in almost every class in many parts of the world.

These opportunities must be grasped with both hands as there is still a great deal of business being placed in the market at inadequate rates. While we feel that in our major classes of business a lot of the hard work has been done, the market must realise that further action must be taken before rates are sufficient to ensure underwriting profits. As long as worldwide capacity continues to shrink it should be possible to impose the necessary rates, terms and conditions on insureds and reinsureds.

I would stress that while these are exciting times and opportunities do exist in many areas, because of the return to rate and form integrity and the shortage of 'innocent capacity' we are very much back in the business of taking on and retaining a substantial degree of risk. The silly reinsurance which encouraged so many insurers to take on business at inadequate terms is no longer available and we will all stand or fall by our ability to charge the right rate and to control policy form.

Finally, I would like to thank the team for all their hard work over the last few traumatic years, at a time when adverse market conditions have made their tasks more difficult and when the return to profitable underwriting has seemed at times a distant project.

R. J. R. Keeling

Underwriter
7th June 1985

Example 4

R.E.THOMSON & OTHERS
NON-MARINE SYNDICATE NO. 484

Underwriter's Report

[Extract – discussion not reproduced]

	US dollar %	Other %	Total %
Fire etc. (direct & reinsurance)	11.8 (10.0)	9.5 (12.0)	21.3 (22.0)
Livestock/bloodstock	9.2 (8.0)	5.1 (6.5)	14.3 (14.5)
Catastrophe (e.g. windstorm, earthquake, flood, etc)	10.2 (8.5)	2.3 (2.5)	12.5 (11.0)
Personal accident/sickness	3.3 (3.0)	1.3 (1.5)	4.6 (4.5)
Hail/frost etc.	2.0 (1.5)	0.6 (0.9)	2.6 (2.4)
Mainly SHORT Tail Total	36.5 (31.0)	18.8 (23.4)	55.3 (54.4)
Professional indemnity	15.6 (16.5)	13.8 (13.0)	29.4 (29.5)
General liability	2.0 (2.0)	2.1 (2.5)	4.1 (4.5)
Railroad (liability & physical damage)	1.4 (2.0)	—	1.4 (2.0)
Liability treaty (motor & general)	1.4 (1.3)	0.5 (0.6)	1.9 (1.9)
Mainly LONG Tail Total	20.4 (21.8)	16.4 (16.1)	36.8 (37.9)
Miscellaneous (e.g. drilling rigs, satellites, motor, fire, theft, collision, directors & officers' liability, boiler/machinery, extended warranty, film producers' indemnity, contingency, nuclear, etc.)	6.6 (6.0)	1.3 (1.7)	7.9 (7.7)
Total	63.5 (58.8)	36.5 (41.2)	100.0 (100.0)

Figures in brackets represent the applicable percentage for previous year. The only noteworthy point about the above is the general increase in the US dollar figures and the reduction in the remainder – this is largely due to rate of exchange fluctuations.

R.E.Thomson
April 1985

M. GARDNER-ROBERTS AND OTHERS   Example 5

NON-MARINE SYNDICATE 396

UNDERWRITER'S REPORT
31st December, 1984

1978-1981 ACCOUNTS
   These years are running off reasonably satisfactorily and there is a small reduction in the overall incurred claims figure as compared with last year.

1982 ACCOUNT
   Not quite the result I was hoping for at this stage last year but a fair outcome at a time when underwriting results generally are poor and the investment result was disappointing.

1983 ACCOUNT
   I am afraid I cannot maintain the optimism that I ventured to indicate in my report last year. A significant deterioration in the 7th and 8th quarters leaves me unable to forecast a profit of any appreciable size on the close of this year. A £20,000 share should sign approximately £16,000.

1984 ACCOUNT
   The indications as to final outcome are not unattractive at this stage although I anticipate that I will have overwritten to a certain extent. I estimate that a £20,000 share will sign in the region of £25,000.

[Further discussion not reproduced]

   The following statistics show the year by year incurred claims loss ratios by Geographical Area and by Risk Category for the first 12 months as at the end of 1984 and (as at the end of 1983).

1.	Geographical Area	Year	12 months	1984	(1983)
	U.K.	1978	60%	74%	(78%)
		1979	62%	75%	(80%)
		1980	56%	67%	(78%)
		1981	24%	76%	(81%)
		1982	25%	104%	(60%)
		1983	38%	66%	(38%)
		1984	23%	23%	—
	Rest of the World	1978	36%	64%	(66%)
		1979	20%	63%	(61%)
		1980	18%	74%	(61%)
		1981	15%	68%	(57%)
		1982	39%	49%	(27%)
		1983	12%	30%	(12%)
		1984	31%	31%	—

2.	Risk Categories	Year	12 months	1984	(1983)
	RC1				
	CAR Annual Policies	1978	76%	89%	(95%)
		1979	62%	90%	(98%)
		1980	53%	74%	(98%)
		1981	49%	91%	(105%)
		1982	58%	118%	(83%)
		1983	52%	82%	(52%)
		1984	68%	68%	—
	RC2				
	Building and Civil Engineering	1978	40%	89%	(101%)
		1979	32%	69%	(92%)
		1980	23%	69%	(71%)
		1981	21%	81%	(74%)
		1982	14%	60%	(42%)
		1983	15%	24%	(15%)
		1984	19%	19%	—

...

M. GARDNER-ROBERTS AND OTHERS

NON-MARINE SYNDICATE 396

UNDERWRITER'S REPORT (continued)
31st December, 1984

2. Risk Categories continued	Year	12 months	1984	(1983)
RC3				
Engineering Industry	1978	28%	**66%**	(68%)
	1979	93%	**40%**	(44%)
	1980	78%	**110%**	(71%)
	1981	12%	**54%**	(74%)
	1982	396%	**33%**	(107%)
	1983	0%	**27%**	—
	1984	27%	**27%**	
RC4				
Construction Industry Liability	1978	32%	**39%**	(39%)
	1979	34%	**61%**	(49%)
	1980	36%	**60%**	(49%)
	1981	8%	**51%**	(49%)
	1982	34%	**49%**	(24%)
	1983	6%	**27%**	(6%)
	1984	7%	**7%**	—
RC5				
Non Construction Liability	1981	1%	**78%**	(46%)
	1982	18%	**45%**	(25%)
	1983	10%	**27%**	(10%)
	1984	8%	**8%**	—
RC6				
Miscellaneous Non Construction	1978	63%	**119%**	(116%)
	1979	40%	**99%**	(106%)
	1980	20%	**136%**	(137%)
	1981	2%	**119%**	(95%)
	1982	10%	**121%**	(37%)
	1983	34%	**69%**	(34%)
	1984	39%	**39%**	—

The following figures show the division of premium income between U.K. and the Rest of the World as at the end of 1984. The second set shows the division by Risk Category as at the same time.

Area Premium Income

Year	U.K.	Rest of World
1978	27%	73%
1979	32%	68%
1980	33%	67%
1981	21%	79%
1982	15%	85%
1983	19%	81%
1984	40%	60%

Risk Category Premium Income

	Contractors All Risks	Construction Liability	General Liability	Miscellaneous Non Liability
1978	55%	40%	—	5%
1979	52%	26%	—	2%
1980	47%	48%	—	5%
1981	37%	41%	19%	3%
1982	19%	52%	23%	6%
1983	21%	35%	28%	16%
1984	22%	32%	34%	12%

M. GARDNER-ROBERTS
May, 1985   *Underwriter*

Example 6

GEORGE MILLER UNDERWRITING AGENCIES
LTD
L. C. TAYLOR AND OTHERS   MARINE SYNDICATE No. 527/379

UNDERWRITER'S REPORT

[Extract – discussion not reproduced]

There now follows a series of charts, which this year includes a comparison between 1981 and 1982 Years of Account. The chart listing major claims has been discontinued as I now intend to comment on any significant claims within each particular Year of Account. The downard plunge in the value of the Pound to the U.S. Dollar makes statistical tables difficult to compile, particularly when different rates of exchange are used for monitoring performance in different areas for the same Year of Account. I must emphasise that these charts are perhaps, too abbreviated, but I can assure you that you are comparing "like with like". I should bring to your notice the apparent overwriting for 1984. Needless to say, a close watch is being kept on our premium income during 1985.

SYNDICATE STAMP CAPACITY AND NET PREMIUM INCOME

	CLOSED YEARS		OPEN YEARS		NEW YEAR
	1981	1982	1983	1984	1985
(A) CAPACITY	£992,000	£2,026,000	£3,167,000	£3,530,000	£3,120,000
RATES OF EXCHANGE	US$ 2.39 C.$ 2.85	1.91 2.26	1.62 1.99	1.45 1.81	1.16 1.53
NET PREMIUM INCOME AT 31.12.84			£2,457,647	£2,145,742	
NET PREMIUM INCOME AT CLOSE	£882,073	£1,720,645			
(B) ESTIMATED NET PREMIUM INCOME AT CLOSE			£2,692,000	£4,088,250	£3,120,000
B/A %	89%	85%	85%	115%	100%

...

GEORGE MILLER UNDERWRITING AGENCIES

LTD

L. C. TAYLOR AND OTHERS   MARINE SYNDICATE No. 527/379

1982 (inc. 1981 A/C in 1984)
NET PREMIUM INCOME ANALYSED IN AUDIT CATEGORIES
(rates of exchange U.S.$ 1.16, C.$ 1.53)

AUDIT CODE	£ EQUIVALENT IN 000's	TECHNICAL RESULT PROFIT/(LOSS) (IN £000's)
T = TIME (Hull, all risks)	1,934	147
B = TIME (Hull, total loss only)	128	32
V = VOYAGE (cargo)	398	(162)
W = WAR	134	19
G = MARINE LIABILITIES	147	47
MISCELLANEOUS	97	54
TOTAL	2,838	137

EXCESS LOSS REINSURANCE PROGRAMME
(excluding facultative reinsurance)

CLASS	COVER		RETENTION	COST AS % of NPI	
	1981	1982	BOTH YEARS	1981	1982
	U.S.$	U.S.$	U.S.$		
TIME	180,000	380,000			
VOYAGE	180,000	180,000			
RIG	525,000	930,000	20,000	16	19
X/L	480,000	980,000			
WHOLE A/C	980,000	1,980,000			

Analysis of Net Premium Income into main classes as Percentages of Whole Account
at end of third year of Account

	HULL	RIGS	CARGO	WAR	LIABS	MISC
1981	47	31	10	5	4	3
1982	47	25	15	7	5	1

Split of business between direct risks (Including Covers) and Reinsurance; as Percentages

	DIRECT	EXCESS LOSS	PROPORTIONAL TREATY
1981	71	17	12
1982	77	14	9

Split of currencies as percentages. This does not necessarily indicate the countries where our business originated

	U.S.$	£	C.$
1981	67	29	4
1982	71	27	2

...

GEORGE MILLER UNDERWRITING AGENCIES
LTD
L. C. TAYLOR AND OTHERS   MARINE SYNDICATE No. 527/379

[Further discussion not reproduced]

                                                            L.C.Taylor
April 1985   Marine Underwriter

Example 7

Analysis of Premium Income

Year of Account	1981	1982
Class of Business		
Time	43.19	42.59
T.L.O.	6.44	6.45
Marine Liability	12.02	13.70
Voyage	12.88	9.35
War	24.00	24.50
Yachts	0.36	0.36
Livestock	0.25	0.15
Aviation	—	2.10
Incidental Non-Marine	0.86	0.80
	100.00%	100.00%

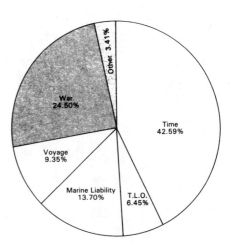

Division of Currency		
Sterling, including converted non-dollar currency	27.34	22.78
US dollars	71.21	75.60
Canadian dollars	1.45	1.62
	100.00%	100.00%

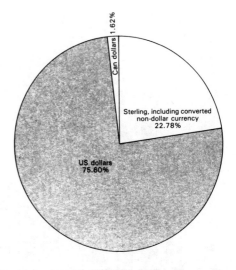

...

[Table not reproduced]

Closed Year Settlements

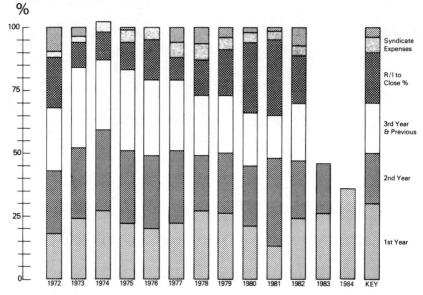

Results of Syndicate 284: 1972-1982 Closed Year Settlements.
Each year of account includes all previous year's claims after the end of the 24th month.

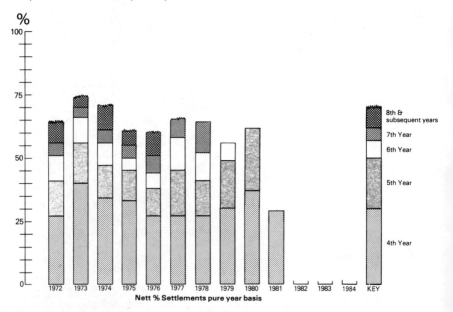

Shows the settlements of each pure year of account as a percentage of the original
assessment of outstanding liabilities thereon at 36 months.

CHAPTER 17
AUDIT REPORTS AND THE TRUE
AND FAIR VIEW

INTRODUCTION

The traditional solvency audit at Lloyd's is described in Chapter 2 above. For the 1983 syndicate accounts no special developments in auditing were required apart from the Chairman's request that auditors review clients' compliance with the proposed accounting policies set out in PAM. The two significant changes were still to come.

The first major change has been that, beginning with the 1984 accounts filed in 1985, the audit has to cover the disclosures of interests. The second is that for the accounts filed in 1986 and onwards the auditors will have to state whether the accounts give a true and fair view of the result of the closed year (i.e. starting with the 1983 underwriting account) and whether the personal accounts give a true and fair view of each Name's net result – although in fact the majority of the accounts filed in 1985 received such an opinion.

Disclosures of Interests

With regard to disclosures of interests, the auditors now have to confirm as part of their audit that the disclosures give a fair presentation of the relevant transactions and arrangements in which there are material interests. The comparable requirement in relation to companies is the duty of auditors (now in CA1985, section 237 (5) – cf. Section 343 (6) and (7)) to see that disclosures are made in the financial statements (if necessary by providing the disclosures themselves) about loans to directors and other transactions and arrangements in which directors, or connected persons, have material interests.

The major audit problem is, of course, that of being satisfied that the information disclosed is complete. Auditors have to review as far as possible the adequacy of the managing agents' systems for obtaining the necessary information, but there is necessarily some element of reliance on the honesty and care taken by those with an obligation to disclose. There is disagreement

209

among the auditors as to whether their duties under the Lloyd's byelaw are more onerous than under the Companies Act. The Companies Act gives some recognition to the difficulty of ensuring completeness by saying that where a company's or group's accounts do not comply with the disclosure requirements, it is the auditors' duty to include in their report a statement giving the required particulars, only in so far as they are reasonably able to do so (section 237 (5)); and the Disclosure of Interests Byelaw has a similar provision (para.7(e)). However, there is no requirement in the Companies Act (unlike the Disclosure of Interests Byelaw) for a 'nil return' i.e. a statement, where appropriate, that no disclosures fall to be made. On the other hand, section 343 (6) and (7) does require a company's auditors, in certain circumstances where the statement of disclosures has to be made available to shareholders but not included in the accounts, to report specifically on whether or not in their opinion the statement does contain the required particulars. It may therefore be held that in the general case it is implied by section 237 (4) and (5) that a 'clean' report also effectively gives an opinion that the accounts do contain the necessary particulars (or, if no disclosures are made, that none need to be made), and that, as in respect of other aspects of a company's or group's accounts, the auditors have obtained all the information and explanations they believe necessary to form this opinion.

Reflecting this disagreement about the extent of the auditors' responsibilities, two firms' reports on the 1984 annual reports of the syndicates they audited stated that 'according to the information and explanations we have received' the reports complied with the Disclosure of Interests Byelaw (see Example 3). Some of the difficulties of 'fair presentation' of the disclosures are discussed further in Chapter 14.

The True and Fair View

SAB sets out the accounting procedures and record-keeping required of syndicates in order for their accounts to give a 'true and fair view' of the results of the closed year and of Names' personal results. It will not, however, be mandatory for auditors to give their opinion on this until the 1985 accounts.

What are the difficulties in giving a 'true and fair' opinion? They may be divided into the 'philosophical' and the 'practical'. The philosophical difficulty relates to whether it is possible for an auditor to give an opinion on results which require, with regard to the estimate of the reinsurance to close the account, the exercise of very considerable amounts of expert judgement often in the face of great uncertainties.

One might point to the fact that auditors are not required to give a true and fair opinion on insurance companies' accounts (CA1985, section 262). However, the prevailing view in the profession is that this derogation from true and fair only applies insofar as insurance companies are exempt from certain specific disclosure requirements. Thus the fact that they may include 'reserves' with provisions is not regarded so much as allowing them to put any amount they like aside to cover future liabilities (as long as it seems at least enough), but as allowing them, having decided how much they need to provide, and how much may be regarded as free reserves, not to disclose this breakdown. In other words, their accounts should be drawn up as if a full true and fair view was going to be given, and then the disclosure exemptions may be applied. Auditors are therefore prepared to give a true and fair opinion on the insurance companies they audit (where a view after only one year is needed); and similarly give opinions on other businesses where there are major uncertainties relating to future outcomes, such as long-term contractors (see, e.g., Watts, 1984, p.136).

The difficulties at Lloyd's are therefore practical rather than philosophical, and relate mainly to the nature of the record-keeping. The transactions and commitments of a syndicate originate at the underwriting box. Some authority may be delegated through 'binding authorities' to coverholders, but this does not alter the ultimate responsibility of the underwriter. In principle, if adequate records are kept at the box of all signings and claims notifications, it should be possible to trace through to see that they are fully and accurately reflected in the accounts for the relevant underwriting years. There is however considerable difference of opinion among auditors not only as to how far this is possible at present (given that the rules on accounting procedures and records have only come into force from 1 January 1985), but also as to how far it can ever be possible.

It is, for example, accepted practice for underwriters not to keep records of 'small' claims notifications; on the other side, it may be that some details of policy terms are by choice or necessity left to the broker to finalise so that only when the advice comes through LPSO does the underwriter know the precise details. The amount of non-proportional reinsurance premiums may not be determinable until certain future events are notified.

Risks are normally allocated to underwriting years on the basis of the date on which the policy is signed through LPSO (see also Chapter 4). Insofar as the underwriter relies on LPSO, the question arises of how accurate LPSO's own processing is. While the three year accounting helps by allowing time for transactions to be completed, the particular problem in relation to the audit arises with regard to the reinsurance to close and in tying up the underwriter's statistics on premiums and claims development with the accounting figures. Without having attempted to audit a range of syndicates myself it is not possible for me to give an authoritative view of the size of this problem or what will finally be needed to resolve it before the 1985 accounts are due. In this regard one may note:

(a) that in the notes to the accounts of 25% of the 1984 sample of annual reports (1983: 19%) it was stated that 'the underwriter relies on LPSO for the accuracy of processing' (or similar wording) (see Chapter 5, Table 1);

(b) that three firms of auditors normally expressed their opinion on the closed year underwriting account in terms that it gave a true and fair view of the result 'on the basis of the accounting policies' (ninety reports, being 20% of all 1984 reports, received this form of audit opinion – see Example 2);

(c) that Lloyd's has agreed that its own auditors should give an assurance on the completeness and efficiency of the processing by LPSO, commencing with the year ended 31 December 1985.

Qualifications

One interesting aspect of the coming into force of the new reporting requirements will be whether qualifications become more common. For the purposes of the solvency audit qualifications are extremely rare – Names must have a clean report if they are to continue underwriting, and therefore all possible steps are taken by agents to ensure that no qualifications will arise. However, the introduction of the new accounting rules and disclosures raises the possibility of qualification on technical accounting points, or for some non-disclosure, or even on the 'true and fair view' overall, without there being any necessary implication that Names' solvency is in doubt. As analysed below, there were more qualified audit reports on the 1984 syndicate reports than on the 1983 reports, and it will be interesting to see in future, when an opinion on 'true and fair' is mandatory, how many cases arise where the syndicate accounts have to be qualified even though it has been possible to sign the solvency certificates. However, if audit problems result from uncertainty relating to the calculation of the reinsurance to close, this will lead instead to more accounts having to be run off to avoid unacceptable qualification.

REQUIREMENTS

SAB requires that the syndicate audit covers:

(a) the underwriting accounts, balance sheet and notes thereto, together with the seven year summary that is now also a part of the annual report (see Chapter 12);

(b) the consistency of the managing agent's and underwriter's reports (or combined report) with the annual report to which they have to be attached;

(c) the personal accounts (which are not filed).

Point (b) requires comment in the report only if the auditor has a qualification to make.

With regard to (a), the requirements of the Disclosure of Interests Byelaw (No. 3 of 1984) have been incorporated into SAB and the disclosures (or statement that there are none to be made) are thereby required to be filed as part of the annual report and so are subject to audit.

As already noted, the requirement that syndicate accounts shall give a true and fair view of the result of the closed year is not obligatory until the 1985 accounts are filed in 1986.

The ICAEW Insurance Industry Subcommittee and the APC's draft Audit Brief on Syndicate Audits have suggested a suitable form of audit report in the following terms (although alternative wordings would be acceptable):

REPORT OF THE AUDITORS TO THE MEMBERS OF SYNDICATE XXX
We have audited the annual report set out on pages (   ) and the personal accounts relating thereto in accordance with approved Auditing Standards.
In our opinion:

(a)   the annual report, which has been drawn up on the basis of the accounting policies set out in note (   ), has been properly prepared in accordance with the requirements of the Lloyd's syndicate accounting rules and gives a true and fair view of the profit/loss of 19xx closed year of account; and
(b)   the personal accounts have been properly prepared in accordance with the Lloyd's syndicate accounting rules and give a true and fair view of each member's net result.

There has, however, been some difference of opinion among auditors as to whether specific mention needs to be made of the disclosures of interests. Under SAB the disclosure requirements of Byelaw 3 are (for the 1984 and subsequent reports) part of the annual report and are therefore deemed to be covered by the audit report's reference to the 'Lloyd's syndicate accounting rules'. However, as the original Byelaw 3 of 1984 (which required the filing in 1984 of a disclosure of interests statement in regard to the 1983 accounts and its audit in subsequent years), referred to the need for the audit reports filed in 1985 onwards to refer to compliance with its requirements, several firms of auditors take the view that it is at least desirable to make specific reference to the disclosures in the audit report. While this does not seem to be strictly necessary, it may be desirable if only to draw attention to the nature of the opinion being given in a situation which ultimately requires reliance on the adequacy of the disclosures made by the relevant parties and because the true and fair opinion itself is limited to the closed year account.

In making comparisons between the audit reports on the 1984 and 1983 accounts, it should be remembered that for the 1983 accounts the audit report only had to cover the underwriting accounts, balance sheet and notes. There was no expectation of a true and fair view opinion. The seven year summary and the managing agent's and underwriter's reports (or combined report) were optional attachments to the filed accounts. While a disclosure of interests statement had to be filed, it did not have to be audited. (See also Chapter 1.)

ANALYSIS

Because the instances of qualification are relatively rare, but individually significant, examination has been made of all syndicate accounts filed rather than of the sample. Because of the different nature of the requirements for the audit of the 1984 and 1983 annual reports they are analysed separately. The analysis deals with the aspects of the audit report relating to the filed annual reports, and not to the private personal accounts.

1984 Reports

With regard to the 1984 reports, Table 1 sets out the number of syndicate reports receiving true and fair opinions on their 1982 underwriting accounts and Table 2 the number in which specific reference was made to the disclosures of interests required under Byelaw 3 of 1984.

Table 1. Audit opinions on closed year (1982) accounts

	Number of reports	%
True and fair (notes 1 and 2)	315	69
Qualified relating to true and fair (note 2)	14	3
	329	72
Other syndicates only having open years (i.e. commenced after 1982) or run-off accounts (cf.note2)	60	13
Other syndicates' reports	68	15
Total reports	457	100

Notes
1. All audit firms generally gave true and fair opinions with the exception of Littlejohn de Paula, although practice varied in regard to joint audits. Arthur Andersen's opinion extended to the open year balances and the balance sheet as well (see Example 4).
2. A true and fair opinion is not expected on open years or run off accounts. With regard to the 28 syndicates commencing after 1982, in two cases a true and fair opinion was expressed and in one case a qualified opinion on the accounts as a whole. With regard to the 50 syndicates having only run-off accounts, in three cases a true and fair opinion was expressed on the run-off year and in twelve cases a qualification was given.
    In the case of one other syndicate which was qualified in respect of the closed year account, the managing agent subsequently decided to keep the account open as a run-off account.

Table 2. References to Byelaw 3 disclosures in 1984 audit reports.

	Number of reports	%
Compliance with disclosure requirements mentioned (note 1)	284	62
Qualified on grounds of lack of disclosure (note 2)	18	4
Other reports (i.e. not referring to disclosures)	155	34
	457	100

Notes
1.   Reference was generally made to the disclosure requirements in the audit reports of all firms except Arthur Andersen, Deloitte Haskins & Sells, Ernst & Whinney and Macnair Mason.
2.   The qualifications related to cases where information relating to the activities of certain former directors or executives was not available.

The qualifications given in the 1984 reports are analysed in Table 3. In the explanatory notes to SAB para.3 it is 'strongly recommended' at para.6 that no year of account should be closed before the managing agent determines whether the syndicate auditor intends to give a qualified audit opinion in respect of that year of account. As noted at Table 1 above, in one case where a qualified opinion was given in respect of the reinsurance to close the account it was subsequently decided to keep the account open, and in all the other cases of qualifications in respect of 'true and fair' the accounts had not been closed.

Table 3. Qualifications in audit reports

	Number of reports	%
Qualifications on true and fair (see Table 1)	14	3
Qualifications on compliance with syndicate accounting rules (note 1)	29	6
Qualifications in regard to Byelaw 3 disclosures (see Table 2)	18	4
	61	13
less: multiple qualifications in above	11	2
Qualified audit reports (note 2)	50	11

Notes
1.   Qualifications with regard to the syndicate accounting rules included qualification as regards non-standard formats of accounts; non-provision of comparatives or of seven year summary; lack of accrual for closed year underwriting transactions; non-provision of information with regard to other syndicates managed in the same market. In respect of two qualifications, supplementary audited information about other managed syndicates was subsequently filed in October 1985 giving the required information in accordance with the rules.
2.   The analysis does not include one report which was qualified only in respect of the personal accounts (as to true and fair view).

Emphasis of Matter

Without qualifying his report, an auditor may draw attention in his report to certain matters in the accounts. The CCAB Auditing Standard on the Audit Report (April 1980) notes that 'as a general principle the auditor issuing an unqualified opinion should not make reference to specific aspects of the financial statements in the body of his report as such reference may be misunderstood as being a qualification. In rare circumstances, however, the reader will obtain a better understanding of the financial statements if his attention is drawn to important matters. Examples might include an unusual event, accounting policy or condition, awareness of which is fundamental to an understanding of the financial statements.

In most cases additional discussion in the 1984 syndicate audit reports was a preamble to a qualification. However, in 26 cases of 'clean' reports there was some 'emphasis of matter' as analysed below:

13 cases (3% of all reports) related to the reasons for keeping the 1982 (or another) account open to 'run-off' (see note   )

12 (3%) cases (all relating to one agency group) drew attention to the stated accounting policies (and in these cases the audit firm did not phrase their 'true and fair opinion' as being 'on the basis of the accounting policies' in contrast to their reports on other syndicates) (see Example 6)

 1 case drew attention to the significance of the underwriter's assumptions with regard to the reinsurance to close (see Example 5).

───
26 (6%)
───

Note: In cases where the 1982 or an earlier account was being kept open, practice varied as to whether or not anything was said. In another 27 cases (6%) receiving 'clean' opinions there was no explicit reference in the audit report to the account being kept open (although normally a 'true and fair' opinion was not given) (cf. Table 1 above).

In the case of two reports there was no date on the audit report (see also Appendix III, Table 1a).

1983 Reports

No specific requirements were laid down either in PAM's recommendations, or in Byelaw 2 of 1984 ('1983 Annual Reports of Syndicates') as to the contents of the audit report on the 1983 accounts. However, the Chairman's letter of 14 February 1984 accompanying the Byelaw requested that the audit report should be similar to the following:

> REPORT OF THE AUDITORS TO THE MEMBERS OF SYNDICATE ABC
> We have audited the annual report set out on pages X to Y in accordance with approved auditing standards. We have received all the information and explanations we require.
> In our opinion, the annual report has been prepared in compliance with the accounting policies set out in note Z.
>
> [Note Z should include a statement of the extent to which the annual report complies with Lloyd's Accounting Manual (i.e. PAM).]

Of the 468 syndicate reports filed most received unqualified reports of a kind similar to this. There were, however, some variations, and the other kinds of report given were as follows:

There were eleven qualified reports including three disclaimers of opinion. Attention was drawn to major uncertainties, or to departures from recommended accounting policies.

The reports on fourteen syndicates (managed by two managing agents) referred to a true and fair view being given of the underwriting account balances and the balance sheet (comparable to Example 4 for 1984).

The reports on five syndicates (all managed by the same managing agent) specifically referred to the disclosure of interests statement having been audited. There were no separate audit reports attached to any of the disclosure of interests statements. However, in the case of fifteen syndicates (managed by four agents) the disclosures (and in the case of one other its 'no interests' statement) formed part of the notes to the accounts and were therefore within the scope of the auditors' opinion, although they were not specifically referred to.

The reports on the syndicates of two of these four agents also specifically referred to the investments having been audited (cf. Chapter 7).

In the case of five reports, there was no date on the audit report (see also Appendix III, Table 1b).

Extensions to the true and fair view?
Some auditors consider that the requirement for a true and fair view on the closed year should be seen as only a stepping stone to requiring a true and fair view on the accounts as a whole. This extension would raise a number of additional problems:

1. The amounts in the balance sheet for the open underwriting years do not normally include any provision for outstanding liabilities on these years (although one troubled syndicate whose business had been terminated did provide for estimated losses on the open 1982 year in its 1983 accounts). If 'true and fair' implies 'comparable with a company's balance sheet' disclosure of this situation would not be regarded as sufficient, and it would be necessary to form a view on any necessary provision. While this is done already for 'solvency' purposes the emphasis is different – on ensuring the amount available is at least enough rather than that it is a fair estimate.

2. It would similarly be necessary to consider how far accruals of premiums and claims and other items should be made in regard to the open years, and how far they could be absorbed in the provision for outstanding liabilities.

3. The question of the practice of using LPSO signing dates would acquire additional force – can the balance sheet be true and fair if all risks accepted are not reflected therein (even though by the market's practice those risks will be borne by the succeeding year's syndicate's Names and there is disclosure of the practice)? (In fact, it now seems likely that this practice may be changed – subject to the problem of maintaining

the consistency of the underwriting statistics – in order to remove any danger of manipulation of the allocation of risks to underwriting years.)

4. There would be technical accounting difficulties in regard to any provision for deficiencies on the open underwriting years as Names would not have provided (and not necessarily be required to provide) extra funds to the syndicate at the time. Their assets to cover deficiencies are largely off balance sheet.

Other major practical difficulties could also arise. If a view about future losses could be taken after one year, should Lloyd's move to one year accounting and recognise profits after one year? If this in turn implied distributions to Names after only one year there would need to be a fundamental reappraisal of how policyholders' and continuing Names' interests should be safeguarded (as a syndicate distributes the whole of its profits and retains no 'equity capital') and of the associated tax arrangements for Lloyd's Names.

While the likelihood of a move to one year accounting seems remote, a way forward in providing information to Names comparable to that in other accounts giving an overall true and fair view would be to include in the notes to the accounts:

(a) the amount of any estimated deficiency on the open underwriting accounts

(b) an explanation of the extent to which risks have been accepted that are not yet reflected in the accounts.

An alternative approach to the whole question would focus on the fact that, with regard to a company's accounts, Counsel's opinion has suggested (*Accountancy*, November 1983 pp.154–156) that legally 'true and fair' means essentially 'in accordance with what the readers of accounts may reasonably expect', and so is necessarily conditioned by generally accepted accounting practices. Pursuing this line one would argue that a syndicate's accounts are true and fair if they are honestly prepared according to generally accepted and understood accounting policies at Lloyd's – and given that these (including the three year accounting system, the allocation of risks by LPSO signing date, and the non-provision for open year losses) are also now set out clearly in the notes to the accounts, no one can be misled if a true and fair opinion is given on such accounts. In this context it may be noted that one firm of auditors already gives such an opinion (see Example 4).

Some additional matters that should receive further consideration in regard to providing Names with up-to-date information about the progress and performance of their syndicates are discussed in the final chapter.

EXAMPLES

■   Examples 1 to 3 give a 'true and fair view' opinion on the closed year account. Examples 2 and 3 also refer to the disclosures of interests.

■   Example 4 gives a 'true and fair view' opinion on the accounts as a whole.

■   Examples 5 and 6 have emphasis of matter. (For the matter referred to in Example 5 see Chapter 6, Example 2.)

■   Example 7 gives a qualified report.

See also: Chapter 3, Example 5
W.M.D., 540
R.H.M.Outhwaite, 317
Richard Beckett, 157.

Example I

REPORT OF THE AUDITORS TO THE MEMBERS
OF MARINE SYNDICATE 434, 437/438

We have audited the annual report set out on pages 6 to 22 and the personal accounts relating thereto in accordance with approved Auditing Standards.

In our opinion:

(a) the annual report, which has been drawn up on the basis of the accounting policies set out in notes 1 to 6, has been properly prepared in accordance with the requirements of the Lloyd's syndicate accounting rules and gives a true and fair view of the profit of the 1982 closed year of account; and

(b) the personal accounts have been properly prepared in accordance with the Lloyd's syndicate accounting rules and give a true and fair view of each member's net result.

DELOITTE HASKINS & SELLS
Chartered Accountants

LONDON
28th May, 1985.

Example 2

STENHOUSE EPPS (UNDERWRITING AGENCIES) LTD.
N.F.EPPS & OTHERS LIVESTOCK SYNDICATE 454

Report of the Auditors to the members of Syndicate 454
We have audited the annual report set out on pages 4 to 11 and the personal accounts relating thereto in accordance with approved auditing standards.

In our opinion:
(a)   the annual report, which has been drawn up on the basis of the accounting policies set out in note 1, has been properly prepared in accordance with the requirements of the Lloyd's syndicate accounting rules and gives, on the basis of the accounting policies, a true and fair view of the profit of the 1982 closed year of account;

(b)   the personal accounts have been properly prepared in accordance with the Lloyd's syndicate accounting rules and give a true and fair view of each member's net result; and

(c)   the report complies with the requirements of the Disclosure of Interests Byelaw.

NEVILLE RUSSELL
Chartered Accountants
246 Bishopsgate
London, EC2M 4PB.

15th May 1985

Example 3

Arthur Young

Chartered Accountants
Rolls House, 7 Rolls Buildings,
Fetter Lane, London EC4A 1NH

REPORT OF THE AUDITORS TO THE MEMBERS OF
MARINE SYNDICATE NO. 936/NON-MARINE SYNDICATE NO. 279

We have audited the annual report set out on pages 7 to 23 and the personal accounts relating thereto in accordance with approved auditing standards.

In our opinion:

(a) the annual report, which has been drawn up on the basis of the accounting policies set out in note 1, has been properly prepared in accordance with the requirements of the Lloyd's Syndicate Accounting Rules and gives a true and fair view of the profit of the 1982 closed year of account; and

(b) the personal accounts comply with Lloyd's Syndicate Accounting Rules and give a true and fair view of each member's net result; and

(c) according to the information and explanations received the managing agents have complied with the requirements of the Disclosure of Interests Byelaw (No. 3 of 1984).

ARTHUR YOUNG
31st May 1985

Example 4

Lloyd's underwriting syndicates managed by
C E Heath & Co (Underwriting) Limited

404 NON-MARINE SYNDICATE — No. 1   **31st December 1984**
Auditors' Report to Members of the Syndicate

We have audited the annual report of C. E. Heath & Co. (Underwriting) Limited's 404 non-marine syndicate No. 1, comprising pages 5 to 15 and the statement of interests of the Managing Agent, together with the resulting personal accounts in accordance with approved Auditing Standards.

In our opinion:—

(1)   The annual report, which has been prepared on the basis of the accounting policies set out in Note 2, has been properly prepared in accordance with the requirements of the Lloyd's Syndicate accounting rules and gives a true and fair view of the profit of the 1982 year of account and of the assets less liabilities of the Syndicate at 31st December, 1984 and the open year of account balances at that date.

(2)   The personal accounts have been properly prepared in accordance with the requirements of the Lloyd's Syndicate accounting rules and give a true and fair view of each underwriting Member's net result for the 1982 year of account.

Arthur Andersen + Co
ARTHUR ANDERSEN & CO.
Chartered Accountants

1, Surrey Street,
London, WC2R 2PS.

24th May 1985.

Example 5

Report of the auditors to the members of non-marine syndicate 421

We have examined the annual report of syndicate 421 set out on pages 13 to 31, together with the personal account of each underwriting member. Our audit has been carried out in accordance with approved auditing standards.

We draw attention to the basis on which the reinsurance to close, as set out in note 6, has been provided and the importance of the judgment of the underwriter as to the unlikelihood of material variation.

In our opinion:

(a)   the annual report and personal accounts comply with the Lloyd's syndicate accounting rules;

(b)   the annual report gives a true and fair view of the 1982 closed year of account loss; and

(c)   the personal account for each member gives a true and fair view of that member's net result.

Ernst & Whinney
Chartered Accountants

London

10th June 1985

Example 6

R W STURGE & CO

REPORT OF THE AUDITORS

To the Members of Syndicates 203, 206, 207, 209, 210/204, 212, 293, 428, 925, 960 and 998

We have audited the annual reports (including the summaries of past results and details of the investment portfolio at 31st December 1984, but excluding the related underwriters' reports) set out on pages 13 to 87 and the personal accounts relating thereto in accordance with approved Auditing Standards. We have also reviewed the disclosure of interests of the managing agent contained in the report of the managing agent on page 9.

We draw your attention to principal accounting policy note 1 on page 10 which explains the basis of accounting for underwriting transactions.

In our opinion:

(a) the annual reports, which have been drawn up on the basis of the principal accounting policies set out on pages 10 and 11, have been properly prepared in accordance with the requirements of the Lloyd's syndicate accounting rules and, except in the case of Syndicates 428 and 925 which have no closed year, give a true and fair view of their respective profit for the 1982 closed year of account; and

(b) the personal accounts have been properly prepared in accordance with the Lloyd's syndicate accounting rules and give a true and fair view of each member's net result; and

(c) the disclosure of interests of the managing agent is fairly presented and the requirements of Lloyd's byelaw No. 3 of 1984 relating to disclosure of interests have been complied with.

Neville Russell
Chartered Accountants
246 Bishopsgate
London EC2M 4PB

22nd May 1985

R W STURGE & CO
PRINCIPAL ACCOUNTING POLICIES

The principal accounting policies adopted in respect of the accounts of all syndicates (except where otherwise noted) managed by R W Sturge & Co. which comply with required Lloyd's accounting practice and have been consistently applied in all years covered by this Report, are as follows:

1. Underwriting Transactions

(a) GENERAL PRINCIPLES. In accordance with the normal system of accounting followed at Lloyd's, the underwriting accounts for each year are normally kept open for three years before the underwriting result is determined. This allows account to be taken of claims and adjustments of premiums arising after the end of the first year. At any one time, therefore, there will generally be three sets of underwriting accounts of current relevance to a syndicate. With the exception of motor syndicate 293, where all transactions are notified directly by the relevant brokers and are allocated to the year of account in which the risk incepts, each underwriting account is based on the transactions as processed through Lloyd's Policy Signing Office ("LPSO") up to the balance sheet date and are allocated to the appropriate year of account on the basis of the date on which policies are signed through the LPSO. The underwriters place substantial reliance upon the LPSO for the accuracy of processing the underwriting figures. It is not currently practicable to estimate the amount of originating premium income owing to the syndicates but not reflected in the accounts in relation to risks underwritten but not yet signed through the LPSO by the brokers concerned. In the opinion of the underwriters and the directors of R W Sturge & Co, any such amounts of unrecorded income by the time the accounts are closed at the end of the third year would be wholly immaterial to the overall results of the syndicates.

(b) OPEN YEARS. For open years of account, the syndicate accounts reflect, in addition to LPSO notified transactions, reinsurance recoveries accruing in respect of proportional reinsurance treaties and also, with the exception of the aviation syndicates, reinsurance recoveries accruing in respect of non-proportional reinsurance treaties. Motor syndicate 293 only takes credit for reinsurance recoveries on open years when the cash is received. However, no further adjustments are made to other transactions and accordingly there are material amounts of premiums and claims which are not reflected in the open year syndicate accounts. No provision is made on open years of account for underwriting losses, if any, which may arise.

(c) CLOSED YEARS. Open underwriting accounts are closed by reinsurance into the following year of account. The reinsurance to close comprises a reinsurance contract, the premium for which is calculated by the underwriter, based on estimated outstanding liabilities, including claims incurred but not reported ("IBNR"), net of estimated reinsurance recoveries, relating to the closing year and all previous years. The contract transfers the liability in respect of all claims, reinsurance premiums and return premiums in respect of the closing year and all previous years to the Names on the next year insofar as they have not already been provided for in the accounts and gives the Names on the next open year the benefit of refunds, recoveries and premiums due in respect of those years insofar as they have not already been credited in the accounts.

Example 7

Crowe Underwriting Agency Ltd.

Swan Motor Policies

Report of the Auditors
to the Members of Syndicate No. 953

We have examined the annual report on pages 11 to 23 and the personal account of each underwriting member. Our audit has been carried out in accordance with approved Auditing Standards, except that the scope of our work was limited by the matters referred to below.

The financial statements for the 1982 underwriting year include transactions entered into in 1982 which were reported on by other auditors. The auditors for the year ended 31st December 1982 reported that in their opinion certain aspects of the accounting and underwriting systems were unsatisfactory with particular regard to records of premiums, return premiums, claims and claim refunds. They were however able to complete alternative auditing tests in respect of premiums and return premiums. In these circumstances we are unable to form an opinion on the accounting records maintained during 1982.

In our opinion, the Annual Report and personal accounts have been properly prepared in accordance with the Lloyd's syndicate accounting rules. Subject to the uncertainties referred to above and in note 2a, the personal account gives a true and fair view of the member's net result for those years.

The statement of interests of Crowe Underwriting Agency Ltd. set out on page 7 complies with the requirements of the Disclosure of Interests Byelaw (No. 3 of 1984).

SPICER & PEGLER
CHARTERED ACCOUNTANTS

18th June 1985

CHAPTER 18

CONCLUSIONS – AND THE FUTURE

The requirements and recommendations under which Lloyd's syndicates have published their accounts for the last two years – the 1983 and 1984 accounts that have been reviewed in this survey – reflect a period of transition with regard to publication of the managing agent's and underwriter's reports; audited disclosure of interests; an audited seven year summary statement and a true and fair view of the closed year account.

The last of these requirements will come into force for the 1985 accounts and the developments that have taken place will have put Lloyd's syndicate accounts in many respects ahead of ordinary company accounts with regard to providing useful information. Given the up-to-date valuations of assets, and the necessarily forward looking approach to estimating the reinsurance to close, the accounts are largely free of most of the limitations of historical cost accounting. They aim to provide both a realistic picture of how the syndicate's insurance venture for a given year has turned out, and an equitable basis for dividing the result between the Names who participated in it.

In other respects, however, they must remain behind company accounting. Insurance companies (who are also increasingly moving to a value-based approach to their accounting) include the results of their latest underwriting, or at least make provision for any forseeable losses arising from that underwriting. As long as the three year accounting convention continues at Lloyd's the accounts cannot give a completely up-to-date picture of the syndicate's affairs.

One therefore has to look to other sources of information in the annual report to find information to help assess the overall situation – to the guidance to be obtained from historical patterns (such as the seven year summary may provide) and to the explanations to be found in the managing agent's and underwriter's reports about business policy and how the open years seem likely to develop. (The disclosure of interests statements will hopefully reveal the steady disappearance of situations that could give rise to conflicts of interest.) This in turn suggests that the historical summaries, or underwriters' analyses of results, need to provide both 'pure year' results, and more detailed segmental results, if as full as possible a picture of the returns and risks of a syndicate's business is to be given. It also suggests that the underwriters' reports need to explain fully the assumptions underlying the reinsurance to close in respect of both the pure closed year and the continuing exposure of older years of account (the assessment of which will vitally affect the results of the open years and of years yet to come) as well as give as full an estimate as possible of how the open years will turn out and what changes in business are planned or foreseen. At present there are either no such requirements or only fairly weak requirements in these areas.

If such requirements were made they would go well beyond what is currently required of (or at least practised in) ordinary company accounts in analysing past results and indicating likely future developments (see, for example, C.R.Emmanuel, 'Segmental disclosure', in Tonkin & Skerratt, 1983, pp.139–149; J.H.F.Gemmell & G.S.Morris, 'Long term contract work in progress' in Tonkin & Skerratt, 1984, pp.254–256). It might be argued that the consequent disclosure to competitors, especially with regard to current business and plans for the future, would not be in Names' best interests. One needs to promote further improvements in company accounts generally before turning again to Lloyd's.

On the other hand, the insurance companies are required to provide very detailed information about their past results in their audited returns to the DTI (including class of business analyses and pure year run-offs [SI1983 No.1811, Sch.2]). These returns are available to their policyholders, and similar requirements could be placed on Lloyd's syndicates. Against this, one may point out that the DTI's requirements are imposed primarily to protect policyholders (who in an insurance company have traditionally had only the company's assets to look to, although now the funds made available under the Policyholders' Protection Act 1975 provide an additional guarantee) while Lloyd's policyholders are protected by the steps taken to secure the adequacy of Names' assets (many of which are outside the syndicate accounts) – and there has never yet been a default on a Lloyd's policy. The argument that there is a need for more detailed information to protect Lloyd's policyholders therefore inevitably seems weak; and the case for Names to have fuller information (or rather for that information to be on public record) has to overcome the objection that company shareholders are not generally treated much better.

There are, therefore, two aspects to evaluating the reforms in Lloyd's accounting – what has been achieved and what else might go on the agenda. The reforms achieved so far have aimed to put accountability at Lloyd's as far as possible on a par with the standards of accountability currently expected of companies. These reforms have been given added impetus by the scandals of recent years, and on the evidence of this survey, they are in general being successfully implemented. Whether accounting reforms can help prevent future scandals cannot definitively be answered, as there is often no clear relationship between a requirement for disclosure of a particular kind of information, or a requirement for the adoption of a particular accounting method, and ensuring that clever and determined individuals are unable to conceal their activities and reap illegal or unacceptable rewards. Every new rule creates a new loophole.

The major contribution here is perhaps that the accounting and reporting reforms are symptomatic of a new climate at Lloyd's in which openness and disclosure are now the order of the day as against exclusiveness and secrecy. In this climate it should be harder for 'fringe' activites to remain undiscovered or pass as acceptable. It also reflects a climate in which participation in Lloyd's is to be seen primarily in its proper economic function of providing the capital needed to share risks efficiently, rather than being suspected of being merely a tax-haven for the wealthy. It should be a well-publicised activity, so that the role of the market and the importance of its business to the UK economy may be better understood generally.

The second aspect of evaluating the reforms is to ask how Lloyd's syndicates' accounts could further improve the measurement and presentation of past results and the provision of useful information about the risks and prospects that Names face. Some additional improvements may come as the transitional regulations finally work through: by the 1985 reports, the 'true and fair' requirement for the closed year will be in force. Some further reforms are already under consideration: for example, it seems likely that there will be moves to eliminate the practice of allocating business to underwriting years by LPSO signing date rather than by when the risk is incurred, which will remove any danger of manipulation of the time of signing.

Some possible further improvements in practice that have been suggested in the chapters of this survey have been:

(a) There should be fuller explanation in the notes of the way in which the fundamental accounting concepts underlying the preparation of accounts are modified for Lloyd's syndicates (in particular in regard to the non-applicability of the going concern concept and the importance of equity between Names).

(b) Explanations of how underwriting transactions are accounted for should be clearer and, in particular, should explain why the closed year result is unaffected by the choice of accounting method.

(c) There should be more emphasis in the notes on explaining the factors that have entered into the calculation of the reinsurance to close as a 'best estimate' and less on the considerations that are relevant to assessing adequacy of reserves for solvency purposes.

(d) Further information could be given about expense allocations, calendar year expenses, the extent of accruals and the various charges that have arisen during the calendar year. In particular, an estimate of the current audit cost should be given (whether or not it has been accrued). Executive remuneration could also be disclosed.

(e) There should be disclosure of the way in which prior closed years have subsequently developed, at least in their total effect on the current result if not by individual years.

(f) The use of ratios and percentages in the seven year summary should be extended.

(g) There should be further consideration of how to provide the calendar year information that would be provided by a Source and Application of Funds statement.

(h) Any analysis of individual investment holdings, where provided, should be included in the scope of the audit report.

There are other, more fundamental items that are not yet on the agenda. Consideration should be given to providing a note of any estimated losses on open years. In common with the rest of the insurance industry, Lloyd's needs to research the best treatment of future expenses and future investment income in assessing how much to provide for future liabilities in the reinsurance to close; and how the impact of inflation on results might be measured. Pure year accounting; greater segmental analysis; fuller explanation of assumptions; and provision of forecasts for open years, should also be on the list of topics to be considered.

Once the market has digested the effects of the present 'catching up' under the new regime of disclosure introduced so far, it will be interesting to see if Lloyd's becomes converted to the idea of being a leader in setting the standards of accountability to which companies should also aspire.

AGENTS AND SYNDICATES

For 1984 a total of 457 reports were filed for 446 syndicates (see Chapter 3). The agents managing the syndicates, and the syndicate numbers are listed below.

For 1983 a total of 468 reports were filed for 455 syndicates. No 1983 reports were filed in 1984 for two syndicates (nos. 954 and 986) managed by Richard Beckett Underwriting Agencies Ltd, but the 1984 reports for these syndicates were filed in 1985.

The market codes used, together with the number of reports filed by syndicates in each market, are as follows:

		1984	%	1983	%
S	Marine	175	38	178	38
N	Non-marine	161	35	164	35
A	Aviation	50	11	50	11
C	Motor	52	11	53	11
L	Life	8	2	8	2
O	Other	11	3	15	3
		457	100	468	100

The abbreviations used in the listing are:

U/W Underwriting
U/A Underwriting Agencies

The syndicates marked with an asterisk are those included in the random sample of one hundred reports described in Appendix IV.

Agent	Joint Agent	Syndicate/Market
A.B.Dick-Cleland (U/W Agencies) Ltd		640N
A.R.Mountain & Son Ltd		856S
A.R.Mountain & Son Ltd (a)		855S*
A.R.Mountain & Son Ltd (aa)		855S
A.R.Mountain & Son Ltd (au)		800A
A.R.E.Chambers U/W Agency Ltd		176S
A.R.E.Chambers U/W Agency Ltd		505S
A.W.Groom & Co. Ltd		455S*
Alexander Howden U/W Ltd		216N
Alexander Howden U/W Ltd		270A
Alexander Howden U/W Ltd		544N
Alexander Howden U/W Ltd		657O
Alexander Howden U/W Ltd		696S
Alexander Howden U/W Ltd		697S*

Agent	Joint Agent	Syndicate/Market
Alexander Howden U/W Ltd		831S*
Alexander Howden U/W Ltd		833S
Alexander Howden U/W Ltd		836S
Alexander Howden U/W Ltd		866C
Alexander Howden U/W Ltd		868S
Alexander Howden U/W Ltd		945S
Alexander Howden U/W Ltd		947N*
Alexander Howden U/W Ltd		949S
Alexander Syndicate Management Ltd		126N*
Alexander Syndicate Management Ltd		127S
Alexander Syndicate Management Ltd		923N
Andrew Drysdale U/W Ltd	C.T.Bowring (U/W Agencies) Ltd	043N*
Andrew Drysdale U/W Ltd	C.T.Bowring (U/W Agencies) Ltd	802A
Anton U/W Agencies Ltd		179N
Anton U/W Agencies Ltd		264S
Antony Coster U/W Agencies Ltd		125S
Aragorn Agencies Ltd		384N
Aragorn Agencies Ltd		808A
B.F.Caudle Agencies Ltd		760N
B.F.Caudle Agencies Ltd		780N
B.P.D.Kellett & Co Ltd		993N
Bain Dawes (U/W Agency) Ltd (xx)		675C
Barder & Marsh		601S
Barder & Marsh		630S*
Barder & Marsh		633S
Barder & Marsh		635A
Barder & Marsh		636N
Bates Cunningham U/W Ltd		877C
Beaumont U/W Agencies Ltd		446S*
Bellew & Raven (U/W Agencies) Ltd		180S
Bellew & Raven (U/W Agencies) Ltd		498N*
Bellew & Raven (U/W Agencies) Ltd		689S
Bellew & Raven (U/W Agencies) Ltd		691S
Bellew & Raven (U/W Agencies) Ltd		718N
Bellew & Raven (U/W Agencies) Ltd		973N*
Birrell Smith U/W Agencies Ltd		363S
Birrell Smith U/W Agencies Ltd		660N
Bolton, Ingham (Agency) Ltd		662S
Bolton, Ingham (Agency) Ltd		787S
Bolton, Ingham (Agency) Ltd		926S
Bolton, Ingham (Agency) Ltd (ba-ca)		231N
Bonnalie & Partners		490N
Bonnalie & Partners		491N
Bonnalie & Partners		916N
Bradley Gascoine U/W Agencies Ltd		901S
Bradley Gascoine U/W Agencies Ltd		921N*
Bradstock, Barker & Ashley (U/W Agencies) Ltd		183N
Brooks & Dooley (U/W) Ltd		861S*
Butcher & Hall Ltd		627O
C.D. U/W Agencies Ltd		529N
C.E.Heath & Co (U/W) Ltd		401S
C.E.Heath & Co (U/W) Ltd		404N
C.E.Heath & Co (U/W) Ltd		606S
C.E.Heath & Co (U/W) Ltd		942A
C.E.Heath & Co (U/W) Ltd		965O
C.E.Heath & Co (U/W) Ltd		969N
C.J.W. (U/W Agencies) Ltd		553N*

Agent	Joint Agent	Syndicate/Market
C.T.Bowring (U/W Agencies) Ltd		028S
C.T.Bowring (U/W Agencies) Ltd		030S
C.T.Bowring (U/W Agencies) Ltd		031S
C.T.Bowring (U/W Agencies) Ltd	Bartleet Coles Macpherson & Co Ltd	040S
C.T.Bowring (U/W Agencies) Ltd		182N
C.T.Bowring (U/W Agencies) Ltd	Fairway U/W Agencies Ltd	362N*
C.T.Bowring (U/W Agencies) Ltd		403S
C.T.Bowring (U/W Agencies) Ltd	Fairway U/W Agencies Ltd	820N
C.T.Bowring (U/W Agencies) Ltd	Fairway U/W Agencies Ltd	824A
C.T.Bowring (U/W Agencies) Ltd		825N
C.T.Bowring (U/W Agencies) Ltd		852N
C.T.Bowring (U/W Agencies) Ltd	Fairway U/W Agencies Ltd	913C
C.W.F. (U/W Agencies) Ltd		006N
Cassidy, Davis Ltd		226N
Cassidy, Davis Ltd		582N*
Cassidy, Davis Ltd		739N
Cassidy, Davis Ltd		779L
Castle U/W Agents Ltd		463O
Castle U/W Agents Ltd		835C
Chandler Graham Ltd		309S
Chandler Graham Ltd		496A
Chandler Graham Ltd		602N
Chandler Graham Ltd		675C
Charles Howard U/W Ltd		268O
Charles Howard U/W Ltd		398A
Charles Howard U/W Ltd		666N*
Christopherson Coan & Heath	Equity U/W Agencies Ltd	218C
Christopherson Coan & Heath		693N
Clifford Palmer U/W Agencies Ltd		314N*
Cornwell & Holliday (U/W Management) Ltd		374N
Coster & Mark	Antony Coster U/W Agencies Ltd	195C
Cotesworth & Co. Ltd		535S
Cotesworth & Co. Ltd		536S*
Cotesworth & Co. Ltd		896N
Craven Farmer U/W Agents Ltd		375S*
Craven Farmer U/W Agents Ltd		478A
Creegate U/W Agencies Ltd (50%)	Brooks & Dooley (U/W) Ltd	089 S
Crescent Underwriting Agencies Ltd		936S
Crowe U/W Agency Ltd		349N*
Crowe U/W Agency Ltd		577A
Crowe U/W Agency Ltd		953C
Crowe U/W Agency Ltd		963O
Crump & Cackett Agencies Ltd		957A
Crump & Johnson U/W Agencies Ltd		744S
Cunliffe-Fraser, Bruce & Co. Ltd	Peter F. Wright & Co. Ltd	707S
Cunliffe-Fraser, Bruce & Co. Ltd	Peter F. Wright & Co. Ltd	719S
D.E.C. (U/W Agency)		288S
D.P.Mann Underwriting Agency Ltd		435N
Dann Kiln & Co. U/W Agencies Ltd		955A
David Holman & Co. Ltd		343C
David Holman & Co. Ltd		892C
David Holman & Co. Ltd		976C
Dawson, Mackinnon, Hayter & Co Ltd		134N*
Dawson, Mackinnon, Hayter & Co Ltd		184N
Dugdale (U/W) Ltd		063S*
Dugdale (U/W) Ltd		217N
Dugdale (U/W) Ltd		508C*

Agent	Joint Agent	Syndicate/Market
Dugdale (U/W) Ltd		702N
Dugdale (U/W) Ltd		939N
Dugdale (U/W) Ltd		959A*
Dugdale (U/W) Ltd (50%)		089S
E.R.H.Hill (Agencies) Ltd		800A
Eamonn Murphy & Co. Ltd		242N*
Eamonn Murphy & Co. Ltd		794N*
Eamonn Murphy & Co. Ltd		240L
Edward Lumley & Sons (U/W Agencies) Ltd		247S
Edward Williams Coutts & Ptnrs Ltd		044L
Edward Williams Coutts & Ptnrs Ltd		235N
Edward Williams Coutts & Ptnrs Ltd		383N
Edwards and Payne (U/W Agencies) Ltd		192N
Edwards and Payne (U/W Agencies) Ltd		219N
Edwards and Payne (U/W Agencies) Ltd		304S*
Edwards and Payne (U/W Agencies) Ltd		330C
Ernest Blackmore & Son Ltd		785S*
Ernest Blackmore & Son Ltd (a-aq)	Chandler Graham Ltd	675C
Eversure Underwriting Agency Ltd		554C*
Eversure Underwriting Agency Ltd		740S
Fenchurch U/W Agencies Ltd		156O*
Fenchurch U/W Agencies Ltd		260C
Fenchurch U/W Agencies Ltd		370N
Frank Bradford & Co (U/W) Ltd		061N
Frank Bradford & Co (U/W) Ltd		100N
G.P.Eliot & Co. Ltd		053A*
G.W.Hutton & Co. (U/W Agency) Ltd		331A
G.W.Hutton & Co. (U/W Agency) Ltd		803S
Gammell Kershaw & Co Ltd		102S
Gardner Mountain & Capel-Cure Agencies Ltd		002S*
Gardner Mountain & Capel-Cure Agencies Ltd		558N
George Miller U/W Agencies Ltd		527S
George Miller U/W Agencies Ltd		598N
Gilliat, Scotford & Hayworth Ltd		056N
Glanvill Enthoven & Co. (U/W) Ltd		464N
Gooda & Partners Ltd		298S
Gooda & Partners Ltd	W.G.Gooda & Sons Ltd	299S*
Gooda & Partners Ltd		514S
Gooda Walker Ltd		164N
Gooda Walker Ltd		290N*
Gooda Walker Ltd		295A
Gooda Walker Ltd		296A
Gooda Walker Ltd		387N
Gorsuch Underwriting Agencies Ltd	Gardner Mountain&Capel-Cure Agencies Ltd	087S
Gravett & Tilling (U/W Agencies) Ltd		397N
Gravett & Tilling (U/W Agencies) Ltd		340A
Gray MacKay Forbes (U/W) Agencies Ltd		432A
Grayston, Rust & Salt Ltd		724S
Grayston, Rust & Salt Ltd		749S
Grayston, Rust & Salt Ltd		815C
Guest Barnes (U/W Agencies) Ltd		225N
H.Pitman (U/W) Ltd		195C
H.G.Chester & Co Ltd		065S

Agent	Joint Agent	Syndicate/Market
H.G.Chester & Co Ltd		067S
H.G.Chester & Co Ltd		072S
H.G.Chester & Co Ltd		475S
H.G.Chester & Co Ltd		485S
H.G.H. U/W Management Ltd		262C
Hampton Evens & Berkeley (U/W Agents) Ltd		358S*
Hampton Evens & Berkeley (U/W Agents) Ltd		460N
Hardcastle U/W Agencies Ltd		318A
Hardcastle U/W Agencies Ltd		319N
Hardy (U/W Agencies) Ltd		382S
Harman Gardner-Roberts Ltd		468N
Haynes & Clack U/W Agencies Ltd		424N
Haynes & Clack U/W Agencies Ltd		497N
Haynes & Clack U/W Agencies Ltd		782N
Higgins & Doble Ltd		284S
Holman Franklin Ltd		313S
Holman Franklin Ltd		687S*
Holman Macleod Ltd		307N
Holman Macleod Ltd		962O
Holman Managers Ltd		804S
Holmes, Hayday (U/W Agencies) Ltd		694N
Holmwoods&Back&Manson (U/W Agencies) Ltd		144N*
I.C.Agnew U/W Ltd		672S*
J.D.Boyagis (U/W Agencies) Ltd		227N*
J.D.Boyagis (U/W Agencies) Ltd		681S*
J.D. U/W Agency Ltd		081C
J.H.Davies (U/W Agency) Ltd		256A
J.H.Davies (U/W Agency) Ltd		257N
J.H.Minet Agencies Ltd	Foden-Pattinson U/W Agencies Ltd R.D.Robertson U/W Agency Ltd	322N
J.H.Minet Agencies Ltd		458A
J.H.Minet Agencies Ltd		887C*
J.H.Minet Agencies Ltd		919N
J.H.Minet Agencies Ltd		920S
Jago Venton U/W Agencies Ltd		205N
Jago Venton U/W Agencies Ltd		376N
Janson Green Ltd		386N
Janson Green Ltd		932S
Janson Green Ltd (a-ad)		231N
Jardine Matheson U/W Agencies Ltd	Lloyd-Roberts & Gilkes Ltd	612N
Jardine Matheson U/W Agencies Ltd		675C
John Hayter Motor U/W Agencies Ltd		253C
John Poland & Co. Ltd		103A
John Poland & Co. Ltd		104N
John Poland & Co. Ltd		105N
John Poland & Co. Ltd		107S
John Poland & Co. Ltd		108S
John Poland & Co. Ltd		560C
John Poland & Co. Ltd		733S
John Poland & Co. Ltd		767N
Johnson Heath Ltd		526N
Joseph W. Hobbs & Co. Ltd	Alan Jackson (U/W Agencies) Ltd	735S
Joseph W. Hobbs & Co. Ltd		816C
K.F.Alder (U/W Agency) Ltd		037C*
K.F.Alder (U/W Agency) Ltd		122N*

Agent	Joint Agent	Syndicate/Market
K.F.Alder (U/W Agency) Ltd		153N
K.F.Alder (U/W Agency) Ltd		429L*
K.F.Alder (U/W Agency) Ltd		503N
K.F.Alder (U/W Agency) Ltd		537N
K.F.Alder (U/W Agency) Ltd		546N
K.F.Alder (U/W Agency) Ltd		950A
K.J.Monksfield (U/W Agencies) Ltd		325C*
K.J.Monksfield (U/W Agencies) Ltd		329S
K.P.H. U/W Agencies Ltd		745S*
K.W.Bickle (U/W) Ltd		221S
L. Hammond & Co. (U/W) Ltd		439C
L.G.Cox & Co. Ltd		590S
L.G.Cox & Co. Ltd		591S
Lambert Brothers (U/W Agencies) Ltd		202S
Lambert Brothers (U/W Agencies) Ltd		437S
Lambert Brothers (U/W Agencies) Ltd		580A
Lambert Brothers (U/W Agencies) Ltd		604N
Langton U/W Agents Ltd		010N
Langton U/W Agents Ltd		011C
Langton U/W Agents Ltd		012N*
Langton U/W Agents Ltd		271A
Langton U/W Agents Ltd		613S*
Langton U/W Agents Ltd		725S
Laurence Phillips (Agencies) Ltd		223S
Laurence Phillips (Agencies) Ltd		710S
Leslie & Godwin (U/W) Ltd		080S
Leslie & Godwin (U/W) Ltd		083S*
Leslie & Godwin (U/W) Ltd (o,p,q)		584N
Link U/W Agency Ltd		603C
Lloyd-Roberts & Gilkes Ltd		055N
Lloyd-Roberts & Gilkes Ltd		806N
London River U/W Management Ltd		711S*
Lovat U/W Ltd		647C
M.C.Winn U/W Agencies Ltd	Gardner Mountain&Capel-Cure Agencies Ltd	674N
M.E.Charlesworth (U/W Agents) Ltd		024S*
M.E.Charlesworth (U/W Agents) Ltd		678C
M.E.Charlesworth (U/W Agents) Ltd		734A
M.F.K. U/W Agencies Ltd		396N
M.F.K. U/W Agencies Ltd		457S
M.F.K. U/W Agencies Ltd		904S*
M.F.K. U/W Agencies Ltd		958N
M.H.Cockell & Co Ltd		269N
M.J.Tullberg & Co Ltd		350C
M.W.E. U/W Agencies Ltd		275S*
M.W.E. U/W Agencies Ltd		575S
Mackinnon Butcher & Hall Ltd		927S
Mander, Thomas & Cooper (U/W Agencies) Ltd		552S
Mark Loveday U/W Agencies Ltd		573S
Mark Loveday U/W Agencies Ltd		656S
Mark Loveday U/W Agencies Ltd		705S
Merrett Syndicates Ltd		417N
Merrett Syndicates Ltd		418S
Merrett Syndicates Ltd		421N
Merrett Syndicates Ltd		799N*
Merrett Syndicates Ltd		863A
Merrett U/W Agency Management Ltd		522S

Agent	Joint Agent	Syndicate/Market
Michael J. Marchant (U/W Agency) Ltd		282S*
Morgan, Fentiman & Barber		991N*
N.T.Evennett & Partners Ltd		658S
N.T.Evennett & Partners Ltd		728S
Newgreen (U/W Agencies) Ltd		685S
Newgreen (U/W Agencies) Ltd		747C
Newgreen (U/W Agencies) Ltd		860N
Norman Frizzell U/W Ltd		850A
Norman Frizzell U/W Ltd		975N
Norman Frizzell U/W Ltd		979C*
Oakeley Vaughan (U/W) Ltd		420S
Outhwaite & Green Ltd		321S
P.&M.Crowe U/W Agency		917N*
P.B.Coffey (U/W Agency) Ltd		902S
Peter Pepper (U/W Agencies) Ltd		228S
Peter Pepper (U/W Agencies) Ltd		851S
Philip N. Christie & Co. Ltd		145S
Philip N. Christie & Co. Ltd		254C
Philip N. Christie & Co. Ltd		469N
Philip N. Christie & Co. Ltd		764S
Pieri (U/W Agencies) Ltd		872S
Posgate & Denby (Agencies) Ltd		488S
Posgate & Denby (Agencies) Ltd		489N
Posgate & Denby (Agencies) Ltd		609S
Posgate & Denby (Agencies) Ltd		700S*
Posgate & Denby (Agencies) Ltd		701N
Posgate & Denby (Agencies) Ltd		839N
Pulbrook U/W Management Ltd		090N*
Pulbrook U/W Management Ltd		312A
Pulbrook U/W Management Ltd		332L
Pulbrook U/W Management Ltd		334S
Pulbrook U/W Management Ltd		533C*
R.A.F.Macmillan & Co. Ltd		843S
R.D.Robertson U/W Agency Ltd		977N*
R.D. U/W Agencies Ltd		272S
R.F.Kershaw Ltd		675C
R.H.M.Outhwaite (U/W Agencies) Ltd		317S
R.J.Kiln & Co. Ltd		510N
R.J.Kiln & Co. Ltd		557N*
R.J.Kiln & Co. Ltd		807N
R.K.Harrison & Graves Ltd		451A*
R.K.Harrison & Graves Ltd		471N
R.K.Harrison Motor Agencies Ltd		587C
R.K.Harrison, Graves & Austin Ltd		722N*
R.L.Glover & Co. (U/W Agents) Ltd		162S
R.M.Pateman U/W Agencies Ltd		052S
R.M.Pateman U/W Agencies Ltd	Willis Faber & Dumas (Agencies) Ltd	042S
R.P.Milligan (U/W Agencies) Ltd		305N
R.P.Milligan (U/W Agencies) Ltd		521O
R.W.Sturge & Co.		203S
R.W.Sturge & Co.		206S
R.W.Sturge & Co.		207S
R.W.Sturge & Co.		209S
R.W.Sturge & Co.		210N
R.W.Sturge & Co.		212N
R.W.Sturge & Co.		293C
R.W.Sturge & Co.		428S
R.W.Sturge & Co.		925A

Agent	Joint Agent	Syndicate/Market
R.W.Sturge & Co.		960A
R.W.Sturge & Co.		998A*
Richard Beckett U/W Agencies Ltd		157N*
Richard Beckett U/W Agencies Ltd		493S
Richard Beckett U/W Agencies Ltd		810S*
Richard Beckett U/W Agencies Ltd		859A
Richard Beckett U/W Agencies Ltd		869S
Richard Beckett U/W Agencies Ltd		893S
Richard Beckett U/W Agencies Ltd		900S
Richard Beckett U/W Agencies Ltd		918N*
Richard Beckett U/W Agencies Ltd		940N
Richard Beckett U/W Agencies Ltd		954S
Richard Beckett U/W Agencies Ltd		986N
Robert Napier Ltd		168A
Robert Napier Ltd		423N*
Robert Napier Ltd		551N
Robert Napier Ltd		862A
Roberts & Hiscox Ltd		033N
Roberts & Hiscox Ltd		624N
Roberts & Hiscox Ltd		625S
Robt. Bradford (U/W) Ltd		093C*
Robt. Bradford (U/W) Ltd	Gray McKay Forbes (U/W Agencies) Ltd	250N
Robt. Bradford (U/W) Ltd		389L*
Robt. Bradford (U/W) Ltd	Gray McKay Forbes (U/W Agencies) Ltd	431A*
Robt. Bradford (U/W) Ltd	Gray McKay Forbes (U/W Agencies) Ltd	443A
Rose Thomson Young (U/W) Ltd		234C
Rose Thomson Young (U/W) Ltd		255S
Rose Thomson Young (U/W) Ltd		259S
Rose Thomson Young (U/W) Ltd		345S
Rowbotham de Rougemont Agencies Ltd		112S
Rowbotham de Rougemont Agencies Ltd		113N
Rowbotham de Rougemont Agencies Ltd	Barder & Marsh	248S
Rowbotham de Rougemont Agencies Ltd		732N*
Rowbotham de Rougemont Agencies Ltd (af)		675C
Roy Hill U/W Agencies Ltd	Gardner Mountain&Capel-Cure Agencies Ltd	372S
S.A.Meacock & Co.		399L
S.A.Meacock & Co.		727N*
S.A.Meacock & Co.		956N
Safeguard (Managing Agency) Ltd		758C*
Safeguard (Managing Agency) Ltd		897C*
Salter & Outhwaite (U/W) Ltd		518N*
Savill, Gough & Hay Ltd		388C*
Scimitar U/W Agencies		079S
Secretan (U/W Agencies) Ltd		366C
Secretan (U/W Agencies) Ltd		367S
Secretan (U/W Agencies) Ltd		411S*
Secretan (U/W Agencies) Ltd		545A*
Sedgwick Forbes (Lloyd's U/W Agents) Ltd		047N

Agent	Joint Agent	Syndicate/Market
Sedgwick Forbes (Lloyd's U/W Agents) Ltd		048A*
Sedgwick Forbes (Lloyd's U/W Agents) Ltd		483S*
Sedgwick Forbes (Lloyd's U/W Agents) Ltd		484N
Spicer & White (U/W Agencies) Ltd		895S
Spratt & White Ltd		161S
Spratt & White Ltd		287S
Spurr Kiln & Co. U/W Agencies Ltd		765N*
Stenhouse Epps (U/W Agencies) Ltd		454O*
Stenhouse Harman (U/W Agencies) Ltd		310A
Stenhouse Harman (U/W Agencies) Ltd		456N
Stenhouse Harman (U/W Agencies) Ltd		561N
Stenhouse Harman (U/W Agencies) Ltd		566S
Stenhouse Harman (U/W Agencies) Ltd		584N
Stenhouse Harman (U/W Agencies) Ltd		809A
Stenhouse Harman (U/W Agencies) Ltd		982L
Stenhouse Patrick (U/W Agencies) Ltd		197N
Stenhouse Patrick (U/W Agencies) Ltd		726S
Stenhouse Reed Shaw (U/W Agencies) Ltd		034S
Stenhouse Reed Shaw (U/W Agencies) Ltd		045N
Stenhouse Reed Shaw (U/W Agencies) Ltd		177O
Stenhouse Reed Shaw (U/W Agencies) Ltd		342N
Stenhouse Reed Shaw (U/W Agencies) Ltd		980C
Stewart & Hughman Ltd		004S
Stewart & Hughman Ltd		015N
Stewart & Hughman Ltd		017S
Stewart & Hughman Ltd		142S
Stewart & Hughman Ltd		172A
Stewart & Hughman Ltd		337S*
Street (U/W Agencies) Ltd		123S*
Three Quays U/W Management Ltd		190N
Towergate U/W Agencies Ltd		588S*
Towry Law (U/W Management) Ltd		453N*
Towry Law (U/W Management) Ltd·		827C
Trojan Underwriting Agency Ltd		378C*
Vanguard U/W Agencies Ltd		500S
Verrall Turner (U/W Agency) Ltd		888S*
W.M.D. U/W Agencies Ltd		174S
W.M.D. U/W Agencies Ltd		540S
W.M.D. U/W Agencies Ltd		847N
W.R.B. (Aviation Agencies) Ltd		801A
Warren Barber U/W Agencies Ltd		512N*
Warren Barber U/W Agencies Ltd		530N*
Wigham-Richardson & Bevingtons U/A Ltd		062S*
Wigham-Richardson & Bevingtons U/A Ltd		631S*
Wigham-Richardson & Bevingtons U/A Ltd		632S
Wigham-Richardson & Bevingtons U/A Ltd	B.P.D.Kellett & Co. Ltd	878N

Agent	Joint Agent	Syndicate/Market
Wigham-Richardson & Bevingtons U/A Ltd	Morgan, Fentiman & Barber	990N*
Wigham-Richardson & Bevingtons U/A Ltd		992N
Willis Faber & Dumas (Agencies) Ltd		051N
Willis Faber & Dumas (Agencies) Ltd		097A
Willis Faber & Dumas (Agencies) Ltd		263N
Willis Faber & Dumas (Agencies) Ltd		406S*
Willis Faber & Dumas (Agencies) Ltd		447S*
Willis Faber & Dumas (Agencies) Ltd		448S*
Willis Faber & Dumas (Agencies) Ltd		449S
Willis Faber & Dumas (Agencies) Ltd		570N
Willis Faber & Dumas (Agencies) Ltd		595A
Willis Faber & Dumas (Agencies) Ltd		648A
Willis Faber & Dumas (Agencies) Ltd		846N
Willis Faber & Dumas (Agencies) Ltd		999C

SYNDICATE AUDITORS

The auditors who reported on the 457 1984 accounts and 468 1983 accounts were as follows:

Firm	1984		1983	
	Sole audits	Joint audits	Sole audits	Joint audits
Arthur Andersen & Co.	19	1	5	13
Arthur Young	59	25	60	38
de Paula, Turner, Lake & Co.*	—	—	18	33
Deloitte Haskins & Sells	4	—	4	—
Ernst & Whinney	95	9	90	16
Futcher, Head & Gilberts	11	9	15	9
Kidsons	1	—	1	—
Littlejohn de Paula*	55	30	38	—
Macnair Mason	5	—	4	—
Neville Russell	85	34	86	45
Pannell Kerr Forster	14	41	14	47
Peat, Marwick, Mitchell & Co.	8	—	9	—
Price Waterhouse	6	—	4	—
Robson Rhodes	—	2	—	3
Spicer and Pegler	19	1	16	3
Touche Ross & Co.	—	—	—	1
	381	152	364	208

---

* The numbers for 1983 are for the two firms of de Paula, Turner, Lake & Co. and Littlejohn & Co. The numbers for 1984 are for the merged firm of Littlejohn de Paula.

STATISTICS ON ANNUAL REPORTS

All reports were made up to 31 December, and were due to be filed by 15 June in each year. Tables 1a and 1b analyse the dates of signing shown on the accounts and audit reports.

Table I a

Date of issue – 1984 reports	Number of reports			
	Annual report date	%	Audit report date	%
February	1	—	—	—
March	—	—	1	—
April	20	4	16	4
May	186	41	175	38
June (before 15th)	213	47	206	45
June (15th)	1	—	1	—
June (after 15th)	8	2	16	4
June (unspecified)	4	1	23	5
July	12	3	12	3
August	2	—	3	1
September	2	—	2	—
Undated	8	2	2	—
	457	100	457	100

Notes
1. Undated annual reports are those not dated on the balance sheet in accordance with SAB.
2. The first two syndicates were motor syndicates but so were three of the eight syndicates with specific dates after 15 June.

Table 1b

Date of issue – 1983 reports	Number of reports			
	Annual report date	%	Audit report date	%
February	2	1	2	1
March	—	—	—	—
April	15	3	18	4
May	151	32	165	35
June (before 15th)	139	30	156	33
June (15th)	24	5	27	6
June (after 15th)	11	2	9	2
June (unspecified)	65	14	71	15
July	—	—	—	—
August	14	3	14	3
November	—	—	1	—
Undated	47	10	5	1
	468	100	468	100

Notes
1. Not all reports counted in this table were dated on the balance sheet itself (e.g. the date might be in the managing agent's report).
2. The first four syndicates were motor syndicates, but so were three of the last six syndicates with specified dates in June.

Table 2a. Size of 1984 reports

Size of annual report (pages)	1984 %
30 or more	3
25 – 29	8
20 – 24	32
15 – 19	38
10 – 14	17
‹10	1
	99

Note
These data relate only to the random sample of 100 reports

Table 2b. Size of 1983 reports

Size of annual report (pages)	Number of reports 1983	%
30 or more	18	4
25 – 29	22	5
20 – 24	32	7
15 – 19	91	20
10 – 14	198	43
‹10	95	21
	456	100

Notes
The major factors producing the differences in size were the length of the disclosures of interests and, in the 1983 reports, the inclusion or non-inclusion of a managing agent's and underwriter's report. Some of the larger reports resulted from the inclusion of a number of syndicates in one set of accounts (see Chapter 3) which is why the 1983 total is less than the total of 468 reports analysed elsewhere in the survey and the 1984 total is less than 100%.
    Size has been measured by the number of pages included on the Central File microfiche for the syndicate.

Rounding of figures
In the 1984 and 1983 accounts the syndicates used whole £, except for seven which used figures rounded to the nearest £000. One of these was the syndicate with the largest gross premium income for 1981 and 1982.

Table 3a. Syndicate allocated capacity and size of gross premium income for 1982 underwriting year given in 1984 accounts

	Syndicate allocated capacity		Gross premium income	
	Number of syndicates	%	Number of syndicates	%
£100 million or more	—	—	4	1
50m – 99.9m	7	2	11	3
30m – 49.9m	9	2	16	4
15m – 29.9m	33	8	44	11
10m – 14.9m	33	8	35	9
6m – 9.9m	47	11	56	13
2m – 5.9m	133	32	119	28
1m – 1.9m	60	14	54	13
500K – 999.9K	43	10	36	8
100K – 499.9K	38	9	27	7
Less than £100K	12	3	13	3
	415	100	415	100

Notes

The largest amount of allocated capacity was £90,195,000, and this syndicate also had the largest gross premium income, which was £179,900,000 (it was the second largest syndicate by number of Names).

The smallest amount of allocated premium income was £12,000. The smallest amount of gross premium income (for an active syndicate) was £11,000.

The total number is less than the 446 syndicates filing accounts as 3 of these had ceased business before the 1982 account, and 28 had started afterwards.

Table 3b. Size of gross premium income for 1981 underwriting year given in 1983 accounts

	Number of syndicates	%
£100 million or more	1	—
50m – 99.9m	8	2
30m – 49.9m	14	3
15m – 29.9m	36	9
10m – 14.9m	41	10
6m – 9.9m	43	11
2m – 5.9m	123	31
1m – 1.9m	53	13
500K – 999.9K	37	9
100K – 499.9K	31	8
Less than £100K	15	34
	402	100

Notes
The largest amount was £146,540,000 (the second largest syndicate by number of Names).

The smallest (for an activate syndicate) was £17,000 (the smallest syndicate by number of Names).

The smallest (for an active syndicate) was £17,000 (the smallest syndicate by number of Names).

Only 25% of syndicates gave the syndicate allocated capacity in their 1983 accounts for the closed year 1981, so this information is not given in this table.

Table 4a. Numbers of Names shown on syndicates for 1982 underwriting year

	Number of syndicates	%
Over 3000	2	1
2000–2999	4	1
1500–1999	4	1
1000–1499	14	3
500– 999	49	11
400– 499	19	4
300– 399	39	9
200– 299	55	12
100– 199	95	21
Under 100	124	28
	405	91
'Incidental' and 'mirror' syndicates	3	1
No 1982 underwriting year	31	7
Number of Names not shown	7	1
	446	100

Notes
The numbers of Names have normally been taken from the seven year summaries filed with the 1984 accounts. In seven cases, although syndicates had a 1982 underwriting account, they had not included a seven year summary, or did not include information for 1982 in the table.
    The largest syndicate had 3557 Names. The smallest active syndicate had one Name.

Table 4b. Numbers of Names shown on syndicates for 1981 underwriting year

	Number of syndicates
Over 2000	4
1500–1999	2
1000–1499	7
500– 999	18
400– 499	10
300– 399	12
200– 299	27
100– 199	40
Under 100	33
	153

Notes

The total number is much less than the 455 syndicates filing 1983 accounts as many of them did not state the number of Names in their annual report, or had ceased business before the 1981 account, or started afterwards. (This table is therefore not a reliable guide to the actual size distribution of syndicates for that year.)

The largest syndicate showed 2924 Names. The smallest active syndicate showed one Name.

SAMPLE CHARACTERISTICS

The following tables analyse, for comparison with the data about the whole population given in Appendix III, the characteristics of the random sample of 100 syndicate reports chosen for detailed analysis. The reports included in the sample are identified by an asterisk in the listing in Appendix I and were chosen at random by reference to their syndicate number.

Where both sample and population data are available, comparison shows it is rare for an individual percentage in the sample to differ from the percentage in the population by more than seven percentage points (e.g. it is rare for 50% in the sample to represent a range wider than 43%–57% in the population as a whole).

Table I

Date of issue – 1984 reports	Annual report date % of sample	Audit report date % of sample
February	—	—
March	—	—
April	4	4
May	36	34
June (before 15th)	54	51
June (15th)	—	—
June (after 15th)	1	6
June (unspecified)	2	2
July	3	3
Undated	—	—
	100	100

Table 2. Size of annual report

See Appendix III, Table 2a.

Table 3. Size of syndicate allocated capacity and gross premium income for 1982
underwriting year given in 1984 accounts

	Syndicate allocated capacity	*Gross premium income*
	% of sample	*% of sample*
£100 million or more	—	2
50m – 99.9m	1	4
30m – 49.9m	5	9
15m – 29.9m	11	5
10m – 14.9m	6	8
6m – 9.9m	9	8
2m – 5.9m	24	26
1m – 1.9m	17	16
500K – 999.9K	14	10
100K – 499.9K	6	6
Less than £100K	4	3
	97	97
Started after 1982	3	3
	100	100

Notes
The largest amount of allocated capacity was £63,300,000, and this syndicate also had the
largest amount of gross premium income in the sample, which was £106,818,000.
   The smallest amount of allocated capacity was £60,000, and this syndicate also had the
smallest amount of gross premium income in the sample, which was £65,000.

Table 4. Numbers of Names shown on syndicates for 1982 underwriting year

	% of sample
Over 3000	1
2000–2999	2
1500–1999	1
1000–1499	2
500– 999	15
400– 499	5
300– 399	7
200– 299	10
100– 199	23
Under 100	29
	95
Started after 1982	3
Syndicate not giving 1982 on seven year summary	1
No seven year summary	1
	100

Notes
The largest number of Names in the sample was 3557 (also the largest syndicate in the population).
    The smallest number of Names was six.

Table 5. Market

		% of sample
S	Marine	39
N	Non-marine	38
A	Aviation	7
C	Motor	12
L	Life	2
O	Other	2
		100

Table 6. Syndicate auditors for the 1984 reports

Firm	% of sample	
	Sole audits	Joint audits
Arthur Andersen & Co.	3	—
Arthur Young	15	6
Deloitte Haskins & Sells	—	—
Ernst & Whinney	21	2
Futcher, Head & Gilberts	2	4
Kidsons	—	—
Littlejohn de Paula	14	4
Macnair Mason	2	—
Neville Russell	18	10
Pannell Kerr Forster	3	6
Peat, Marwick, Mitchell & Co.	—	—
Price Waterhouse	1	—
Robson Rhodes	—	1
Spicer and Pegler	4	1
	83	34

LLOYD'S GLOBAL ACCOUNTS 1984 – ALL CLASSES COMBINED

LLOYD'S OF LONDON

NOTES TO THE ACCOUNTS

1. BASIS OF PREPARATION OF GLOBAL ACCOUNTS

The global accounts represent the aggregation of the results of all syndicates operating at Lloyd's. At 1st January, 1984 there were 23,438 members participating in 457 syndicates. The global accounts are compiled from returns which have been prepared by accountants approved under section 83(4) of the Insurance Companies Act, 1982.

The following generally accepted accounting practices at Lloyd's have been adopted in the preparation of the global accounts:

(a) Three year accounting method

The revenue accounts for all classes of insurance business underwritten at Lloyd's are prepared using the "three-year" accounting convention. Under this method the revenue accounts are usually held open for three years from the commencement of each underwriting year. By that time a sufficiently accurate determination of outstanding liabilities can generally be made to permit the account to be "closed" and the underwriting profit or loss determined.

An account is usually closed by paying a premium to the same syndicate for a later underwriting year. For example, at 31st December, 1984, the 1982 year of account of most syndicates was closed by the Names on the 1982 syndicate paying the 1983 syndicate a premium to insure all outstanding liabilities of the 1982 year of account (and all previous years reinsured therein). The 1983 syndicate will have many of the same Names as the 1982 syndicate but some may have left and new Names may have joined. This premium is commonly referred to as the "reinsurance to close".

The profit, once determined, is paid out to the Names who participated in that syndicate during the closed year. The accounts of the two most recent years remain "open" under this method. The open years are subject to further premium and claim transactions up to the dates of closure. The global accounts do not include any estimate of these future transactions. The balances on the open years do not purport to give any indication of the likely profit or loss that may be determined when these years of account are closed.

(b) Premiums

In general, premiums are allocated to a year of account by reference to the date of notification of each risk to the syndicate by Lloyd's Policy Signing Office. Premiums are gross premiums less commissions and brokerage, and are net of reinsurance premiums.

(c) Claims

Claims are allocated to the same year of account as the premium for each risk. Claims include fees and related costs less salvages, and are net of reinsurance recoveries.

(d) Reinsurance to close

As stated in 1(a) above, a year of account is normally closed by reinsurance to the following year of account at the end of the third year. The reinsurance to close comprises estimated outstanding liabilities including claims incurred but not yet reported, net of estimated reinsurance recoveries on such liabilities, relating to the closed year and to all previous closed years.

Where outstanding liabilities cannot be arrived at with sufficient certainty to close a year of account and hence determine the final profit or loss, that year of account is left open and is not reinsured into the subsequent year of account. An amount is however retained as at each 31st December to meet all known and unknown outstanding liabilities until the account is finally closed. In presenting the global accounts, amounts retained as at 31st December are included in reinsurance premiums paid to close the account. Subsequent transactions are reflected in the global accounts prepared in respect of the calendar year in which the transactions arise.

(e) Investment income

Investment income arising in each calendar year is allocated to a year of account in proportion to the balance of funds for the year after making provision for income tax at the basic rate.

(f) Investment appreciation

The funds of syndicates are invested in a variety of securities and investments. In the preparation of syndicate returns, investments held at the end of the year are stated at market values ruling at that date. Realised gains and losses on sales of investments and unrealised capital appreciation computed at the end of each calendar year are allocated to underwriting accounts in proportion to the balance of each underwriting account. The figure for investment appreciation is arrived at after making provision for capital gains tax.

(g) Syndicate expenses

The expenses incurred in the administration of syndicates are generally charged to the year of account during which they are incurred.

(h) Profit commission

Amounts charged by underwriting agents in respect of profit commission are not included in the global accounts.

2. BASIS OF CURRENCY TRANSLATION

Underwriting business at Lloyd's is recorded in three separate currencies, being sterling, United States dollars and Canadian dollars. The syndicates maintain separate records in respect of each of these currencies. Items expressed in United States and Canadian dollars are translated into sterling at the rates of exchange ruling at the end of the year. Items brought forward from the previous year are therefore revalued at those rates. The following exchange rates have been adopted in the translation into sterling of transactions in United States and Canadian dollars:

	US dollars as at 31st Dec			Canadian dollars as at 31st Dec		
	1982	1983	1984	1982	1983	1984
1982 account	1.62	1.45	1.16	1.99	1.81	1.53
1983 account	—	1.45	1.16	—	1.81	1.53
1984 account	—	—	1.16	—	—	1.53

Transactions during the year in other overseas currencies are translated into sterling at the rates ruling at the time transactions are processed through the Lloyd's central accounting system.

3. TAXATION
Syndicate profits are distributed to individual members in proportion to their participations and these profits are subject to United Kingdom, United States and Canadian taxation as appropriate by assessment on each member as an individual. There is therefore no provision for taxation in the global accounts, except as indicated in 1(e) and 1(f) above.

Indirect taxes, such as payroll taxes and irrecoverable value added tax on expenses, are included in syndicate expenses.

4. REINSURANCE PREMIUMS PAID
TO CLOSE THE ACCOUNT
The reinsurance premiums paid to close the 1982 year of account of £3,779.7m include approximately £647.8m (1981 year of account £110.8m) representing amounts retained to meet known and unknown outstanding liabilities in respect of accounts which have not been closed — see note 1(d).

These amounts arise in respect of syndicates associated with the following agencies:

	£m
Richard Beckett Underwriting Agencies	283.4
RHM Outhwaite (Underwriting Agencies) Ltd.	97.4
Alexander Howden	77.5
Posgate & Denby (Agencies) Ltd.	75.3
	533.6
Others	114.2
	647.8

The total profit of £57.0m is arrived at after providing for losses of £129.4m (1981 year of account £19.0m) in respect of these unclosed accounts. £73.2m of these losses are attributable to syndicates associated with Richard Beckett Underwriting Agencies Ltd.

5. SYNDICATES MANAGED BY RICHARD BECKETT UNDERWRITING AGENCIES LTD
The 1982 account and 1981 account comparative figures reflect losses reported in the annual reports of the above syndicates. No account has been taken in preparing the global accounts of amounts recovered by Names pursuant to an offer dated 21st June, 1984 by Richard Beckett Underwriting Agencies Ltd and W.M.D. Underwriting Agencies Ltd.

In determining the assets and underwriting liabilities of members participating on the above syndicates as at 31st December, 1984 and in preparing the 1984 global accounts no account has been taken of any adjustments which might arise were certain unsubstantiated allegations made during 1985 to be sustained. These allegations relate, inter alia, to the presentation of information in accounts sent to Names during 1978-81 and to the basis of the offer referred to above. Nevertheless the relevant assets have been valued and underwriting liabilities calculated by professional underwriters, where appropriate with additional expert advice, using the best information available and taking account of all the circumstances in accordance with Lloyd's rules. In view of the matters referred to in this note and other uncertainties affecting the determination of a final profit or loss no year of account of the syndicates in question was closed as at 31st December, 1984.

ALL CLASSES COMBINED
Global Accounts at 31 December 1984

1981 year of account £'000	INCOME	Notes	1982 year of account £'000	Incurred in 1982 £'000	Incurred in 1983 £'000	Incurred in 1984 £'000	1983 year of account £'000	Incurred in 1983 £'000	Incurred in 1984 £'000	1984 year of account £'000
—	Balance brought forward		—	—	1,184,625	3,849,374	—	—	1,203,083	—
2,255,026	Reinsurance premiums received from previous account		3,215,899	11,239	2,716,533	488,127	3,765,113	4,187	3,760,926	4,201
2,258,249	Premiums		2,892,476	1,677,567	771,601	443,308	2,917,861	1,824,631	1,093,230	2,445,385
105,533	Investment income on syndicate funds		128,451	11,899	27,756	88,796	39,247	10,774	28,473	12,410
255,864	Appreciation of investments		313,529	43,037	54,858	215,634	87,662	21,116	66,546	28,798
17,285	Profit on currency exchange	2	17,995	465	2,124	15,406	7,421	206	7,215	(234)
1,388	Other items		947	792	87	68	838	755	83	526
4,893,345	TOTAL INCOME		6,569,297	1,744,999	4,757,584	5,100,713	6,818,142	1,861,669	6,159,556	2,491,086
	EXPENDITURE									
2,708,428	Reinsurance premiums paid to close the account	4	3,779,746	—	—	3,779,746	—	—	—	—
1,848,363	Claims		2,516,570	379,673	890,682	1,246,215	1,572,283	453,758	1,118,525	540,487
157,692	Syndicate expenses		186,023	154,919	16,494	14,610	189,296	169,266	20,030	196,916
26,869	Annual subscriptions and levies		28,430	24,469	1,707	2,254	35,306	34,973	333	48,997
113	Other expenses		1,515	1,313	(673)	875	821	589	232	969
—	Balance carried forward		—	1,184,625	3,849,374	—	5,020,436	1,203,083	5,020,436	1,703,717
4,741,465	TOTAL EXPENDITURE		6,512,284	1,744,999	4,757,584	5,043,700	6,818,142	1,861,669	6,159,556	2,491,086
151,880	PROFIT	4&5	57,013			57,013				

LLOYD'S GLOBAL ACCOUNTS 1984 – STATEMENT OF SECURITY UNDERLYING LLOYD'S POLICIES

LLOYD'S OF   LONDON

SECURITY UNDERLYING POLICIES ISSUED AT LLOYD'S

The Lloyd's security system comprises two main elements; first, the financial resources of members and, second, the controls exercised by Lloyd's — the latter being designed so that any weaknesses are detected at the earliest possible moment thus enabling corrective action to be taken.

The financial resources may be divided between those belonging to or held in trust for the individual members and those held centrally under the supervision of the Council of Lloyd's.

A. FINANCIAL RESOURCES

1. RESOURCES OF MEMBERS

(a) Technical reserves
The technical reserves of a syndicate, which are broadly comparable with those of an insurance company, comprise:

— the reinsurance to close (loss provisions) in respect of the closed year and prior years; and

— underwriting balances in respect of the two open years.

The assets supporting the technical reserves must be held in a trust fund in accordance with the provisions of a trust deed approved by the Secretary of State. These assets are available in the first instance for the payment of claims, expenses and other outgoings of the member's underwriting business. Whilst the underwriting balances will largely be used to meet these payments they will, in the meantime, produce substantial investment earnings to increase further the funds available. It is not until these payments have been made and provision has been made for outstanding liabilities that the profit (if any) may be released to the members.

At the end of 1984, the value of the assets comprising the total underwriting balances of members of Lloyd's was £6,724 million (1983 £5,052 million). The assets were in the form of cash and investments (including the American and Canadian Trust Funds held in New York and Toronto respectively, totalling approximately US$4,848 million (1983 US$4,400 million) and C$417 million (1983 C$360 million)) and amounts due for payment to underwriters by Lloyd's brokers through the central accounting system.

(b) Member's personal resources
These consist of:

Lloyd's deposits
The Lloyd's deposit which each member must provide before commencing underwriting is held in trust by Lloyd's as security for that member's underwriting. The amount of the Lloyd's deposit which each member must lodge is related to the member's permitted level of underwriting. A member's Lloyd's deposit is not released until his underwriting liabilities have been fully reinsured by other Lloyd's underwriters. The market value at 31st December,

1984 of members' deposits was £1,212 million (1983 £983 million).

Members' personal or Special Reserve Funds
Most underwriting agents require their members to establish underwriting reserves in addition to their Lloyd's deposits. These funds may be in the form of personal reserves held in trust by the underwriting agent or may be held in trust by the agent and Lloyd's in the Special Reserve Fund scheme approved by the Inland Revenue. For the purposes of the annual solvency test at 31st December, 1984 members' personal reserves with a market value of £212 million (1983 £170 million) were available. The market value at the end of 1984 of members' special reserve funds was £231 million (1983 £205 million).

Personal wealth
Members of Lloyd's accept insurance business solely for their own account and their liability in respect of such business is unlimited. Consequently, each member's total wealth is available as security to support that member's share of underwriting liabilities.

Each prospective member must provide independent verification to the Council of Lloyd's that he or she has a minimum level of wealth (known as "qualifying means") which varies according to the status of the individual (ie whether or not the Name is a member of the Lloyd's community). Members of Lloyd's who wish to increase their level of underwriting are required to produce a current confirmation of their means. Furthermore members are required to provide a periodic confirmation that their means have not fallen below the prescribed level.

Only certain assets qualify for inclusion as means, the object being to ensure that a high proportion is in the form of readily realisable assets. Based on the most recent information available, the amount of members' means confirmed to Lloyd's in support of their permitted level of underwriting totalled in excess of £3,480 million (1983 £2,914 million).

As many members include their deposits and/or reserve funds in their means figure the whole of the value of the Lloyd's deposits (£1,212 million) has been deducted to arrive at the figure of £2,268 million (1983 £1,931 million) shown on page 38, in order to arrive at a conservative estimate of members' means which are not held in trust. Since the object of the means test is to demonstrate a *minimum* level of wealth it may reasonably be inferred that the actual wealth of members of Lloyd's exceeds this figure, probably by a substantial amount.

The total resources of the members of Lloyd's, either in the form of assets held in trust at Lloyd's or representing their means confirmed to Lloyd's are £10,647 million (see item (VII) on page 38) (1983 £8,341 million). As this figure includes only the amount of the members' qualifying means, it represents a very conservative valuation of the total resources of the members of Lloyd's.

2. CENTRAL RESOURCES OF LLOYD'S

Individual members are liable for their own underwriting commitments but should the assets held on their behalf at Lloyd's or their personal resources prove insufficient to meet their liabilities, the resources held centrally by Lloyd's are available to meet their underwriting obligations. These resources comprise the central fund, to which all members pay an annual levy, and the assets of the Corporation of Lloyd's. As at 31st December, 1984, the net value of the central fund and Corporation assets were £167 million (1983 £134 million) and £141 million (1983 £114 million) respectively.

It should be emphasised that the central fund (and indeed the assets of the Corporation of Lloyd's) exist as the ultimate safeguard and protection for the Lloyd's policyholder.

The possibility of individual members failing to meet their obligations is, however, minimised by the stringent security controls exercised by the Council of Lloyd's as explained below.

B. SECURITY CONTROLS

1. PREMIUM INCOME LIMITS

The volume of business members may accept in any year is calculated on specified ratios of their Lloyd's deposits and qualifying means. If members' premium income should exceed their authorised premium limits, they must provide further deposits in proportion to the amount of overwriting; alternatively, they may increase their overall premium limits by an amount at least equal to the amount overwritten, provide any additional deposit required to support the new level of underwriting and, where appropriate, show new means levels. Failure to meet these requirements would be followed by a reduction in their permitted level of underwriting or by their being required to cease underwriting altogether. New requirements have recently been introduced to improve the monitoring of syndicate premium income under which gross premium income processed through Lloyd's is measured against estimates of premium income provided by each syndicate.

2. STATUTORY SOLVENCY TEST

Members are required to hold at all times sufficient assets at Lloyd's to meet their estimated future liabilities (calculated in a manner prescribed by the Council and approved by the Secretary of State for Trade and Industry) and to undergo an annual solvency test, as at 31st December, to demonstrate that they have achieved this.

When estimating future liabilities an additional amount must be set aside if reinsurance ceded outside Lloyd's exceeds 20% of the gross premiums on an underwriting account (30% where reinsurers have undertaken to provide acceptable further security).

In the case of assets held in members' premium/trust funds, only cash and readily realisable assets may be taken into account for the purpose of the solvency test.

Should members hold insufficient assets within Lloyd's to meet these solvency requirements, they are required to provide additional assets from their own resources to cover the shortfall. Members who fail to comply are suspended from underwriting and amounts sufficient to cover the shortfall are earmarked from the central fund.

C. SECURITY RATIOS

Each member underwrites solely for his own account and the liability for his underwriting commitments is, therefore, several rather than joint. The following ratios must be considered in this light when comparing them with those of an insurance company.

SECURITY RATIOS	
Ratio of premium income (before ceded reinsurance) to surplus	approx 1.4:1
Ratio of premium income (after ceded reinsurance) to surplus	approx 1.1:1
Ratio of technical reserves to premium income (before ceded reinsurance)	approx 1.3:1
Ratio of technical reserves to premium income (after ceded reinsurance)	approx 1.5:1
Ratio of technical reserves to surplus	approx 1.7:1

The figures in the above ratios have been arrived at as follows:

(a) Premium income is the total premium income accounted for in calendar year 1984. It excludes the reinsurance premiums received to close prior years of account, and US and Canadian dollars are translated into sterling at the rates of exchange applying on 31st December, 1984.

The market premium income declared to Lloyd's is after deduction of commissions and brokerage and, in order to equate this to the normal insurance company definition of gross written premiums, the Lloyd's figures have been grossed-up to take account of an average commission and brokerage figure across all markets and lines of business, estimated at 18.7%.

(b) The total of members' capital and free reserves has been regarded as the equivalent of a company's surplus. The total represents members' Lloyd's deposits, personal reserves, special reserve funds and personal wealth and has been conservatively estimated at £3,923 million (1983 £3,289 million) (see para A1 (b)).

(c) The technical reserves are equivalent to the underwriting balances which totalled £6,724 million at the end of 1984 (1983 £5,052 million) (see para A1 (a)).

These ratios are based on premiums received in the year 1984. Whilst the proportion of premiums underwritten to permitted capacity will vary from syndicate to syndicate, the capacity of Lloyd's as a whole in 1984 was substantially in excess of the actual premium income underwritten in that year. The ratios shown would be subject to amendment in the event of notional total capacity being applied.

D. STATUTORY SOLVENCY MARGIN

Lloyd's as a whole completes a solvency margin statement as part of its statutory return to the Department of Trade and Industry. The return to be filed as at 31st December, 1984, shows that the assets available are some five times the required margin of solvency.

LLOYD'S STATUTORY RETURN 1984 – FORM 9

FORM 9   CONSOLIDATED STATEMENT OF ASSETS AND LIABILITIES OF
UNDERWRITING MEMBERS OF LLOYD'S

		As at 31st December 1984 £000	As at 31st December 1983 £000
UNDERWRITING ACCOUNTS (GENERAL BUSINESS)			
Assets held in premium trust funds plus amounts due from Lloyd's brokers (Note 1)	1	6,932,916	5,220,351
Provision for estimated future liabilities	2	7,001,824	5,220,623
Sub-total (1 – 2)	3	(68,908)	(272)
Lloyd's Deposits (general business) (Note 2)	4	1,210,530	981,120
Lloyd's Special Reserve Funds (excluding any amount shown at line 11) (Note 3)	5	230,683	205,478
Total (3 + 4 + 5)	6	1,372,305	1,186,326
UNDERWRITING ACCOUNTS (LONG TERM BUSINESS)			
Assets held in premium trust funds plus amounts due from Lloyd's brokers (Note 1)	7	3,372	2,702
Provision for estimated future liabilities	8	3,177	2,252
Sub-total (7 – 8)	9	195	450
Lloyd's Deposits (long-term business) (Note 2)	10	1,954	1,669
Lloyd's Special Reserve Funds applied to long term business (Note 3)	11		
Total (9 + 10 + 11)	12	2,149	2,119
OTHER ASSETS			
Underwriting members' qualifying assets (note 4)	13	2,267,964	1,930,896
Lloyd's Central Fund (Note 5)	14	167,210	134,216
Corporation of Lloyd's: total net assets (Note 6)	15	141,060	114,180
Total (13 + 14 + 15)	16	2,576,234	2,179,292
GRAND TOTAL (6 + 12 + 16)	17	3,950,688	3,367,737

NOTES

1. A premium trust fund is a fund to which, in accordance with the provisions of a trust deed approved by the Secretary of State under section 83(2) of the Insurance Companies Act 1982, are carried all premiums received by, or on behalf of an underwriting member in respect of any insurance business.

2. A Lloyd's Deposit is a deposit by an underwriting member and held in trust by Lloyd's by way of security for the member's underwriting obligations.

3. A Lloyd's Special Reserve Fund is a fund maintained under arrangements to which Schedule 10 to the Income and Corporation Taxes Act 1970 applies.

4. Underwriting members' qualifying assets have been assessed by reference to the Lloyd's means test applicable to individual members' level of underwriting.

5. The Lloyd's Central Fund is a fund to which underwriting members contribute and which is held on trust by Lloyd's to be applied in or towards paying and making good or purchasing such of the claims and returns on contracts of insurance and guarantee underwritten by members of Lloyd's in respect of which they have been declared by the Council of Lloyd's to have made default.

6. The total net assets of the Corporation of Lloyd's are as shown by the audited accounts of the Corporation.

BIBLIOGRAPHY

Lloyd's Publications

Fisher Working Party, *Self-regulation at Lloyd's*, May 1980.
Consultative Document: *The Annual Financial Report for Underwriting Members of Lloyd's (Report of Fisher Task Group 4)*, December 1982.
Consultative Document: *Disclosure of Interests by Underwriting Agents (Report of Plaistowe Working Party)*, August 1983.
Consultative Document: *Lloyd's Syndicate Audit Arrangements*, July 1984.

Comments of Accountancy Bodies

CCAB Memorandum on 'The Fisher Report on Lloyd's', March 1981 (ICAEW, TR 428).
CCAB Memorandum on 'Lloyd's Accounting Manual', March 1983 (ICAEW, TR 501).
ICAEW Memorandum on 'Lloyd's Syndicate Accounts and the True and Fair View', October 1984 (ICAEW, TR 558).

Other Publications

About Lloyd's
Doody,B.K., *Lloyd's of London: A Detailed Analysis of Results 1950–1977* (London: Lloyd's of London Press, 1979).
Cockerell, Hugh, *Lloyd's of London – A Portrait* (Cambridge: Woodhead-Faulkner, 1984).
Hodgson, Godfrey, *Lloyd's: A Reputation at Risk* (London: Allen Lane, 1984).
Chartered Insurance Institute Tuition Service, *Management II (Lloyd's)* (London: Chartered Insurance Institute, 1981) and Supplementary Notes 7/82 (1982).
Rew, J. & Sturge, C. (eds.), *Lloyd's League Tables – 1982*, Parts 1 & 2 (London: Chatset, 1985).

About Insurance
Harte, G. & Macve, R.H., 'Lessons of the V&G crash', in D.Flint & P.McMonnies, *Business Failure and Auditing Standards* (George Allen & Unwin, 1986 – forthcoming).
Macve, R.H., 'Inflation accounting and the accounts of insurance companies', a series of four articles in *The Post Magazine & Insurance Monitor*, Vol. CXXXVIII, Nos. 35–38 (September 1977), pp.2097–2101, 2173–2178, 2225–2226, 2291–2295.
Peat, Marwick, Mitchell & Co., *UK Accounting Principles and Presentation: Insurance. A Survey of Major Composites – 1983* (London: Peat, Marwick, Mitchell & Co., 1984).

General

ASC, *The Corporate Report: A Discussion Paper* (London: ASC, 1975).

Edey, H.C., 'Why all-purpose accounts will not do', *Accountancy* (October 1978), pp.108–109, reprinted in Harold C. Edey, *Accounting Queries* (New York & London: Garland, 1982).

Financial Accounting Standards Board (FASB), *Statement of Financial Accounting Concepts No.1: Objectives of Financial Reporting by Business Enterprises* (Stamford, Conn.: FASB, November 1978).

Macve, R.H., *A Conceptual Framework for Financial Accounting and Reporting: The Possibilities for Developing an Agreed Structure* (London: ICAEW, 1981). A report prepared at the request of the Accounting Standards Committee.

MacNeal, K., 'What's wrong with accounting?' *The Nation* (New York: October 1939), reprinted in W.T.Baxter & S. Davidson (eds.), *Studies in Accounting* (London: ICAEW, 1977), pp.168-178.

Sandilands, F.E.P. (chairman), *Inflation Accounting: Report of the Inflation Accounting Committee*, Cmnd 6225 (London: HMSO, 1975).

Tonkin, D.J. & Skerratt, L.C.L. (eds.), *Financial Reporting 1983–84: A Survey of UK Published Accounts* (London: ICAEW, 1983).

Tonkin, D.J. & Skerratt, L.C.L. (eds.), *Financial Reporting 1984–85: A Survey of UK Published Accounts* (London: ICAEW, 1984).

Watts, Tom, 'British Accounting Standards and the EEC – experiences in the search for the objectives of financial statements', in B.Carsberg & S.Dev (eds.), *External Financial Reporting: Essays in Honour of Harold Edey* (London: Prentice/Hall & LSE, 1984), pp.135–147.

ABBREVIATIONS

ALM   The Association of Lloyd's Members

APC   The Auditing Practices Committee of the CCAB

ASC   The Accounting Standards Committee of the CCAB

CA   Companies Act, e.g. CA1985=The Companies Act 1985

CCAB   The Consultative Committee of Accountancy Bodies

CII   The Chartered Insurance Institute

CPP   Current Purchasing Power

ED   Exposure Draft of SSAP

DTI   The Department of Trade and Industry

IBNR   'Incurred but not reported' claims

ICAEW The Institute of Chartered Accountants in England and Wales

LPSO   Lloyd's Policy Signing Office

PAM   Author's abbreviation for 'Provisional Accounting Manual',
       i.e. the *Lloyd's Accounting Manual: Accounting to
       Underwriting Members of Lloyd's, Provisional* (November 1983)

SAB   Author's abbreviation for The Syndicate Accounting Byelaw,
       i.e. Lloyd's Byelaw No.7 of 1984

SI   Statutory Instrument

SLAP   Statement of Lloyd's Accounting Practice (Provisional)

SSAP   Statement of Standard Accounting Practice

INDEX

This subject index does not include the material reproduced in the examples or in Appendices V – VII. For the abbreviations used see Appendix IX (p.263). Cited authors are not included here but full titles are given in the Bibliography (Appendix VIII, p.261).